CAROLINA VOICES

CAROLINA VOICES

Two Hundred Years of
Student Experiences

EDITED BY

Carolyn B. Matalene and
Katherine C. Reynolds

UNIVERSITY OF SOUTH CAROLINA PRESS

Published by the University of South Carolina Press in cooperation
with the University of South Carolina Bicentennial Commission

UNIVERSITY OF SOUTH CAROLINA *BICENTENNIAL*

Published in Columbia, South Carolina, by the
University of South Carolina Press

Manufactured in the United States of America

05   04   03   02   01   5   4   3   2   1

Library of Congress Cataloging-in-Publication Data

Carolina voices : two hundred years of student experiences / edited by
Carolyn B. Matalene and Katherine C. Reynolds.
    p.   cm.
Includes bibliographical references and index.
ISBN 1-57003-429-X
1. University of South Carolina—Students. 2. University of South
Carolina—History. I. Matalene, Carolyn B., 1941– II. Reynolds, Katherine
C., 1945–
LD5036 .C37   2001
378.757'71—dc21   2001001180

Dedicated to all those
University of South Carolina students
who turned in their papers on time

Contents

List of Illustrations / ix

Preface / xi

1   A Boys' College in a Small Town: The Antebellum Years / 1

2   Students in Battle: The Civil War and Its Aftermath / 37

3   Struggling to Survive: The Old College from 1880 to 1906 / 66

4   A Whole of Many University Parts: Confronting the
    Twentieth Century / 104

5   Nothing the Same Again: World War II and Beyond / 144

6   Years of Protest, Years of Growth / 170

7   Going Global, Getting Wired: Carolina Prepares for a
    Third Century / 202

Bibliography / 231

Index / 237

Illustrations

Following page 36

Pres. William Howard Taft speaks from the steps of the old President's House, 1909.

The Class of 1900 during their junior year

The 1896 USC football team

The student engineering club, 1900

The 1896 USC baseball team

"Co-ed Follies" of 1927

A student instrumental group, 1906

The Darlington County club, 1911

In 1911 students drew well water for their rooms.

Student artists on the Horseshoe, 1935

1942 dormitory scene

In the chemistry laboratory, 1943

The competition never dies.

In 1944, ROTC was a large and welcome presence on campus.

Wartime socializing, 1945

Following page 150

1947 Commencement on the Horseshoe

Registration bottleneck, 1935

"Miss Venus" contest, 1955

Frisbee on the Horseshoe, 1978

Demonstrators protest the war in Vietnam, 1969.

Pope John Paul II on the Horseshoe, September 1987

Officers of the ROTC Association, "Compass and Chart," 1942

Remembering Gamecock football

Remembering Gamecock basketball

Army v. Marine ROTC skirmish on the Horseshoe, 1999

USC Women's Club lacrosse scrimmage, 1999

Students in Preston Residential College, 1996

Theater production, Department of Theatre and Speech, 1998

Men's soccer team, USC v. Davidson, 1997

Music laboratory, School of Music, 1996

Women's softball team, 1998

Student researcher in chemistry laboratory

USC mascot, Cocky, on parade

Pres. John Palms helps a student move into Preston Residential College, 1997.

Preface

"Time is the avatar of each individual consciousness," said William Faulkner, and so too is each student's experience of the University of South Carolina a personal collection of memories, a unique combination of encounters never to be foreseen, forever to be relished. From joining in heated classroom debates and surviving intricate lab sessions to combing the shelves of the library and producing late-night papers, from throwing frisbees on the Horseshoe and celebrating in Five Points to cheering the Gamecocks and falling in love, being a college student is one of life's most intense experiences. Few have wished it shorter.

Nothing more clearly reveals the personal nature of Carolina than the voices of thousands of students, past and present. The texts they have left behind for two centuries testify to their willingness to learn and grow, while they also create a rich tapestry of campus history. In this volume we have let students tell their own versions of USC's story, allowing them—and only rarely teachers, parents, and other observers—to report their activities and ideas and opinions in their own words. Their letters and journals and diaries, their news stories and editorials and poems, their oral histories and e-mails provide intimate illustrations of life on and around, and sometimes beyond, the campus.

We have used primary sources and provided only brief explanations in order to foreground students as the authors. Thus, this work does not constitute a history. Others have written scholarly, institutional histories of USC, from Maximilian LaBorde and Edwin L. Green to Daniel Walker Hollis and Henry H. Lesesne, and we have depended heavily on their insights and conclusions. We have tried to tell instead the human story, capturing the color and spirit of the times, revealing attitudes and opinions, issues and passions. Nor have we checked the veracity of our sources since hyperbole is the favorite trope of the college student. Letters home are meant to maintain communication, not necessarily to tell the truth. Thus, this book is intended to interest and amuse, to rekindle memories and perhaps offer insight as it presents the perceptions of some who have brought vigor and meaning to the University of South Carolina for the past 200 years.

Beginning with the legislation that created South Carolina College in 1801, we have searched family papers, collections of letters, presidential archives, autobiographies and histories, journals and diaries, student newspapers and literary magazines, oral histories and e-mails. The materials we collected fell naturally into seven chronological chapters with clear themes emerging in each, sometimes living conditions and classroom practices and social life, sometimes larger historical events. In some decades students left campus and wrote home from service in war; in others alums reflected on campus happenings.

Both the genres and the media of students' texts have changed as the technologies of communication have evolved. In the nineteenth century students were limited to the one-on-one communication of letters and journals. Faculty and administrators added institutional reports and occasional newspaper stories. In the twentieth century, students gradually took to the telephone, and those living nearby, now equipped with cars, drove home and talked things over. However, as student publications like the *Gamecock* and *Garnet and Black* and a series of literary magazines were established, students found new forums for public expression. By the 1970s and 1980s telephones were so accessible that few students wrote letters. Then in the 1990s electronic mail brought back quantities of written words in a breezy and staccato new style.

In our search for all kinds of communication, we were aided by archivists and librarians who guided us to dozens of collections, by colleagues who made suggestions, by alumni who searched their memorabilia and memories, by students who shared their personal lives, and by University of South Carolina Bicentennial Commission and staff members who gave our project a cheerful home and generous nurturing.

Among the superb archival administrators who assisted us at the South Caroliniana Library were: Elizabeth Bilderback, Robin Copp, Sam Fore, Henry Fulmer, Thelma Hayes, John Heiting, Mark Herro, Thomas Johnson, Megan Moughan, and Allen H. Stokes, Jr. Elizabeth Cassidy West guided us through relevant University archives and presidential papers, and Herbert J. Hartsook gave us access to the Modern Political Collections. At the University of North Carolina–Chapel Hill, John E. White assisted our research at the Southern Historical Collection; and at Emory University's Robert W. Woodruff Library, Pat Clark searched the Dickey Archives, Special Collections. Graduate assistants Karan Romaine, Natasha Chisholm, and Jon Pope carried out numerous, sometimes tedious, tasks.

We also acknowledge the individuals who gave us permission to use their personal oral histories and items from their private collections, especially those who rummaged through attics, boxes, e-mails, and recollections on our behalf, including: Elisabeth Alford, Mary C. Anderson, Crys Armbrust, William C. Barksdale, Jr., Daisy Boatwala, Erin Bush, Mary King

Butler, Thorne H. Compton, Bruce Coull, Joanna Daiwo, Dan D'Alberto, Yang Deyou, Bert Easter of Easter Antiques, Walter Edgar, James Fant, Vicki Sox Fecas, Toni Metcalf Goodwin, Johnny Gregory, Sarah Hammond, Kristen Harrill, R. B. Haynes, Betty Hodges, Rhett Jackson, Ed Madden, Alexa Maddox, Jessica Mann, Dennis Myers, Caroline Parler, Michael Safran, Thomas and Linda Salane, Alice Skelsey, Allison Smith, Selden K. Smith, Stephen E. Stancyck, Larry M. Stephens, Carl Sessions Stepp, Emily Streyer, Arthur Tai, Henrie Monteith Treadwell, Helen Anderson Waring-Tovey, Othniel Wienges, Jr., Frank Williams, and Martha Wright.

We are grateful to Pat Conroy for allowing us to quote passages from his novel *Beach Music*.

Early encouragement to start the project was provided by: Dennis Pruitt, Bicentennial Commission member and Vice President for Student and Alumni Services; Catherine Fry, USC Press Director; and Alex Moore, USC Press Acquisitions Editor.

As our research got underway, members of the Bicentennial staff provided ongoing and invaluable assistance that moved the book from idea to reality: Sally T. McKay, Executive Director; Harry H. Lesesne, Associate Director and Bicentennial Historian; and Jill E. Grantz, Administrative Assistant. Finally, we offer our esteem and gratitude to Thorne H. Compton, Chairman of the Bicentennial executive committee, who could be counted on for expert guidance and a lively wit when we most needed it.

A Note on Archival Editing

The letters, journal entries, and other written records appearing in this volume generally are excerpted versions of the originals in order to allow space for numerous documents. Salutations and closings of letters are retained only when their wording connotes something of interest about the sender or recipient. Dates and locations of origin, when included in the original, are worked into introductory head notes.

As editors, we retained as much of authors' original writing styles as possible in the excerpts. We silently corrected only those spelling errors and small grammatical mistakes that appeared to be careless, one-time occurrences and might cause confusion for readers.

When writers referred to themselves or to others by last names or by initials only, we added full names in brackets when identification was possible. Additionally, for students, we added class years and hometowns when these were available and would assist in identification.

Carolyn B. Matalene Katherine C. Reynolds
Department of English College of Education

CAROLINA VOICES

1

A Boys' College in a Small Town

THE ANTEBELLUM YEARS

In 1801 young men in America attended college to attain a classical education. They learned Latin and Greek, read the classical texts, and studied theology and philosophy as well as mathematics and some science in their pursuit of the seven liberal arts. They also mastered the canons of rhetoric and practiced oratory, for in the Ciceronian tradition an education in eloquence was essential training for the *vita activa*. As Isocrates had insisted, "By speech we refute the wicked and praise the good. By speech we educate the ignorant and inform the wise."

The founders of South Carolina College wanted to provide the young men of the state with just such a classical education in order to prepare them for citizenship as politicians or lawyers, educators or ministers. The common curriculum, specified in the initial legislation and followed by the first students, did, in fact, prepare them for public life as the alumni records prove and as the letters in this volume reveal. Students learned how to speak with authority as they participated in hours of classroom recitation, then debated each other after school. Thus, young men from the Piedmont and the lowcountry turned into gentlemen—not into tradesmen or farmers.

Such a confirmed belief in the transforming power of the literature and languages of the ancient past may seem antiquated in our electronic culture, but as we listen to the voices of our forebears, we need to understand their deep commitment to and belief in both a different set of texts and a different technology of learning. From the worried words of a first-year student to the sophisticated syntax of a senior, we can hear how well immersion in the classics worked its way on the language skills and political effectiveness of South Carolina College's first sons.

Founding Visions

At its December 1804 meeting the Board of Trustees heard the Report of the Committee on the Rules and Regulations of the College, establishing the rigorously classical curriculum and emphasizing excellence in oratory as a paramount objective for the future leaders of South Carolina.

SECTION 1. There shall be established in the college four classes, which in their succession shall bear the usual titles of Freshman, Sophomore, Junior and Senior.

SECTION 2. For admission to the Freshman Class, a candidate shall be able to render from Latin into English, Cornelius Nepos, Sallust, Caesar's Commentaries and Virgil's Aeneid; to make grammatical Latin of the exercises in Mairs' Introduction; to translate into English any passage from the Evangelist St. John, in the Greek Testament; to give a grammatical analysis of the words, and have a general knowledge of the English Grammar; write a good, legible hand, spell correctly, and be well acquainted with Arithmetic as far as includes the Rule of Proportion.

SECTION 3. Candidates for admission to any of the higher Classes, in addition to the foregoing qualifications, shall be examined in all the studies that have been pursued by that class since the commencement of the Freshman year.

SECTION 4. The studies of the Freshman year shall be the Greek Testament, Xenophon's Cyropedia, Mairs' Introduction, Virgil, Cicero's Orations, Roman Antiquities, Arithmetic, English Grammar, and Sheridan's Lectures on Elocution. A part of every day's Latin lesson shall be written in a fair hand, with an English translation, and correctly spelled.

SECTION 5. The studies of the Sophomore year shall be Homer's Iliad, Horace, Vulgar and Decimal Fractions, with the extraction of Roots, Geography, Watts' Logic, Blairs' Lectures, Algebra, the French Language and Roman Antiquities.

SECTION 6. The studies of the Junior year shall be Elements of Criticism, Geometry Theoretical and Practical, Astronomy, Natural and Moral Philosophy, French, Longinus de Sublimitate, and Cicero de Oratore.

SECTION 7. The studies of the Senior year shall be Millots' Elements of History, Demosthenes' Select Orations, and such parts of Locke's Essay as shall be prescribed by the Faculty. The Seniors, also, shall review such parts of the studies of the preceding year, and perform such exercises in the higher branches of the Mathematics as the Faculty may direct.

SECTION 8. From the time of their admission into College, the students shall be exercised in Composition and public speaking, for which purpose such a number as the Faculty shall direct shall daily, in rotation, deliver orations in the College Hall. There shall also be public exhibitions; and competition in speaking and other exercises, held at such times and under such regulations as the Faculty shall require; and every member of the Senior Class shall, at least once each month, deliver an oration of his own composition, after submitting it to be perused and corrected by the President.

William Harper, Class of 1808 and member of the Board of Trustees in 1813, explained that the College's origins were inspired by differences between the upper and lower regions of the state.

This measure originated in the contest which had arisen between the *upper* and *lower* country of the State, with respect to representation in the Legislature. The upper country, which at the adoption of the Constitution of 1791 was comparatively poor and unpeopled, had allotted to it by the provisions of the Constitution a much smaller representation. It had now grown in wealth, far out-numbered the lower country in its population, and imperatively demanded a reform in the representation. This the people of the lower country feared to grant on the ground of general deficiency of education and intelligence in the upper country, which would render it incompetent to exercise wisely and justly the power which such a reform would place in its hands. It was to remedy this deficiency that it was proposed to establish a College at Columbia.

State representative Henry W. DeSaussure exemplified the lowcountry view.

We of the lower country well knew that the power of the State was thence forward to be in the upper country, and we desired our future rulers to be educated men.

William Grayson, Class of 1809, writing his autobiography at the end of his life, concluded that the College's founders had indeed realized their intentions.

The great merit of the South Carolina College is that it has tended to make the State one people. At the Revolution and for some years after it, the Upper and Lower country were two communities with little intercourse and less sympathy with each other. . . . The traces of these former differences between the two portions of the State are still discernible in their civil division and their names. The lower or older part is a region of parishes and saints; the upper, of districts and less holy men. Below we find spiritual chiefs, St. George, St. John, St. Peter, St. Paul. Above, secular worthies only, Sumter, Pickens, Pendleton and Anderson. But the real differences of which these names are signs were removed or weakened by the influence of the College, by its establishing cordial and enduring friendships between the young men from every part of the State.

BOYS INTO SCHOLARS

The students who entered South Carolina College in 1805 were white males barely beyond adolescence. Although many were as young as fourteen or fifteen, few entered as freshmen. Instead they achieved status as sophomores or juniors based on their performances on entrance examinations. In fact, for six of the first ten years, there were no freshman classes. This pattern persisted throughout the early years of the College—an era when private tutoring and preparatory academies helped students exceed the limited freshman requirements before arriving at South Carolina College.

William C. Preston, later president of South Carolina College (1845–1851), entered the institution in 1809 as a fourteen-year-old sophomore after traveling south from Richmond, Va., for his health. In his autobiography he recalled the experience.

Mounted on horse-back with a negro servant to wait on and take care of me, I proceeded on my lonely journey. Columbia, So. Ca., lay in my way. There I put up at a tavern situated on the spot now occupied by the high sounding Congaree House then bearing the most characteristic appellation of Goat Hall. There I met with several young men, Charleston boys, who had come up to join the South Carolina College. These youngsters, whose address and manners were very attractive, easily persuaded me that I was far enough South for my health, and that the new and flourishing College which they were about to enter was a fit place to obtain an education. . . .

. . . No questions were asked as to my age. In College I took and maintained a good stand. The state of discipline nor the course of instruction at that time were much calculated to confer a high education. I graduated with distinction in 1812. . . . When I graduated I was not quite 18 years old.

William J. Grayson of Beaufort, a graduate in 1809, described his missing freshman year as a fortunate combination of preparation and perfunctory admissions standards as he recalled his first taste of college life.

My instruction hitherto had been confined to a little French and to what is called an English education. At sixteen I became ambitious of learning to read Homer and Virgil in their own language. At this time two brothers of Dr. Jonathan Maxcy the first President of South Carolina College opened a school in the town of Beaufort. . . . [There] I read the ordinary Latin authors, made some progress in Greek, and at the end of eighteen months became a candidate for admission into the Sophomore class in Columbia College.

I was examined by the Reverend Doctor Maxcy. The examination was not half as formidable as I had supposed. A letter from his brother had somewhat macadamized the way. I construed an ode in Horace. The Doctor made a few critical remarks on the exquisite beauty, the *curiosa felicitas* of the poet's diction and the work was done. . . .

Before my formal initiation, during the first night of my arrival in Columbia, I was introduced by an acquaintance to the mysteries of college life. In one of the recitation rooms we found an assemblage of students engaged in a scene of great jollity and good humor. Some were singing; some talking; some mounted on benches and making set speeches; some interpolating critical remarks on the orators, while the young freshmen performed the part of silent and admiring auditors. . . . At this period a rage for the French Revolution was the popular sentiment. It had convulsed the Republic during Washington's administration and was still prevalent in the country. The Gallic propagandists of liberty were all patriots and heroes. The "Rights of Man" and the "Age of Reason" were the great books of the day. Their author was the most admired genius. Men who had never heard of Shakespeare or Milton were deep in the pages of Paine. On the night of my introduction to the social life of Alma Mater the song sung was one in celebration of the French convention and the rights of man. It announced that in America these rights first began and a noisy repetition of "viva las" for the convention, the rights of the race and America, closed every stanza and was shouted out by all voices in full chorus. The scene differed as much as possible from that of the pale student, the midnight lamp and the classic pages.

Faced with a classical curriculum that emphasized ancient languages and liberal arts subjects, students could be highly serious as they prepared for oral classroom recitations or composed their written assignments. While letter grades did not yet appear during those early years, class rank and the possibility of suspension or expulsion were among the motivating pressures.

John Palmer, a fifteen-year-old freshman, wrote on January 18, 1819, to his mother in Pineville of his full schedule.

Perhaps you will not dislike to know everything which our class does at present; every morning we recite a Xenophon lesson to Mr. [Thomas] Park, at eleven o'clock a Latin lesson and at four PM we cipher to one of the tutors. I dare say when you look at this you will think that I have very little to do, but I assure you I find sufficient employment in these few things and in reading.

William McIver, always earnest and self-disciplined, catalogued his academic pursuits to his father in Darlington in a letter of January 11, 1836.

Monday and Tuesday, recitations before breakfast. Every Wednesday and Thursday, we recite in Cicero and the other days of the week in Homer. These are heard at 4 p.m. by Mr. [Isaac] Stuart. We recite regularly in mathematics every day at 11 a.m. I have been called upon several times in mathematics and Greek and have always been prepared. Every Friday is devoted to hearing lectures on History from Dr. [Francis] Lieber.

. . . After reading the history of Greece, I believe I will stop reading in English and read in the original, as by so doing I will accomplish a twofold purpose, improve myself in the languages and learn history besides, although my advance will be but slow.

Our class will speak on the stage next month. We are at liberty either to memorize a piece and write a composition besides or by speaking our own composition to do both in one. Which would you advise me to do?

Charles W. Hutson, a freshman from Beaufort, shared with his mother his worst academic fears (February 10, 1857).

I am very busy now, and was wool'd [found out] this morning by [Robert] Barnwell and mean to study to make up. And that wasn't the worst of it, for he called me immediately after recitation to ask me about my composition on "Lyric Poetry," to which he paid a very equivocal compliment. He told me that he wished to find out how original it was, so as to know how to mark me, as he said, "it showed an older hand, and more information, than he thought consistent with my years." I don't like his suspecting me of copying, for a suspicion it is clearly.

Hutson was more relaxed when he later corresponded with his father (February 17, 1857).

I do not find the studies at all difficult, although to make a good recitation requires rather more study than I have been doing of late. I am getting gradually to study a little harder than at first. Everything here seems to teach extemporizing, except the Classics. In the [Euphradian] Society it is something of an evil, for there seems to be rather more extempore speaking than preparation of any kind. Personalities and rhetoric occupy a much higher place than sound reasoning. However, I am much pleased with it, although I did not expect so much of this sort of thing.

. . . As for study, I can study as hard as any one else on an emergency; it is an extensive bore to be obliged to study steadily, and on an uncertainty too, whether one will be called up or not [to recite from lectures or books]. I will be almost satisfied, if I come off no worse this term than last.

Families offered academic encouragement long distance, with Mama generally leading a large pack of advisors and supporters. James Blanding found ample advice in a letter from his mother, who wrote from Charleston on May 9, 1840.

Where you stand in your class is a very important matter, and I would have you ask yourself this question: "Do I stand in my class as high as I am entitled to? If not, am I exerting the talents God gave me to their utmost?" If not, you are doing yourself the grossest injustice and giving regret to your friends. But I know this is not the case. You are too aware of your circumstances and the importance of devotion to your studies for this to be the case.

Daniel Wallace of Union, S.C., had the highest expectations for his son, William Henry Wallace, Class of 1849, when he wrote a letter in 1846 (n.d.).

Dismiss from your mind once and forever the fatal delusion that you have come into the world to enjoy indolence and ease; such thoughts are the delusive songs of the syrens that would lead to your destruction. It is labor only that can bring up to the light of day the priceless jewels from the unfathomable depths of the mind. If you cannot labor then with the head, you must with the hands. In fact, if you cannot labor with both, your fate is sealed, and mark the word, degradation is your sure destiny. Then burn your lamp at night—upon the right use of time much depends—form no intimate friendships with those who may appear not to be gentlemen. All is not gold that shines. Keep in a condition to say NO when morality and duty alike demand it. Industry and perseverance conquers all things. Then do your duty, your whole duty and you will have your reward.

Older brother, William, added his counsel to James Blanding on June 2, 1840.

You are doing right in staying at College and not coming down. You take the proper view of it in your letter. You prepare yourself the better to enjoy manhood by diligently devoting youth-season to study. That is the true time for enjoyment; at the time of ripe manhood the mind delights in nobler pleasures, which are firmer and more lasting than those of youth. The consciousness of superior intellect, of a highly cultivated mind, and of an honest upright character confers more happiness than the vivacity and carelessness of youth can ever do.

At least some parents found their sons unable to succeed in the academic life. For example, in a letter of December 14, 1847, Charles Heyward of Charleston appealed to Pres. William C. Preston after his son, Joseph Heyward, received an academic warning.

I acknowledge receipt of your letter in regard to my son Joseph, in consequence of his deficiency in the 'different branches studied in his class.'

As you may well suppose, this circumstance gives me much concern, but I can't help hoping that the President's exhortations and some gentle advice of his friends will induce him to apply himself more diligently to his studies this winter, and by next June he may be prepared to bear an examination satisfactory to the faculty.

Joseph Heyward never got past his sophomore year, leaving South Carolina College in 1848.

OVERWHELMED BY ORATORY

When Joshua H. Hudson of Chester, S.C., arrived on campus in 1849, he joined the Euphradian Society, one of two college "literary" clubs engaged in debates, speech making and social activities. In 1905, after serving as a Confederate Army colonel, a state legislator, and a circuit court judge, he attended the Centennial Celebration of South Carolina College and recalled with awe the inspired speeches and debates he witnessed in Euphradian Hall (the upper floor of Harper College).

The hall was then newly furnished and equipped, and presented a beautiful, attractive, brilliant and imposing appearance. The impression upon a boy from the back country upon beholding the gaudy and dazzling spectacle on being conducted into the hall was simply overwhelming.

The president was James M. Carson, from Charleston, a handsome youth, who initiated the candidates with a dignity unsurpassed. The hall was filled with nearly a hundred Euphradians, all attentive, dignified and deeply interested spectators.

I have since then sat before many presiding officers of deliberative bodies, but never before one who presided with more dignity and ability than James M. Carson—not even excepting the Hon. James Simons, the then Speaker of the House of Representatives, in the Legislature of South Carolina.

For decorum, dignity and the orderly transaction of business I believe I can truthfully say that throughout my college course the Euphradian Society was not surpassed by the Senate or the House of Representatives of South Carolina, and this is saying much; for I have been told that the Legislature of South Carolina was then, if not now, more dignified than Congress in session, and the Congress of the United States more orderly and dignified than the Parliament of Great Britain. It should also be remarked that the Euphradian Society in numbers was almost as large as the House of Representatives of South Carolina. . . .

The ablest argument I ever heard delivered, and I heard many before and more afterwards, was delivered in the Euphradian hall by R. W. Barnwell. Never before and never afterwards, up to the final crisis in 1860, did I hear a more able argument against the doctrine of secession by a single State or by the solid South. Young though he was, he spoke as one inspired and as a prophet. But who can stem the tide of fanaticism and madness? Who in times of great political excitement will listen to reason? Very few, and those are scorned.

I wish I could give the outline of the inspired argument of this gifted man against the expediency of secession, but time does not permit. Its prophecies have been fulfilled. . . .

It must be borne in mind that the literary societies, Euphradian and Clariosophic, embraced the entire student body of the College, nearly equally divided between them, and moved on, year after year, with a generous and most praiseworthy rivalry, each glorying in the applauding the brilliant achievements of the members of the other.

But how was it that raw recruits from the back country could in these societies get on and hold a hand with their fellows from the cities, and in fact often and in the main set the pace and take the lead? The answer is that from the time they were small boys in village academies and old field schools they were taught to write compositions and declaim extracts from the best poets and orators. They were never permitted to write silly and frivolous pieces, nor to read aught but original compositions, and in their public examinations, they were compelled and trained to stand up before trustees and large audiences and recite their oral examinations, not always by rote, but more often in answer to questions propounded by trustees and committees. And so it was that the raw student from the back country, as soon as the first shock passed and he could catch his breath and compose himself in the brilliant Euphradian hall and learn the course of exercises, not only could venture to speak and to read, but entered upon the trying duty with more zeal and ambition than his fellow student from the city.

While Joshua Hudson's euphoria about the Euphradians may seem extreme, he added a list of eminent alumni to support his rhetoric. From 1806 to 1816 the Euphradian Society initiated students who would later become governors of South Carolina (Stephen D. Miller and John P. Richardson); North Carolina (William A. Graham); Alabama (John Murphy); and Mississippi (William McWillie); five U.S. senators (William Harper, Stephen D. Miller, William C. Preston, William A. Graham, and Josiah J. Evans); and four U.S. representatives (Stephen D. Miller, John Murphy, William McWillie, and John Campbell).

These and others apparently were well prepared for their positions by their literary society experiences. Oratory among members of the Euphradian and Clariosophic Societies was serious educational business that could be intimidating, as a nervous sophomore, Giles Patterson of Spartanburg, noted in an 1847 journal entry.

This evening I have to speak tonight in Society. Can I do it? May God help me.

Charles W. Hutson wrote home to Beaufort on February 2, 1857, of his first literary society experience.

Saturday night I joined the Euphradian Society, and W__ M__ [probably William Hutson Martin] the Clariosophic. The subject on debate in our society was one very interesting to me, and as I had something to say on it, I rose to say it; but words were wanting and I hesitated and stammered dreadfully at first, but got through at last. I will not soon again venture extempore speaking.

Members of the Clariosophic and Euphradian literary societies, who together accounted for nearly all students on campus in the antebellum years, practiced debate as both entertainment and intellectual exercise.

Debate topics ranged from current political and social questions to philosophical and religious questions. Votes taken after presentations on both sides of the issues reflected both the skill of the student debaters and the political and social context of the time. The societies demonstrated shifting opinions, especially on the issue of slavery, in arguments and decisions throughout the early years of the College.

1807, Clariosophic:

"Who had a greater right to America, the Aborigines or the Europeans?" (Decided in favor of the Aborigines)

"Have women as great genius by nature as men?" (Decided in the negative)

"Is the abolition of slavery in this country a thing practical?" (Decided in the affirmative)

"On the whole, does refinement of manner produce happiness?" (Decided in the affirmative)

"Could time spent acquiring dead languages be better spent?" (Decided in the affirmative)

"Are theatrical performances on the whole advantageous?" (Decided in the negative)

"Will the monies expended on the South Carolina College be more advantageous if they had been appropriated to the creation of academies in the several Districts?" (Decided in the affirmative)

1808, Clariosophic:

"Is drunkenness or gaming attended with the most evil consequences?" (Decided in favor of drunkenness)

"Has love more influence on the mind than ambition?" (Undecided: tie vote)

1809, Clariosophic:

"Would it be disadvantageous for the country for the several states to become independent?" (Decided in the affirmative)

"Does justice require the manumission of slaves?" (Decided in the affirmative)

"Has the introduction of slavery been advantageous to South Carolina?" (Decided in the negative)

"Ought a man who instigates the death of another to suffer death?" (Decided in the affirmative)

"Ought divorces to be permitted?" (Decided in the negative)

"Does the study of history instill a love of war?" (Decided in the affirmative)

1826 Euphradian:

"Is it politic to permit owners of slaves in this country to emancipate them?" (Decided in the negative)

1827 Euphradian:

"Could South Carolina provide for the emancipation of her slaves in any manner beneficial to them so emancipated?" (Decided in the negative)

1833, Euphradian:

"Ought persons of the female sex be permitted to participate in government?" (Decided in the negative)

1834, Euphradian:

"Is visiting, admiring, and looking at the girls compatible with the collegiate duties of a student?" (Decided in the negative)

1837, Euphradian:
"Should waiting with the arm around the lady's waist be considered decent?" (Decided in the negative)

1842, Clariosophic:
"Would the admission of the border states be beneficial to the Southern Confederacy?" (Decided in the affirmative)

"Ought South Carolina to establish a military school in connection with the Arsenal [military preparatory academy]?" (Decided in the affirmative)

"Should beauty and personal accomplishments have more influence on the choice of a wife than riches?" (Decided in the affirmative)

"Ought toleration by government to extend to all sects of religion?" (Decided in the affirmative)

"Which is the greater villain, John Q. Adams or Joe Smith?" (Decided in favor of Mormon leader Joseph Smith)

1845, Clariosophic:
"Should restrictions be placed on the education of slaves?" (Decided in the negative)

"Is public opinion a good criterion of right?" (Decided in the negative)

1848, Clariosophic:
"Is it likely that slavery will be eventually abolished?" (Decided in the negative)

1849, Clariosophic:
"Ought divorces to be permitted?" (Decided in the affirmative)

1852, Euphradian:
"Should slaves be allowed to learn trades?" (Decided in the negative)

1856, Euphradian:
"Is it politic that we should educate our slaves?" (Decided in the negative)

1859, Clariosophic:
"Should an individual be compelled to support a war which he believes to be unjust?" (Decided in the affirmative)

1860, Clariosophic:
"Might South Carolina pass a law requiring free negroes to leave the state or become enslaved?" (Decided in the affirmative)

1861, Clariosophic:
"Will England or France take part in the conflict between North and South?" (Decided in the affirmative)

"Should military achievement influence the election of the next President of the Confederate States?" (Decided in the negative)

Commencement, which took place each December, provided community entertainment, student recognition, and still more oratorical display. Edward Hooker, a tutor at the College, described the December 7, 1807, commencement in his journal.

The exercise of the day began between 11 and 12 o'clock. The pieces were few but tolerably good. There were five regular graduates. The music was instrumental and very good; the performers being four or five of the best in the state. The degrees were conferred with considerable form. The President came down from the pulpit and addressed the Trustees briefly in Latin and introduced the candidates. Then [he] took an arm chair which stood a little forward on the stage and I took another chair at his left hand, holding a handsome gilt duodecimo volume of French. They came on 2 by 2. The President addressed them in Latin, sitting. Then [he] presented the book; which they held while he said another sentence, and then returned to me. They being then bachelors, the President acknowledged them as such, in Latin. . . . The President then pronounced a degree conferred on one of the class who was absent, and on one Master, a Mr. King of Darlington. He then went back to the pulpit and pronounced the honorary degree of L.L.D. conferred on J[ohn] Drayton, Esq., of Charleston and D.D. on the Rev. Messrs [Richard] Furman and [William] Percy of Charleston, [Moses] Waddel of Vienna and [Joseph] Alexander of York. After this the President made a handsome parting address of about 15 or 20 minutes. The valedictory followed and music closed the exercises.

STUDENT EVALUATIONS

From the beginning, College faculty ranged from the respected to the reviled among students.

The first president of the College, Jonathan Maxcy, relied more on oratorical appeals than on harsh discipline to keep his young students in line. William J. Grayson described in his autobiography a typical Maxcy pronouncement from the chapel steps and its effect on the young men gathering for their required morning prayers.

Perhaps some disorderly conduct of a preceding day or night had required animadversion, and we heard anew the thrilling eloquence with which he appealed to every generous sentiment of his auditors, and rebuked all bare and groveling propensities and passions, while he described the disappointed hopes of parents and friends, and defeated expectation of the proud State of South Carolina, that had endowed so munificently the College in which they stood, as a nursery for virtue and honour and learning and genius to form scholars, orators, and statesmen,

and not as a receptacle and hiding place for sensuality and vice to repro-
duce vile and obscene things, until the conscious culprits hung their heads
in confusion and shame, and good resolutions filled all hearts.

**Typically, approbation mixed with objection when students assessed fac-
ulty, as recalled by James Marion Sims of Lancaster, a graduate of the
Class of 1832.**

[Pres. Thomas] Cooper was a man of great intellect and remarkable
learning. Next to President Cooper, Professor [Robert] Henry was perhaps
the ablest man in the faculty. Professor [Henry J.] Nott was an able man
and a lovely character, but not a man of a great deal of force. The other
professors, of mathematics ([James] Wallace) and languages ([Thomas]
Park) were very ordinary men, very old, and without the confidence and
respect of the class.

**Giles Patterson, a student from Spartanburg, objected to lax faculty
behavior in an 1847 journal entry.**

There has been a great remissness in attending recitations by the professors of late. Two had the mumps for two weeks nearly. [Pres. William
C.] Preston has gone to Washington for a month. [James H.] Thornwell,
as soon as he recovered from the mumps went off to a religious association
in Charleston and has just returned. [Robert] Henry is frequently absent,
and so is [Francis] Lieber. The Trustees will have to take them in hand if
they don't mind.

[I] just now returned from a party given by Dr. Lieber to the Junior
Class in honor of Daniel Webster who graced the room with his presence
but a short while. The old Doctor had provided for us well in lemonade and
cake and claret, ice creams, strawberries, etc.—quite a treat. Preston was
there, also half tight, so I was told. I saw Mrs. Webster also, a noble and
commanding woman. She towered above all the ladies present by a head.

[I] attended Lieber's recitation at 11 o'clock where we were entertained by an excellent lecture by the Dr. He took into consideration the difference between the political state of things in antiquity and modern times.
His terms of explanation are most appropriate and his comparisons,
although seemingly surrounded with rudeness, are nevertheless very good.

**In 1886, thirty-four years after receiving his bachelor's degree, Harry
Hammond of Barnwell wrote about several of his instructors in a letter
to Prof. R. Means Davis (December 9).**

Dr. [Francis] Lieber taught Tyler's History (if I remember aright) in the
freshman and sophomore years. . . . I remember he once asked, "What is

Bologna noted for?." It passed without any one seeming to know. In great surprise the doctor said "for professors and sausages," at which the class, with some confusion, raised a laugh. And the doctor, waving them down said, "Sh jenllemen, you must not laff for where dere is professors and sausages dere is students and hogs." In the junior year we had Lieber's labor and property, and in the senior year his political ethics. As a teacher he was always fresh and suggestive and inspired much interest. His political views as far as the Union was concerned [against secession] were opposed to that of many of the trustees. I believe, however, he was a slaveholder.

As for Dr. Cooper . . . , I don't think anyone can give even a list of his writings since Dr. [Robert W.] Gibbes is dead. My father told me that Dr. Cooper, having a sick horse, went to Dr. Gibbes and asked him if he could refer him to any good work on the veterinary art, to which the doctor replied by taking down a volume from his shelves and saying, "Here is one I have found trustworthy." "Who is it by?" asks Dr. Cooper. "It is," says Dr. Gibbes, "by one Thomas Cooper." He had forgotten he had written the treatise.

Charles Hutson, Class of 1860, recalled several professors in his autobiography.

Professor Robert Barnwell elicited from some of us a singular pleasure in presenting arguments derived from what in later days figures as "research work." He and the LeContes [Drs. John and Joseph] were our favorite professors. It was Dr. Joe LeConte who of all my professors impressed me most. Some of the other professors at times betrayed lapses in general information that made me disposed to doubt their culture. One, for instance, did not know or had forgotten who Charlotte Corday was. Another did not know that when a Latin hexameter line ends in que the sound is to be carried in scanning into the next line. It was I who ventured modestly to remind him of the fact. One, in replying to a speech of welcome, shocked us all by using the phrase *in loco parentorum*. These may seem to be trifles; but they stuck in my memory and prejudiced me.

ADVENTURES AROUND THE TOWN

The youngsters who populated the campus had energy to spare before and after their classroom meetings, and organized extracurricular activities were mostly limited to daily chapel services and weekly literary society meetings. More spontaneous activities, however, ranged from polite social visits to rowdiness with friends.

William Grayson, Class of 1809, later wrote in his autobiography of entertainment among neighbors near the campus.

Among the inhabitants of the neighborhood were two of the famous partisan chiefs of the Revolutionary War, Col. Thomas Taylor and Col. Wade Hampton. He became General Hampton in the War of 1812. They were prosperous, wealthy, and remarkable, among other meritorious acts and qualities, for sometimes inviting a number of the College lads to take part in their good cheer. Their dinners were a great contrast to those of our worthy steward whether at steward's hall or in his own house where bacon and "long collards" constituted the standing dish. We gave our kind entertainers the most convincing proof that we appreciated the difference. Col. Hampton's table was adorned not only with dainties and dishes of substantial excellence but with magnificent cups and vases of silver won by his horses on the turf and set out in compliment to his young guests. He was uniformly courteous to them all and made the day pass very pleasantly.

William McIver, writing to his father in Darlington on May 14, 1836, pursued an extracurricular life with an academic bent.

I paid two dollars in consideration of four lectures which were delivered by a Greek. President [Robert W.] Barnwell recommended us to attend. They were highly interesting. His style was like that of the ancient orators of Greece. His descriptive powers are very good. The circumstances of events described was vividly drawn and presented to the mind with perfect clearness. He used the English language with elegance, ease and correctness.

By 1840 Columbia's population had increased to 4,340, and the variety of amusements had grown as well, among them a horse-racing track. Giles J. Patterson of Chester insisted in a journal entry that he was an observer rather than a participant (January 19, 1847).

Friday morning after eleven o'clock recitation R. Henry and Seibles proposed to go to the races, Henry offering to pay my entrance fee. I accepted, never having in my life witnessed such a display of human folly. We arrived there without anything remarkable except a long and tiresome and dirty walk. On entering we met a horse which was said to have been an old race horse named "Steel." We walked on around the track which was very level and raked the last night since the races on the day before. The course was in the form of an ellipse, the center being cultivated in corn, the stalks still standing. The first house we arrived at was what is called the Gambling House, where there was the bar room, and the numerous modes of losing money arranged around the room to suit every man's taste, or so that no man could go home with any money in his pocket with an excuse. Around all but one of which, by the way, was chuck-a-luck man, was a crowd of men betting and looking, the roulette rolling, pharo-pharo dealers, etc. I spent about an hour here with some interest, watching the emotions evinced by the winners and losers.

Nor did Patterson partake in the common practice of drinking too much (October 24, 1846).

Last night I went up town to an oyster supper treated by Fresh. [Robert] Henry and when there I witnessed a most pitiful spectacle. A young man of my class, very young, drunk. Alas, for the manners of the age. I cannot record all that I saw then; two [*sic*] revolting. May I never be the victim of pride of alcohol.

Pres. Robert Barnwell, reporting to trustees in May 1841, saw no cure for the excesses of students.

We have still too much idleness, too much disorder and too much vice, but as these are not new evils, and I confess myself unable to suggest any sufficient remedy for them, we must continue to lament and strive to mitigate them.

The lamentation continued in Pres. Robert Henry's report of May 7, 1845.

For a few nights we have been greatly annoyed by the riding of horses and blowing of horns, between the conclusion of the hours of study and usual time of retiring to rest. I am happy to say, that these disorders continued for no great length of time and seem to have been indulged in more in sport and from embrace of animal spirits than from any set design to invade the order and quiet of the institution. Some instances of intoxication have also occurred and whenever detected, have been punished with suspension for a longer or shorter period, according to the degree of intent manifested and the publick scandal arising out of it.

Nights on the town, however, inspired student poet James R. Chalmers of Mississippi, Class of 1851, to provide his classmates with their favorite drinking song about their favorite drinking spot run by Billy Maybin in the Congaree Hotel.

Billy Maybin's Oh!

Come, doff your gowns, good fellows, don't put your
    coats on slow,

For a drinking at old Billy's we are ready for to go;
Above he serves good suppers, good liquors down below,
And many a time we've had a spree at Billy Maybin's, O!
Though we love all wholesome fellows and approve of
    drowning cares,
Don't forget still to be moderate and think of morning
    prayers,
Lest when the bell is chiming to matins for to go,
You should think 'twas clanking of the plates at Billy
    Maybin's, O!
Next Monday morning surely old Sheriff comes around,
And you're up before the faculty for going up the town,
"Did you go into an eating house?" "Did you take a
    drink or no?"
Oh, yes, sirs; took a drink or two at Billy Maybin's O!

Not all singing was by boys in bars; sometimes a duet constituted a date— even for the straitlaced William McIver (May 24, 1836).

I have never seen a young lady with whom I was so much pleased as with Miss H. She is not one to strike with admiration at first sight, but as your acquaintance increases, so does your esteem. She has not that beauty which exists in the imagination and is seen in the productions of painters and sculptors, but her features glow with that light of the soul which the skills of the pencil cannot portray. . . . She plays admirably well the guitar and pianoforte. I accompanied her by singing the second. In this way I employed hours of pleasure.

Writing to his brother on October 24, 1851, Nathan Whetstone revealed perhaps a more typical student's point of view.

Everytime a speech is delivered at the college at night, there is no recitation the next day. . . . But I am sorry to say that I did not attend [Dr. James H. Thornwell's temperance speech] last night as there was a circus in town. I went to that. . . .

I'm corresponding with only one lady at present. Who is Miss S. Smith. She writes a very good & neat letter. It seems you visit the young ladies there very frequently, which is very good. This place does not suit me as well as Old Cokesbury as regards ladies.

John O. Rigby, writing from Orangeburg April 17, 1849, to his "Dear friend" at South Carolina College, offered some questionable social advice in a gradually deteriorating style.

It is with the utmost pleasure, that I now occupy my seat, to answer your kind and affectionate Epistle, which came to hand some few days previous. . . . You wrote to me that you had not been out to visit the ladies. I hope you have gone out amongst them before now for you could not do a better thing than to visit the Ladies in that. It is the very place to learn the manners of young ladies. You need not be ashamed of them for fear of being a little green; for you do not expect to marry them no how. Go out and visit them and I do not think you will ever regret it. You said that you expected me most married not so yet I am grown coal [*sic*] in love with the ladies, for some time prior. As soon as I find one now to suit me I think I will court her. If I go to get married I will send you a letter. . . .

The common punishment for misbehavior was suspension. Writing to Pres. William C. Preston from Winnsboro on February 19, 1848, Robert E. Johnston, a sophomore, begged for readmission.

As it is my own wish and that of my Father that I should return to College, I deem an apology due the Faculty and yourself as President. My misconduct was the result of thoughtlessness rather than disrespect of the laws of the College and I hereby show my regret for it and a promise that should I be again received as a student to be circumspect in my conduct and to abide strictly by the regulations of the college.

Robert's father, Sam Johnston, wrote to the College president as well, March 13, 1848.

Your kind favour of the 19th bringing three charges against my son Robert, came duly to hand. I was then so ill and confined to bed that I did not read your letter for some days afterward. As to Robert's youth, I claim no indulgence for him on that score. If he was prepared to enter college he must be bound to conform to the bye laws and regulations of the college as much so as those of riper years, or not be there. I think, and I do hope, that if yourself and the faculty of the college, think proper to receive him and reinstate him in his class, that he will see the error of his ways and in future give you no troubles.

But Robert seems not to have been reinstated.

Visiting dignitaries provided occasions for somewhat more sedate socializing, as well as much-loved "fire balls." Occasionally the guests disappointed their audiences, as Giles Patterson revealed in his account of Daniel Webster's May 13, 1847, visit.

Webster on his tour through the South arrived here yesterday evening. His arrival was celebrated by a party at the President's house, the Senior Class alone of the students being invited, by music in abundance in the campus by the German band, but their sweet notes were often drowned in the most discordant sounds of the pestiferous horns in the hands of Fresh. A general illumination throughout college together with lighted stands in the campus and fire balls thrown by the students presented a magnificent spectacle. I should add also the torch light procession which had the effect to bring Webster in the campus and ultimately extracted a short speech from him. The speech was merely a get-off for if I did not look on it as such I should be forced to call it a perfect failure.

In a letter dated February 2, 1860, Charles Hutson described another night on the town laced with speeches.

Last night we went up to the Congaree House and serenaded [U.S. representative Lawrence M.] Keitt [a former student at the college], who gave us a very fine speech not in the least political, but relating almost entirely to the College, and full of rich classical allusions. I'm inclined to think 'twas not entirely extemporaneous. He spoke a good deal against turning the College into a University. We came back, and serenaded old Mc [Pres. Charles F. McCay], who told us that the Trustees had forbidden him to give us extra holidays on such occasions. Upon which we marched in front of his house in a groaning procession, the music playing a dead march. Afterwards we danced a grand "College reel" in front of the Chapel and took exercise if we did nothing else.

STUDENTS BEING STUDENTS: FOR BETTER AND WORSE

It could be argued that South Carolina College students have not changed—they have just expanded their repertoire of vices. Breaking or stealing the College bell became popular since, according to College regulations, only if the bell were rung could students be summoned to classes—and they enjoyed insisting on the letter of the law.

The Standing Committee beg leave to report,

That sometime in February last, an insurrection broke out among the students in the college, a number of whom proceeded to attack the houses of one of the professors and one of the tutors, demolished the windows; took down the College bell and broke it to pieces; and committed other outrages, with great disrespect to the faculty and some of the trustees who were present. The outrages were so violent, and the families of the faculty were so terrified that application to the civil authority was deemed necessary, and the intendant of the town, took such measures in concert with the faculty and Trustees, as restored order, and submission. A number of the students who appeared to be the most active ringleaders were suspended by the faculty whose cases wait against several of the young men. The trials were however postponed, that the Board might consider what was proper to be done in the business.

The Bell having been broken it is necessary that a new one should be provided, or the exercises of the College are conducted irregularly for want of a bell.

The Committee submit to the Board the propriety of making some additional regulations for the enforcement of better discipline of the college.

Henry DeSaussure
Chairman of Standing Committee
April 27,1814

Pres. Thomas Cooper, outspoken proponent of free trade and atheism, seemed to inspire students to especially riotous behavior. His letter of February 14, 1822, to Thomas Jefferson revealed both his frustration and their favorite tricks.

Dear Sir

I send you the history of a College rebellion (an annual case here) which may be put by among the memoirs pour servir a l'histoire du gouvernement academique; facts that furnish some useful conclusions. You are to consider as true in addition the following facts: viz That the Professors have never been absent from a single recitation, so far as I know, since I have been at this College. That the students are repeatedly invited & requested to apply to any of the Professors at any time for a repetition of instructions, or a solution of difficulties in the course of their Studies. . . .

The Senior Class have adopted as their guiding system of morality, that they are under no obligation to obey the Laws of the College, but merely to abide by the punishment inflicted on disobedience if they should be discovered.

Every student in College, holds himself bound to conceal any offense against the Laws of the Land as well as the Laws of the College: the robbing of hen roosts, the nightly prowling about to steal Turkies from all the houses in the neighbourhood are constant practices, among a set of young men who would never forgive you, if you doubted their honor, altho' I know this form of declaration is little else than an insolent cover for falsehood among many of them.

After consenting to refer the dispute to the Trustees convened by the Governor, they were guilty the next night of every outrage that they had the power to commit. The Professors were threatened, pistols were snapt at them, guns fired near them. Co. John Taylor (formerly of the Senate from this place) was in company with myself burnt in effigy; the windows of my bedroom have been repeatedly shattered at various hours of the night, & guns fired under my window. If we were to ask any young man, who did so, he would feel insulted at the question, and deem his honour injured by being asked if he knew the perpetrator of a crime, altho' he stood near the offender at the time.

Of the junior class we have suspended about 20, and reported for expulsion 4 or 5 others. The senior class, at present knowing our full determination not to give way, are very regular now & probably will continue so.

No professor of any reputation will stay at an institution where their authority is to be disputed inch by inch, and their lives put in jeopardy if they resist the encroachments of a hot headed set of boys, whom no kindness can conciliate, and who regard all exertions made to promote their improvement as mere matters of duty for which no thanks are due. Some of the very young men to whom last year I gave a daily lecture more than I was bound to give —who were incited and tempted to attend that lecture as an extra duty— to whom I continue to give instruction to the last day of their remaining in College, stole my horse out of the stable shaved its tail & mane, and rode it about in the night till it was nearly exhausted. I found them out & forgave them, but it produced no amelioration in some of their accomplices who remained, and are now suspended.

Dr. [Timothy] Dwight [president of Yale College] prophesyed that no collegiate institution could be permanent south of Potowmack. In my own opinion the parental indulgence of the South, renders young men less fit for college government than the habits of the northern people; and the rigid discipline of the northern seminaries must be put in force inexorably in the South, or the youth who are sent for instruction, will permit their teacher to give it them, only when the student condescends to be taught.
. . .

One of the most fiery of President Cooper's many confrontations was with John S. Palmer, a student from a lowcountry plantation family who wrote his mother all about his blameless behavior (May 7, 1822).

Dear mother,

Let me hasten to communicate to you a circumstance which though it has terminated happily was nevertheless disagreeable. A few nights ago a ball was given from which a few of the students returned not altogether sober and as usual with cake and candy. By then, I who had remained at home and awaited their return was invited to partake of the cake. During this time a great noise was made by some who were most intoxicated which caused the faculty (or to be more particular Dr. Cooper and Mr. [Lardner] Vanuxem) to come up. When it was discovered that they were coming, some of the company present proposed holding them off by opposition. This was agreed to but they all except two ran off and concealed themselves, but in the meantime Dr. Cooper and Mr. Vanuxem approached the head of the stairs where was a cot drawn to prevent their access. By the side of this cot stood one (who shall be nameless for the present) holding a chair in an attitude of threat and defiance to the faculty. Opposed as I was in fact to keeping the faculty off by violent measures, still seeing the eminent danger in which this young man was situated in opposing the officers of a college, I ran up, placing myself immediately behind him determined to keep them at a stand, not however by injuring their persons, but rather by means of the cot over which they could not have advanced if held fast. Observing however that we were exceeded in strength and that they were likely to be struck down by the chair, I advised the young man for God's sake not to be too rash and to retire to the room, which we did and with another person. Once there I attempted to keep them out by holding the door, but before we could have time to exert our strength they burst in upon us. I was asked my name by Mr. Vanuxem and refused to give it thinking I might escape unnoticed. Upon this he asked the other person what was his name. He replied that he was a citizen. Dr. Cooper then advanced and in a great rage inquired of me my name. Upon telling him I did not wish to give it he struck me with his cane. There, my dear mother, I could scarce restrain myself so far as to keep from knocking him down, but regarding his gray hairs I instantly demanded his motive for attacking my person. He abused me with language that would have disgraced a jockey and said he had his brains almost knocked out and again asked my name. By this time my blood was warm and retiring a few paces back, positively refused to give it. Upon this seizing me with the assistance of Mr. Vanuxem they forcibly carried me into the antechamber where the latter discovered my name. Never had my feelings been so severely wounded, struck and then abused without the means of redress and on the verge of being suspended or expelled. Then, I must inform you Dr. Cooper acted under the impression that I had thrown the chair at them, but they were much mistaken as they have since been convinced.

On the morning following the night above mentioned circumstances transpired, I called on the faculty individually and stated my case to them and requested an immediate trial which they granted me. Accordingly at 9 o'clock Saturday 4th I was called before their honorable body who after having heard Dr. Cooper's compared it with mine and unanimously agreed in acquitting me of the charge of throwing the chair at Dr. Cooper and Mr. Vanuxem but entered into a resolution (which they have revoked) that for refusing to give my name to the faculty when so ordered, and for being uncooperative to be suspended until December next. They told me that if I had anything to offer in extenuation of the offense which they were inclined to think was not premeditated I might do so, and that they were glad to have it in their power to restore me. Accordingly, the students drew up a petition requesting that as my deportment had been previously good the faculty should revoke their severe decree. I myself addressed a letter to them, the contents of which was sent to them at ten o'clock this morning. The faculty convened and after some consideration annulled their resolution, and I was happily restored. I have demanded satisfaction of Dr. Cooper for striking me, but he refused to give any. I threatened to prosecute him for damages and also to carry him before the trustees. Satisfaction of some kind I must have.

Sometimes students rioted about attending classes. When chemistry professor R. T. Brumby, who had been out sick, asked the juniors to attend make-up sessions, they refused. Pres. William C. Preston recounted the students' reactions on the night of April 10, 1850.

We had hardly adjourned, before I saw unequivocal indications of an approaching commotion. At twilight noise began to arise in the Campus, and large groups to be formed before the Professors' houses. In a short time the mob increased to a multitude. Shouts and riotous yells were heard; and as darkness closed, a bright flame arose from the midst of the crowd. Upon hastening to the spot with some of the Professors, I witnessed a scene of confusion, uproar and turbulence, beyond what I had ever seen. . . . The whole college apparently was assembled—one boy brandishing a sword, but with no indication of murderous intent—though its flashing in the light of the blazing fire looked fearful enough. The fire was consuming a table covered with a pile of books—the chemical Text Books, which the members of the Junior class had devoted as a solemn sacrifice to the flames.

Brumby was nicknamed "Old Fossil" by the student poet of South Carolina College, James R. Chalmers, who wrote a song about the incident.

> Come white folks listen to me a story I'll relate
> Which happened in the valley of the old Carolina State

At South Carolina College Old Fossil he did say
That the Junior Class should go to him on Dr. Thorn-
    well's day.
Old Fossil he said go, but it was no use you know
The Junior Class swore at last:
Be damned if they would go.

A source of much contention, sometimes sparking collective student rebellion, complaints about food began as early as 1806—and haven't stopped since. Cornelius K. Ayer wrote to his brother in Barnwell, May 15, 1819.

Tell father that the food in the stewards hall has been so very bad that I have been forced by hunger to go outside to get something to eat else-where. I have got an account of about 5 or 6 dollars for eating, now it will be 10 or 12 before I leave here, and that I would be very glad that when he sends for me he would send the money to pay for it. I shall also have some washing to pay for.

The "Great Biscuit Rebellion" in 1852 resulted in the suspension of 108 students so that only eleven students graduated in 1853—just before the trustees abolished the compulsory system. Once a food fight escalated into a duel—described by Dr. J. Marion Sims, Class of 1832.

I lived in the age of duelling. I was educated to believe that duels inspired the proprieties of society and protected the honor of women. I have hardly a doubt that, while I was a student in the South Carolina Col-lege, if anything had happened to make it necessary for me to fight a duel, I would have gone out with the utmost coolness and allowed myself to be shot down. But my views on that subject were entirely changed, a long, long time ago.

There was a real duel in the South Carolina College just after I grad-uated. It was between [A. Govan] Roach, of Colleton, and [James G.] Adams, of Richland. Roach was a young man about six feet high and a physical beauty. Adams was no less so though not so tall. Both men were of fine families, and Adams was supposed to be a young man of talent and promise. It occurred in this way: They were very intimate friends; they sat opposite to each other in the Steward's Hall at table. When the bell rang and the door was opened, the students rushed in, and it was considered a matter of honor, when a man got hold of a dish of butter or bread or any other dish, it was his. Unfortunately, Roach and Adams sat opposite each other, and both caught hold of a dish of trout at the same moment. Adams did not let go; Roach held on to the dish. Presently Roach let go of the dish and glared fiercely in Adams's face, and said: "Sir, I will see you after supper." They sat there all through the supper, both looking like mad bulls. Roach left the supper-room first, and Adams followed him. Roach waited outside the door for Adams. There were no hard words and no fisticuffs—all was dignity and solemnity. "Sir," said Roach, "What can I do to insult you?" Adams replied, "This is enough, sir, and you will hear from me." Adams went immediately to his room and sent a challenge to Roach. It was promptly accepted, and each went up town and selected seconds and advisers. And now comes the strange part of this whole affair: No less a person than General Pierce M. Butler, distinguished in the Mexican War as colonel of the Palmetto regiment, and who became governor of South Carolina, agreed to act as second to one of these young men. The other had as his adviser Mr. D. J. McCord, a distinguished lawyer, a most eminent citizen, a man of great talents, whose name lives in the judicial records of the state as being the author of McCord and Nott's reports. Here were two of the most prominent citizens of South Carolina, each of them about forty years of age, aiding and abetting duelling between two young men, neither of them over twenty years of age.

They fought at Lightwood Knot Springs, ten miles from Columbia. They were both men of the coolest courage. . . . They were to fight at ten paces. They were to fire at the word "one," raising their pistols. . . . When the word "Fire" was given, each started to raise his pistol; but each had on a frock-coat, and the flap of Roach's coat caught on his arm, and prevented his pistol from rising. When Adams saw that, he lowered his pistol to the ground. The word was then given a second time: "Are you ready? Fire! One!" They both shot simultaneously.

Both were wounded, Adams mortally; Roach recovered after a long time.

William DeSaussure, a faculty member, wrote to his grandson, William Boykin, on February 24, 1856, about a "town v. gown" riot.

Tell your father we have had a very exciting affair in the College. The Students fell into dispute with the City police, and there were cracked crowns and bloody faces on both sides. But when at the market place two lines, citizens on one side, and Students on the other, armed with guns and bayonets, and frantic with rage stood face to face within 35 feet of each other, the peril of a fatal termination was imminent. We got the Students off to the College Chapel, where they were addressed by Mr. [James H.] Thornwell, Col. Wm Preston, and Col. Maxcy Gregg and myself—and we succeeded at last in quieting them.

The storm is not yet quite over; there is a heavy ground swell, and I shall not be surprised if a large number of students leave the College.

SEND MONEY. . . . SEND CLOTHES. . . . SEND ME HOME!

Material comforts were in very short supply for nineteenth-century college students. Among the hardships was a trio of ongoing concerns: limited money, limited wardrobes, and limited transportation. Even when students and their parents managed to scrape together tuition money, they often could not purchase books, clothes, or meals off campus. Few went home—even when home was no farther than Newberry or Florence—except during the longest winter and summer breaks, for lack of a horse to ride or fare to pay a stagecoach. Letters home often included subtle and not-so-subtle appeals to parents and other relatives concerning these and other needs.

William Bull of Charleston, Class of 1810, shared a tale of woe with his mother in a letter of November 2, 1808.

I am almost bare of shirts and unless I can get some soon I shall be something like the soldiers in the American [Continental] Army who had only sleeves and collars for shirts.

A year later William Bull reported to his mother that he was working out his own budget (September 15, 1809).

I had some idea of keeping my horse here in order to ride out sometimes, as I can get him kept for about 5$. But as I sacrifice my time here for the acquirement of literature, it is proper that I should use every means of obtaining it. I have therefore formed a plan for going through Colledge by only keeping school until January twelve months, and by the utmost stinting and parsimony to save money enough to carry me through the senior year. For the way I go on now I do now enjoy more than half the advantages of Colledge. In order to put this plan into execution I will leave no stone unturned. I am sensible of spending and where the moderate expenditure of a student is thought to be about $500 per year. I must beg you to carry my horse down with you and sell him if you can do it to advantage and apply the money to your own use. If you cannot get $150 for him, keep him for me, as he is a most valuable horse.

. . . I must beg you also to have as much fine homespun made for me as possible at home for winter clothes, mixed with wool as I must wear nothing else. The bed and bedding you promise to send I will want about the 1st of December. Send the price of each article that I may remit you the money for them. Also a flute and musick book if you can get anybody to choose one for you. I hope you will not be angry when I tell you that I cannot accept any present for which you have to pay the money.

Cornelius K. Ayer appealed to his father, Lewis M. Ayer, in Barnwell, S.C., March 3, 1819.

This is the first time that I have attempted to wright to you, but I have wrote to Brother and Sister and have not received any answer from them yet. I am in hopes you will wright the first opportunity. I have been here four months and have never herd from any of you yet, but I am determined to continue wrighting until I do get the answer. The principal reason of my wrighting at this time is, that I am out of mony and I shall have to pay for my tuition shortly and I have not the mony. I was forced to draw the money you left, little sooner than you told me. I had to get some Books which I could not do without, I have paid the steward and for my washing, and that took all the mony that was left. You must know that no one can live here, unless he has someone to weight on him, such as cut wood make fires, and bring water, and unless I get some money in a short time I shall loose him, and he is a boy who I can put confidence in, and If I loose him I shall not get one half so good. I expect when I come home you will say that I have been very extravagant, but I have got me a book and I have sat down every article for which I have spent my money for, it is well for every man to take care of what he has, therefore I have nothing to say against your stinting me, but when you know that the money is not spent foolishly nor carelessly I think you might afford me a little more, than you would if I had spent it foolishly. I am not of the opinion that a man should allow his son as much as he thinks proper to spend, for it just ruins them at once. There are some here whose Fathers do it and they will never learn anything as long as they stay here. They get into all kinds of vice and folly. They think of nothing else but drinking and eating, whereas if they had not this priviledge allowed them they would make smart men. All I want is enough to appear deasent and if I should want any little thing, I can get it. I am in hopes that when I receive an answer that I will get some. You will have to send the money for my tuition by the 2nd of April. I have enjoyed my health very well since I have been here and hope to continue to be so. There are some things which I have great nead of and cannot go on with any ease until I get them. These are the clasical Dictionary an ancient map and a larger Atlas they will cost about 25 or 30 Dollars. These I cannot do well without. Give my complements to Brother Jack and Sister and tell them that I do not intend to wright to them any more, until they wright to me, and also to Brother

Henry. Those I have wrighten to and the other I have not. This I am in hopes will find you all enjoy your perfect health. Wright to me the first opportunity. I have no more but remain your most Obt. and fathful Son

John S. Palmer, a junior from Pineville, alerted his half-brother, Thomas Palmer, to his needs on April 12, 1822.

If it be possible do transmit me as soon as possible 100 dollars as my tuition and steward's bill are not yet discharged. I well know how disagreeable these applications for money are but hope that as I have had but $260.00 yet this session, less than ever before, my request be not deemed altogether unreasonable. Remember me to the family.

Later that year he enumerated his expenditures to his mother (May 1, 1822).

You wish a statement of the monies I have received at different times this year. In October I brought with me 150 dollars. Brother gave me 10 dollars during the session of the legislature. Mr. W[hite] forwarded me 100 dollars on January 25th and 100 dollars on April 12th, making in all received 360 dollars. I shall want in June 100 more dollars which together with what I've already received will be 460 dollars for this year's expenses, exclusive of what I shall want in the vacation if I remain here. But since I have been informed of Brother's [Thomas's] low state of health and S[am]'s [a younger brother] illness and also that I must omit for awhile the study of medicine my desire of remaining here has in a great measure cooled and hope that if Brother's health be no better to be allowed to spend the summer in Pineville. You ask what sum will be necessary for my expense in a vacation spent in Columbia. To the best of my knowledge 80 dollars will be the least that it can be done with.

Palmer wrote from college to his mother on June 3, 1822, to describe the hardships of returning from Charleston to Columbia.

I left Charleston a few hours after you did and at the expected time arrived safely in Columbia, though not without having passed some of the worst roads I ever traveled. We swam three different times in the Edisto Swamp and the bridge at Murray's was in such a dangerous condition that the morning after we crossed it the whole fell in. This we looked on as almost a miraculous escape as it creaked and tottered as we passed it the evening previous. On arriving here I discovered that the class had advanced but little and for that reason did not regret the visit occasioned by the late truly melancholy event.

William Charles, of Charleston, warned his mother in Morristown, N.J., of steep expenses in a March 1, 1823, letter.

You requested me to tell you what my expenses here were. I pay three dollars and a half per week [for board] and forty dollars a year for tuition. Besides this I pay fifty cents a dozen of washing. It is a very expensive place.

. . . You told me to avoid the company of the rich, but the fellows here are upon such an equality that I cannot tell the rich from the poor. You must not be afraid of my becoming dissipated. . . . Riches go a great way with some people, though not with me. I sometimes wish that I was rich that I might get married young, for I expect to marry a poor girl, but when I reflect how much many are worse off than I am, I am content.

John Charles made his appeal for family funds to his brother, Edgar, in Darlington, S.C., February 19, 1826.

I have now a request of a different nature to make you. It is that you will remit me as soon as you receive this some money. We received notice from Professor [James] Wallace the other day that on the 1st March we must pay our board and tuition up to the 1st October. As I have not heretofore been punctual, I should like if convenient to you to be able to be this time.

The condition of students' wardrobes and wallets changed little by 1837, when William McIver wrote to his mother in Darlington (April 20).

When I put on my new shirt I found no buttons on the sleeves. However, I cut two off the night shirts Aunt M. gave me and sewed them on.

I have supplied myself with summer clothing. I have bought four pair of stockings, two pair of pantaloons and two other. I would like to have several shirts made expressly for summer. I believe the fashion is to cut the collars lower—i.e., narrower—and sew them on the shirt. The collars are very pointed and the sharp ends are intended to turn over the collar and be worn with a ribbon. I will look for a reply to this next week.

Clothes from home often came with ample advice from mother on how to wear them and how to care for them, as in this letter to James Blanding from his mother in Charleston, June 7, 1839.

I send you two pair drawers cut by your pattern, one nice vest, 6 pair stockings, three collars, two cravats, worn by all the young men in town. I send you also a frock coat, made by Rea from your pattern. It is a common morning article. I will send you another vest by Will, but the style here is not to wear vests except on Sunday, and button up the frock coat. Don't give away your clothes to the negroes. I call losing them giving them away. Never leave your room without locking up all your clothes—and especially at the springs [Limestone Springs, where James would spend summer break] where there are 100 strange negroes.

I have sewed up your clothes in two yards of linen. Now I wish you to do exactly as I direct with your winter clothes. The moths will cut them all to pieces ere you see them in the fall unless you are very particular. Just take a tie of tobacco leaf, which will cost you 25 cents, and sun your clothes first and then intersperse the leaves through all your clothes, but dry the leaves in the sun first for 2 hours or it will color your clothes, and then sew them up in the linen. Write your name on it and beg Aunt Sarah or Mrs. Green to put them away for you. I would do this immediately, as they are in your way and you will be very likely to have them stolen.

THE RELIGIOUS LIFE

The spiritual realm was an important element of life at South Carolina College. Many pious students spent a great deal of time in church, in solitary Bible study, or in religious discussion groups, some intending to put their college education to use as members of the clergy. Even the less devout young men were required to attend the chapel services every morning.

When Cornelius K. Ayer wrote to his brother on May 15, 1819, he had clearly mastered the spirit of many sermons, if not the letter.

I have something in my mind which I cannot refrain from expressing, it is this, than [sic] when I was at home, I asked something about you, and they told me more than I ever hear before or ever wish to hear again. I never was so much supprized in all my life. I thought shurely you had quit all your vicious practices, and was indeavouring to wipe the stain which was stampt on your character before, but you still continue to make it blacker and blacker, and I am sorry to say that you are ruined for ever to eternity; if Jupeter and all the Gods were to combine they never could restore you that character you once enjoyed. The time you have spent in drinking and frollicking will never return. . . . The mispense of ever minute is a new record against us in heaven. Let us then indeavour to spend the time present in such a manner that we may look back on it with satisfaction, then may we look forward to that great day, when at the dread Tribunal, we are to deliver up an account of all things committed to our care, when we may say, "O Lord of the hours thou hast granted unto me, have I lost none."

Mississippi native James R. Chalmer, Class of 1851, penned a poetic reminder of the daily call to prayer.

Morning Hour

'Tis morning hour, the sun shines bright,
The dew drops blaze beneath his ray,
The twinkling stars their faded light
Have melted into day.
Then sleep no more but upward bound
However much you long to stay;
The Chapel Bell with tinkling sound
Is calling us to pray.
'Tis morning hour, from room to room
The wakeful fellows grumbling roar—
Oh, do get up my sleepy chum,
Ere Jim shall close the door.
Then sleep no more but upward bound
However much you long to stay;
The Chapel Bell with tinkling sound,
Is calling us to pray.

William McIver of Darlington, Class of 1837, exemplified the outer reaches of devotion to religious activity in a letter to his father, April 2, 1836.

I've agreed with a young man named [George M.] Bates from New-berry, a member of the Lutheran church, to go out every Wednesday and Friday evenings and pray together for ourselves and the students. I cannot but hope for a revival [of religious sentiment]. . . . The Tuesday night prayer meeting was well attended last meeting and I hope some good will be done. A young man from the Presbyterian Seminary proposed to Brother Holmes, Cousin A[llen] and myself to try and establish a Bible class of the students to be held every Sunday morning at the Baptist Lecture Room. I've drawn up a subscription list and will try to get as many as I can to join.

McIver continued in a similar vein to his father on November 14, 1836.

I have never received so much comfort to my soul from any of your let-ters, as from the last. Had you been here, and attended me as my shadow, you could not have known my real state more exactly and truly than you did. For the first time an overpowering sense of the goodness of God burst into my soul, in giving me pious parents. I wept when I read that daily I was the subject of your prayers. Never did my heart glow with more ardent affection for my dear parents. I trust that God has forgiven me for sinning against him in that I have caused my kind, beloved parents any pain. I have begun to see the cause of my spiritual desertion. I feel that it was the result of too much conformity to the manner and habits of the students. I trust that God has led me back by his good spirit into the path of duty. Whilst reading the journals of the men of God, I felt fully the missionary spirit animating me to devote my life to the cause of God in efforts for the conversion of the heathen.

I promised the colored members of our church here to continue the Wednesday night prayer meeting on my return this session, but I will not have time to do so until after our examinations.

In 1837 young McIver continued (February 26).

My mind devotes to study, or rather reading, from morn to midnight. I fear becoming careless of the thing respecting religion. The increasing pleasure I find in literary pursuits causes me to give them my almost exclusive attention. Although I daily read the word of God, yet it is at such a time as is least calculated to find me prepared to receive the Sacred Truths and treasure them up.

I have endeavored to analyze my feelings in regard to the ministry to see if the impressions of which I formerly spoke were of a nature which would justify my becoming a preacher. I firmly believe that they were of a sort common to almost every Christian. In times of religious excitement, whether revival of religion in a church or the state of feeling produced by reading powerful affects to the heart, such as those of our East Indian Missionaries, the tone of mind thought about in every Christian must create a desire to become the herald of salvation. I know not but what I may be called to this office in future life I shall be found ready and willing.

Students who failed to take adequate comfort in religious endeavors were likely to be admonished by pious parents. Sarah Charles, with three sons from Darlington at South Carolina College, wrote during a stay in Morristown, N.J., to Hopkins Charles, February 7, 1826.

By all that I can find out religion seems to be no part of your concern in Darlington and much less at Columbia, by having nothing to do but attend balls and orations. But I believe there are serious characters in every College as some go there to prepare for preachers, but some of them had better never preach at all. Let me know how often you hear a sermon and whether you have any religious books to read besides the Bible.

Take care you do not resist the Holy Spirit once too often so that it will take its everlasting flight. Oh what a dreadful thing that would be. You have no reason to expect long life but with great abstinence you may attain middle age. But your constitution seems broke now so you must take care, especially in March. You have all got poor constitutions and ought not to frolic away the few days you have to live. If your brother Edgar had given that money to the poor that he paid for learning you to dance it would do him better. . . .

COLLEGE IN THE TIME OF SMALLPOX

Surviving college meant much more than progression to graduation. Disease and death were very real threats as smallpox, pneumonia, dysentery, scarlet fever, and a wide variety of unspecified illnesses claimed young lives on campus and caused great alarm among those remaining. Students also suffered from frequent colds and infections, perhaps related to weather or sanitation, and they received news of illness and death among family members with disturbing regularity.

William McIver wrote to his mother in Society Hill, May 21, 1836.

I could scarcely believe my eyes when I read of the death of Smiley Gregg. Hawes tells me that he had been troubled with several attacks of cramps in the stomach during the summer. It is an awful lesson to all to see a youth snatched away by death's resistless hand, the more so where that one is unprepared, as I much fear Smiley was. I am afraid that my dear little sister has some consuming disease. God grant that it may be otherwise. . . .

I mentioned in my note that I had a few days before its date a rheumatic affliction in my shoulder. My distress has lasted long. Yesterday was a rainy day and the pain in my side returned with considerable violence. Fearful that going out would increase it and bring it on my shoulder, I remained at home. The weather being fair today, I feel it but slightly.

Charles Woodward Hutson recalled in his memoirs of antebellum student days a close brush with fatal disease.

My roommate [and cousin], Charley J. Hutson [Charles Jones Colcock Hutson], took the scarlet fever. I nursed him through it but did not take it. When he went home, however, his elder brother, Richard Woodward Hutson, rubbing him during the scaling-off period, took it from him, and, alas, died that summer to the great grief of us all.

William Whetstone sent disturbing news to his mother in Kershaw, May 23, 1854.

It is very sickly now in Columbia, the number of deaths this week being about 11 or 12. The disease being principally Dysentery or Diarrhea. I had myself a very severe attack of dysentery, but am glad that I got over it without any difficulty. It appears that dysentery is prevailing all over the country. It was that that Miss Mitchell died with. I never have known it to be so serious before in my life. The Doctors have a plenty to do now, and indeed, I have as much as I care about doing. The School at Barhamville where Miss Mitchell died is broken up altogether. I mentioned in my last letter that Uncle Jerry had come up and he [was] taken very sick that night while here, but got over it soon.

. . . This is the evening for the great eclipse of the sun. It has not come on yet, but I am expecting it every minute. I mentioned something about the sickness of Columbia. It is very sickly indeed. I hear there have been 4 deaths today. I would like very much to come home awhile, but the expense is so great to come on the stage, and as I want to come home 3 weeks in July, I think I will put it off till then, for if I would come now, I would want to come again in July anyhow. Though if I had a chance to come now without coming on the stage, I should be certain to come, and come in July also. But it is very uncertain about my coming now, as I don't think I will have a chance. . . .

As ever, your most affectionate, Love till death.

For faculty and administrators, outbreaks of disease were threats not only to young lives but also to the survival of the College. Pres. Robert Henry reported this concern in a report to the trustees during an outbreak of fatal illnesses in 1843, but he managed to take some comfort in the good student discipline and improved student-faculty relations caused by their collective nervousness.

Since our last annual meeting, the College, notwithstanding some untoward circumstances, arising out of a prevalence of sickness and consequent mortality among the students, has continued to exhibit increased evidences of good order and devotion to study. Owing to the existence of measles, with a marked deterioration to the lungs, joined in some cases by small pox known to have appeared in the neighbourhood, the students began to exhibit a good deal of anxiety for their situation in the latter part of February. Several applications for permission to return home, evidently arising out of alarm, were refused by me. I thought it, however, of great importance to appoint at once a committee of the faculty to confer with physicians of the town and report as soon as practicable concerning any real ground of apprehension. The committee having reported unanimously that after careful inquiry in every quarter from which they could expect to derive information, they believed no real cause of alarm existed, the result was immediately communicated to the college and produced the desired effect of restoring tranquility. The apprehension of contagious disease had hardly subdued when a form of diarrhea made its appearance and, in some instances was obstinate and severe in its type.

The Marshal was instructed to give the most vigilant attention to the state of the apartments and to secure cleanliness in them and throughout the premises, by every means in his power. Notwithstanding every precaution, another death occurred and was immediately followed by a petition on the part of the students for the dismissal of the College. The Faculty, feeling that they had no proper authority in the matter, agreed to refer it to the Board of Trustees.

In a few weeks, however, to the great consternation both of Faculty and Students, another case of mortality occurred. In this exigency, when the alarm of the students had almost assumed the form of panick and in the absence of the Trustees, the Faculty became thoroughly convinced that a restoration to the comforts of home and the benefits of domestick supervision was the only method which would be entirely effectual in arresting the baseness of disease. To a renewed petition of adjournment of the College, they therefore thought it their duty to accede, without further delay. Since the return of the Students in October, another death has taken place among them. The number of deaths in all has been four, comprising in every case those who stood high for their character and attainments.

In the midst of these afflicting scenes, which it has been my painful duty to detail, a source of great consolation has been found in the increased mutual attachment which has grown up between the Professors and the Students. Indeed I have never known the conduct of the Students more exemplary than it has been for the last year.

Pres. William Howard Taft speaks from the steps of the old President's House during a campus visit, 1909.

The Class of 1900 during their junior year. Laura Kershaw Perry (center) was the third woman to graduate from USC.

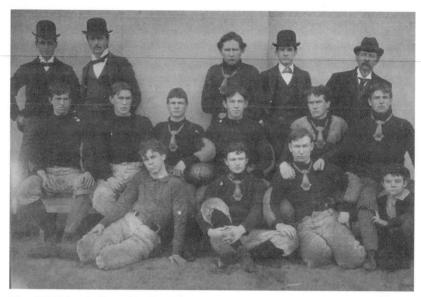

The USC football team of 1896

The student engineering club, 1900

The USC baseball team of 1896

The Coed Follies of 1927

A student instrumental group, 1906

The Darlington County club, 1911

In 1911, without in-dormitory plumbing, students drew well water for their rooms.

Student artists on the Horseshoe in 1935

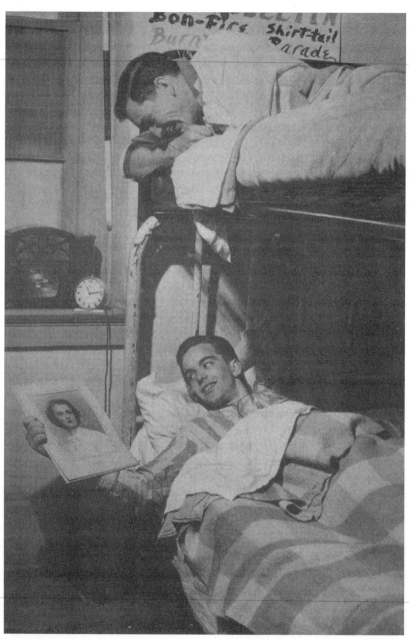

1942 dormitory scene

In the chemistry laboratory, 1943

The competition never dies.

In 1944 ROTC was a large and welcome presence on campus.

Wartime socializing, 1945

2

Students in Battle

THE CIVIL WAR AND ITS AFTERMATH

Secession, war and reconstruction defined the context for perhaps the most remarkable period in the existence of the University—approximately from 1861 through 1877. The students, most of whom joined a student-initiated cadet company, welcomed the possibility of battle in service to the Confederacy. In 1862, when students laid down their books and took up arms, South Carolina College closed its doors. For the next three years alumni soldiers confronted hardship, disease, death, and finally surrender. The campus they left behind served as a hospital for the wounded and sick.

After the final reality of the Confederate defeat in 1865, the College managed to reopen and, from 1866 to 1873, to transform itself into a budding university. Well before it could flower, however, students and faculty of the reviving institution resigned en masse in 1873, protesting the edict of the postwar "Radical Republican" legislature that the University admit African American students. From 1873 to 1877 most of the students of the University of South Carolina were African American men. Some were adults elected or appointed to state government, and others were beneficiaries of generous scholarships provided by the legislature. They were joined by African American female students pursuing teacher training at the State Normal School located on campus.

READY FOR ACTION

Student excitement mounted as the possibility of war drew close, and the students formed the South Carolina College cadet company to prepare for action. In a 1901 memoir Iredell Jones, a junior from York in 1860, described the fervor that permeated the community and the College.

During the year [1860], political conventions were held. The State seceded from the National Union on the 20th of December. The streets of Columbia were at times filled with excited audiences, and speakers from the balconies and porches of hotels hurled back at Northern fanatics threats of resistance against any efforts or action looking to coercion. In the meanwhile the bonfires were lighted and torchlight processions were frequent, and the beautiful patriotic girls of the glorious old city made palmetto cockades and tied them with blue ribbon and presented them with a "God-speed" to the cause of liberty.

How could the gallant young men of South Carolina College fail to be impressed with the patriotic fever now raging over the land? It is not surprising that they hurried to reorganize the College [cadet] company in the fall of 1860. The [approximately 105] members provided themselves with a pretty gray uniform, and were delighted to parade the streets of the city and perform various military evolutions in the presence of an admiring public. . . . If they exulted in their handsome uniforms, the martial step and inspiring drum beat, their inmost thoughts struck deeper and a more serious chord when the threatened hostilities at last broke out.

John Barnwell Elliott, then a junior, described a student celebration of the Confederate cause in a letter to his mother in Beaufort, February 12, 1861.

Yesterday we suspended the exercises of the college in honor of the forming of the Confederacy, and at night the campus and city were beautifully illuminated. Fire works were set off in all parts of the city—and the campus presented quite a brilliant front. The students formed a line and marched around the campus, setting off fire works, etc., and then adjourned to the rooms above the chapel and had a regular "stag dance."

P.S. I would like you to make me some night shirts, exactly like the last, and send them to me. Under drawers you can send later.

Throughout 1861 students were eager to join the action when hostilities broke out at Charleston. Robert Armstrong Harllee's letters to his parents in Mars Bluff, S.C., described his participation in the Fort Sumter bombardment.

April 9, 1861, Columbia

I sustained myself through examinations with more credit than I expected, looking every moment to be called from college to enlist for our country's defense.

. . . Great excitement now prevails in Columbia. One company of Col. Kershaw's regiment left today for Charleston and two will leave tomorrow. All the military together with hundreds of citizens accompanied the company today to the depot. It is needless for me to depict the scene that took place there. Husband and wife, mother and son, sister and brother were there parted probably never to meet again.

It will be with surprise (and I hope agreeable surprise) when I inform you that the probabilities are in favor of my being in Charleston to mingle in the scene of action in a very few days. We [College cadets] have offered our services to the Governor and our Captain has gone to Charleston in behalf of our company to intercede with and ascertain of the Governor and Beauregard the probability of our being accepted and if accepted under what conditions.

P.S. My letter was not mailed on yesterday. Governor Pickens has accepted us upon the condition we get permission from our parents and repair immediately to Charleston. . . . Everybody is excited, the Richland Mounted Riflemen are ordered to Charleston. Professor [Charles E.] Venable is a lieutenant. I hear he will leave tomorrow with his company. We are doing nothing in the way of studying. No recitations, no nothing but students leaving for other companies and everybody talking about Charleston and Ft. Sumter.

April 11, 1861, Sullivan's Island

Shortly after I arrived at this place I was taken with a violent attack of dysentery. I was removed from the Moultrie House to a private dwelling of Drs. Yates and Moore, a short distance from our quarters, through whose kind attention I have almost recovered and will soon resume my position in ranks of the College Cadets.

May 5, 1861, Columbia

As soon as I arrived back in Charleston [after a brief visit home to fully recover] I understood that our company had taken their departure for Columbia. I was very much disappointed and I expect that they were. I arrived in Columbia on a Saturday morning quite well and wrote home immediately but having gone to sleep to make up for lost time as I rode all the night previous on the cars, I did not wake until the mail was made up and my letter was consequently delayed.

College is very dull, there being only about thirty students here, the others having gone home.

May 18, 1861, Columbia

Quite a gloom has been thrown over the whole college by the death of [Tristram B.] McLaurin, a student of the senior class from Marlboro. He was one of the most popular students in college, liked by both students and professors. He contracted the disease on Sullivan's Island, but was able to return to college, but soon after he returned the dysentery could not be checked until it inflamed his bowels of which disease he died.

The number of students are gradually decreasing. Living here is now enormous. Board has got to five dollars a week and everything else in proportion. A great many students are going home to return and apply in October.

Will you please send me fifty dollars as soon as practicable. When I went to Sullivan's Island I did not pay tuition thinking it probable we might be kept in service for some time. No deduction has been made and consequently we are forced now to pay the whole sum of thirty-five dollars. I also need a small amount to pay my board for the time I have been here and one week before I returned.

On November 8, 1861, one day after Union forces captured Beaufort and Port Royal, 51 students signed a petition to Gov. Francis Pickens to volunteer for service.

We the undersigned students of South Carolina College feeling it derogatory to our sense of honor and of our duty to our native state to remain passive spectators of the contest which seems to be pending within our borders while troops are being transported from neighboring states for her protection, do submit to your excellency the following with the hope that it may have the effect of persuading your excellency to provide us with such necessary equipment and transportation as will enable us to assist in repelling the threatened invasion.

Believing as we do that the parents of each and every one of us would in the present emergency grant us their permission to leave college and repair immediately to the scene of action, if the matter should be brought before them. We are willing to and do take upon ourselves all the responsibilities of our going forthwith as a company into the service of the State of South Carolina.

A memorandum from faculty chairman Maximilian LaBorde to the trustees, also dated November 8, 1861, describes the faculty response to war fever among the students.

At the close of the summer vacation, the College exercises were resumed under flattering prospects. All went on well until the attack upon Port Royal, the news of which no sooner reached here than [Joseph John] Fripp, [Thomas Stuart] Rhett and [James Smith] Heyward of the Sophomore Class craved permission to go home as they resided in or about Beaufort. I refused, whereupon they went without permission. Some ten or twelve others I understand followed their example. The next day the students met en masse (without permission) and resolved (the Governor favoring) to leave for the scene of war. At a called meeting of the faculty, the Governor's communication was laid before us. We resolved unanimously that we had no authority to disband the college. The students however left in a body.

Notes from the Field

The war the students confronted when they reached Virginia, Pennsylvania, Mississippi, and elsewhere was, for most, a war against boredom and contagious illness, punctuated by long marches and occasional skirmishes with the enemy.

John Barnwell Elliott, who left South Carolina College in his junior year, wrote to his sister Hester about his early days in the Confederate States Army.

June 11, 1862, Brewton Hill, Ga.

Although we did at one time hold ourselves in readiness to march, there seems to be no hope of our leaving this post, since troops have returned from Charleston to this place, showing that they had as many as they wanted over there. . . . In camp we are having a very slow time, having nothing to do but drill. I have tried so far to keep up a regular course of reading and have nearly completed a third volume of history since our enlistment began. This and my letters to you comprise my list of literary pursuits. I suppose you have heard from Percy. His continued bad health has compelled him to apply for discharge from the service which I suppose by this time he has received.

Charles Hutson, Class of 1860, corresponded with various family members during the three years he served with Hampton's Legion before returning to Columbia and eventually to the University of South Carolina as a graduate student.

January 24, 1862, near Occoquan, Va.

At last, dear mother, I am settled in tolerable comfort. Our boy, Pleasant, cooks for us under cover of an old tent, which we spread like a shed over our kitchen fire and we now get our meals regularly, only going out occasionally to cut and bring in wood for him to cook with. In our tent we are kept comfortable by our warm stove-fire and sociable chat whiles away the monotony of the day. This state, however, is endangered at present by the rumour, terrible to us, which gives us the prospect of a removal. The talk is that the difficulty of transporting supplies may force us to retire to some point nearer Manassas. This we would not like at all, because everything domestic would have to be rearranged.

February 5, 1862, near Occaquan, Va.

Everything seems to be inactive on this line, and I think that matters will remain in status quo until this wet weather ceases and the roads become somewhat improved, which interesting state of affairs we are not likely to have until April. . . . I had a brief note from my old friend and classmate, [William H.] Brawley, who is at Centreville [Va.] in Winder's regiment. He was in the Drainesville battle and writes that he was "mightily scared," but managed to fight pretty well. He deplores the super abundance of mud and the length of the winter and declares himself heartily tired of service. I should like very much to take a little trip to Centreville; so many of my friends are there, including several classmates I have not met since graduation.

We have been several times ordered to hold ourselves in readiness for a night march, the enemy making frequent approaches to Colchester. Our post-Manassas soldiers are very eager for a fight, and much disappointed at the inactivity to which we have been doomed for the past six or seven months.

February 18, 1862, near Occaquan, Va.

Last night we had an alarm. The picquets at Deep Hole, Occoquan Bay, had sent up a courier to announce that the enemy were landing, the picquets having fired upon what was supposed to be their advanced guard. . . . We marched for three or four hours. I was very afraid we would shoot each other in the darkness. But fortunately, no damage was done. We saw not a shadow of the enemy. . . . We returned to camp thoroughly exhausted. I was fortunate enough to get a refreshing draught of whiskey from a friend. Today we have been busy getting wood for our kitchen. I wish very much that I had a good, stout pair of boots. I am almost on the ground.

May 7, 1862, Barhamville

Last night our company was sent forward through the woods to act as skirmishers, and we spent the greater part of the day in moving forward and changing our position from point to point. There was heavy firing immediately on our left without our coming into collision with the enemy until about half past one. Just as they came up, the rest of the Legion drew near and a rapid fire commenced, the men on both sides sheltering themselves behind pines and old stumps. But our heavy fire and loud cheering disconcerted the enemy and the regiment opposed to us broke and fled. Three mounted [enemy] officers were shot by other companies in the Legion. . . . I must say that I lost by the day's action, for my heavy coat and oil cloth incommoded me so much in skirmish that I flung them aside in the woods, and I failed to resupply myself from the Yankee goods and chattels.

Student soldiers witnessed death and suffering among the friends, relatives, and classmates who fought by their sides. Thomas John Moore, who left South Carolina College in 1862, informed his sister in Spartanburg of the death of their older brother, Andrew Charles Moore, an 1858 graduate of South Carolina College.

September 2, 1862, Manassas, Va.

Bud [Andrew Charles Moore] was killed on the field. He was shot in the head with a very small ball. I think it struck him in the right temple. He was shot a little before sundown while charging a battery. I had him buried on Sunday as decently as possible. I dug his grave myself and put him into it about 12 o'clock Sunday night. I could not procure a coffin but wrapped him in two blankets and marked his grave so it could be found in case we wish to remove his remains.

He was fighting bravely when he fell, being near the battery and among the front men. I have preserved a bunch of his hair for you and his wife.

I was knocked down by a grape shot but not seriously hurt. . . . Our regiment suffered terribly. We must have lost nearly 200 men. Our company lost 11 from being killed. Captain Tucker was killed, Col. Cadberry and many others. Willis Brewton was killed and Frank Landrum was wounded in the foot.

John Barnwell Elliott also confronted the grim realities of warfare.

July 8, 1862, Ft. Boggs, Ga.

I have just returned from Charleston, having been sent on there with a detachment of men to convey the remains of Eddie Cheves to his family at that place. We left camp about twelve o'clock at night for Savannah where we met the body and carried it on by the cars that morning. It was indeed a sad duty.

At the funeral I saw Charles Haskell. He said that he had heard from Virginia and that John Haskell [who left South Carolina College in 1861] he feared was mortally wounded . . . was struck in the shoulder by a piece of shell which crushed all the bones about the part. At last accounts they had succeeded in amputating the arm but had very little hopes of his life. Joe Haskell [John's younger brother who left South Carolina College at the end of his freshman year, 1861] I hear acted very gallantly at the battle of Chickahominy—he was acting volunteer aide to Joseph Johnston . . . , being too young to hold a commission. Dr. Stuart's brother I see has died of a wound received in the late battles. He was not more than eighteen years old.

While on sick leave in Savannah in 1864, Elliott managed to put his recent experiences to verse in a poem he sent his sister.

Since my last I have been roughly
Shaken by the hand of fate.
Thin and weak, my state was very
Sad indeed to contemplate.
For unlike the angel visits,
Happ'ning few and far between
Chills are vastly more attentive
Staying longer, too; I ween
But I will not quarrel with them
For they so touched Harley's heart
That he gave ten days' furlough
Saying, "Get thee hence, depart."
So I "Got me hence" and wandered
To the regions of the "blest."
And beneath the roof Paternal,
Sigh "The weary is at rest."
For I deem with bricks and ashes
Mustard plasters and quinine,
Blankets, pepper, teas and blisters,
Backed by tactics feminine
Chills will scarcely dare give battle.
So "the days that are to be"
Have the ring of "life in Life," far
Sweeter than of "Death" to me.
But of this you know already,
And a dearth of other news
Leaves me nothing else to write of
Save the weather and the Jews.

Several picnics have been given
Where the latter were in force.
Robert G., the gay inspector
Being prominent—of course—
Up the river, down the river
On the islands have they been
But your servant for such service
Was too weakly, pale and thin.
And a "Hop" last night was given
Cards for which were handed here
From their fancy style, it must have
Been a grand affair.
I send one, but was not present,
How they prospered cannot tell.
Jews were thick, no doubt as usual,
For the weather suited well.
We have had a real chess fever
Since I came from camp to town
Every night the board is opened
Where content the sword and gown.
But enough—the page is ended
So my trash must cease to pour
Answer quickly, and believe me
Still the same as e'er affectionate your,   Brother John
     B. Elliott

ONE STUDENT'S REALITY

Robert Armstrong Harllee spent the spring of 1861 on campus longing for an opportunity to join troops heading north. He finally found a place in the Eighth South Carolina Regiment of the Confederate States Army and immediately left for Virginia. A prolific letter writer, he recounted his experiences in detailed correspondence to his family in Mars Bluff, S.C.

May 25, 1861, Columbia

It was with great pleasure I received the intelligence that in the event Col. [Ellerbe B. C.] Cash went to Virginia he would probably give me some appointment, and having heard from Charlie Gregg that it was probable he would start soon, I lost no time in informing you to see Colonel Cash for me immediately and say to him I am more than anxious to go to Virginia and any appointment will be thankfully and gratefully appreciated.

I feel I am prompted by every honorable and noble impulse to serve my country in whatsoever capacity I may be competent, and though there be great sacrifice, still sacrifice is necessary to every glorious achievement. . . .

May 29, 1861, Columbia

It was not without some disappointment that I understood my chance for going to Virginia but lately so bright so soon had vanished. If I could not obtain that position, please ascertain if there is any position whatever I might obtain, watch every opportunity and if any is afforded, take advantage of it.

Why I am so anxious to obtain a position immediately is that President Davis has authorized Governor Pickens to order every volunteer from South Carolina to proceed immediately to Virginia, and I wish to have some position secured in time.

June 6, 1861, Camp Beauregard, Richmond, Va.

Col. Cash's whole regiment arrived here on Tuesday tired and hungry. The soldiers were not provident enough in providing provisions and as the Confederate States had prepared no provisions we arrived in Richmond in rather a destitute condition. It has been with the greatest difficulty since that time that our commissary can procure provisions or Gen. [Ellerbe B. C.] Cash can supply us in the necessary conveniences of equipage, clothing, etc.

Capt. Stackhouse, Dr. Pearce and I have been for the last two days getting up a uniform for our company. We understand that the ladies of Richmond were making them for nothing so the Capt. delegated [cousin] Andrew [Harllee] and I to see them on the subject. We called on Dr. Barrows the Baptist minister of Richmond who escorted us to ten different churches. We found at each church no less than twenty ladies and every one of them had been working for six weeks. They said they were anxious to work for any soldiers, but more anxious to work for South Carolinians. Each church took some part of the work, and in less than a week Capt. Stackhouse's company will have a beautiful uniform costing only eight dollars.

Since our arrival here I have been incessantly at work. I commenced as commissary, but I have been promoted to Sergeant. . . .

I am tenting with Honorine McClenaghan, Ross and Pearce, and [their negro slaves] Ned and Mid. We are somewhat crowded. Ned seems to be agreeably disappointed with camp life. He sends "howdy," etc.

My health remains extremely well and I think I will return home fat and heavy. Ladies frequent our camp every evening, but they do not seem so proud of our presence as they were represented by the 1st and 2nd regiments. . . .

July 23, 1861, Centreville, Va.

The Battle of Bull Run is over. I am unhurt. On the 17th we were encamped at Fairfax. Early in the morning we were apprised that a tremendous force was within a few miles of us. . . . Their forces numbered 15,000 (I mean that were advancing against our regiment).

Our wagons were fortunately sent on to Manassas early in the morning and about eight o'clock we began the retreat, the greater part of the time double quicking with our knapsacks upon our backs. We continued the retreat until we arrived at Centerville. . . . We remained there until about 12 o'clock when we became almost surrounded and began retreat again and scarcely arrived at Bull Run before we were attacked by the enemy.

. . . Two days afterwards our forces were attacked by their whole army amounting to seventy-five thousand men. We then flanked them, put them to flight and pursued them. They fled without any order. . . . Thirty pieces of artillery were taken, hundreds of horses were killed and taken. The woods and hills from Bull Run to Centreville are showered with baggage, tents, guns, the dead and dying.

. . . Notwithstanding, I have had no knapsack, no tent, and part of the time no blanket and nothing to eat, exposed part of the time to hard work and rainy weather, still I am in better health than I ever was. But we are all in want of shoes. If the men could get their pay they could buy them, but they have not yet received one cent and a great many of them are in need of shoes.

July 24, 1861, Vienna, Va.

I think one more victory as signal as the 21st will end the contest and our soldiers desire no better and easier task than to flog troops demoralized by cowardice, defeat and disgrace. The Federal Government says that a short war is to be made of it, that it must be short even if desperate, which proposition Jeff Davis and his soldiers are ready to comply with. The Yankees well know that time is killing them worse than bullets and "masterly inactivity" is their worst enemy.

. . . Ned [Harllee's negro slave] acted during the battle like a true Spartan. He kept close to my tent and baggage until the fight was over and afterwards it was all that the officers could do to keep him off the battle field, as he feared I, among many others, had been killed. He wishes that his wife shall know that he is well and wants Big Tom to tell her to use all of his property whatsoever he may have in whatsoever way she desires. He also inquires to know whether she is well.

August 18, 1861, Charlottesville, Va.

Today finds me in the beautiful town of Charlottesville. I arrived here yesterday in obedience to the orders of Gen. Bonham to visit all the hospitals where the sick of the 8th Regiment have been sent and ascertain if any were able to do service and if so to send them to the camp immediately.

I first went to Culpeper where I found many of our sick. Many were low with typhoid. . . . I saw there hundreds of the wounded, some I think will recover but they are convalescing quite slowly. The kind inhabitants seem to be doing everything in their power to facilitate their recovery but many of them linger for weeks and then die. Numbers of South Carolinians were there visiting their friends and I felt quite at home.

About fifteen of the sick of our regiment joined me at Culpeper and I carried them to Charlottesville as I was acquainted with Prof. [Robert W.] Barnwell [Jr., professor of history and political economy, nephew of the third president of South Carolina College] under whose supervision the hospitals had been erected. Upon arriving there I found him and put the sick under his charge. He immediately conducted them to a new house recently fitted up for the sick where every accommodation and convenience that would contribute to their comfort was furnished. I must say that it surpassed my sanguine expectation and reflects credit not only upon him but upon the people of South Carolina. Dr. [Maximilian] LaBorde [a medical doctor and professor of rhetoric, logic, and belles lettres at South Carolina College] and Prof. [of Greek, William J.] Rivers are also engaged in the philanthropic enterprise here.

. . . I have not succeeded in finding either Ed DeBerry or [fellow South Carolina College student John LaRoche] Jenkins. I suppose they are at Richmond. Jenkins left our camp a week ago quite sick. After recovering from measles, he was attacked with dysentery.

December 1, 1861, Charlottesville, Va.

Already the most robust and powerful have fallen victims to pneumonia, but still the Confederate Army of the Potomac remains in dormant inactivity while five are dying from disease when one would be killed with the bullet, even if Washington City itself were to be stormed.

. . . After recovering from mumps I was attacked with cold and diarrhea, completely unable to digest anything, my health became so debilitated that Dr. Pearce advised me to leave as it was impossible to obtain a furlough at that time. I receive every attention here both from my host and Dr. Nelson who visits me occasionally, and I think I will return to camp the latter part of this week.

December 15, 1861, Camp Bonham, near Vienna, Va.

It is now the middle of December and still we are in tents, all preparations for winter have ceased which was owing to an order to hold ourselves in readiness to go into winter quarters near Bull Run. Sad indeed is the spectacle which our regiment presents on parade, almost everybody is sick and new names are added to the sick list every day. The diseases are of the most fatal character always assuming a typhoid type. In the latter part of last summer and fall the regiment received near one hundred recruits and fully one half of them are now dead and discharged.

It was with feelings of the deepest sympathy and regret that we heard of the burning of Charleston. I hope the people of the county will now be more vigilant than formerly. . . .

If we had of been sent to Carolina I do not think there would be a difficulty in revolunteering for the war, but now the proposition of fifty dollars bounty and sixty days furlough will be scorned with contempt by the majority of men in this regiment. In the first place, we have been wronged in not being sent to defend our own state, secondly we will be honor bound to return in sixty days whether we succeeded in getting in an organization that suited us or not, thirdly we will have to return the 1st of March, the most disagreeable month of the year.

January 6, 1862, Camp Bonham, near Vienna, Va.

This is decidedly the hardest service now in the army. We have to walk six miles before coming to the picket post and there remain for three days with no shelter except what the natural position affords. An ambulance is carried out with us and after the first day it is generally kept busy transporting the sick back to camp, the majority of whom are generally attacked by pneumonia and their disease usually proves fatal.

If I remain in good health I do not desire to return home before the middle of April, as I am now acclimated and can stand the service very well, which those coming on here from a southern climate and used to sleeping in warm houses are apt to suffer. . . . The ground is now completely covered with snow, the natives say that it will remain so until March.

January 28, 1862, Camp Van Dorn, near Manassas, Va.

As you have undoubtedly heard we are now at our new camp. The past few days have been occupied in rendering ourselves comfortable as we expect to remain here until April. The season had so far advanced and no material being furnished us but pine poles and no tools but an axe we concluded to live as before and only erect a chimney to our tent.

We found it very inconvenient to have so many members in our mess and we were unable to support the negroes as we were deprived of our provisions allotted to us and it was impossible to purchase provisions for them as none but commissioned officers were allowed that privilege.

. . . The sad defeat of our arms in Kentucky has cast quite a gloom over the army. We begin to believe that unless our soldiers fight harder than they have been doing that the contest is going to be harder than first anticipated. The time has at last arrived when all who are able to bear arms, young or old, should bestir themselves to action. . . .

Do not construe my saying that I was anxious to go home as being in any respect desponding, notwithstanding I am anxious to be at home still I have never desponded but rather in better health and spirits than I have been since I have been in the army.

Circumstances changed quickly and dramatically during war. A month after Robert Armstrong Harllee's mention of good health and spirits, Andrew Turpin Harllee, his cousin in the same regiment, sent a different message home from Camp Van Dorn, Va.

February 27, 1862

There is excitement here now, we are expected to move some way but don't know where. We have sent back all heavy baggage to Manassas and are now on "Light Marching Order."

I am afraid [Robert] Armstrong will not live until night. He grows weaker and weaker and his breathing is very short. I thought he would not stand it until this morning. He has a severe attack of pneumonia. I telegraphed his father yesterday to come for him at once. . . . It would be awful if we had to fall back and leave him here in the hands of the enemy, for he cannot be moved. Dr. Coit has a comfortable house built and he is in that.

The *Marion Star* paid tribute on March 3, 1862.

A meeting was called by his friends to pay a tribute of respect to the memory of Sergeant R. Armstrong Harllee, who died in camp on the 28th of February. As a soldier he was brave, cool and scrupulously faithful in the performance of every duty. His quick sense of honor forbade him to evade anything which duty enjoined. With intellect and education that justified him in aspiring to promotion, he never neglected the humblest duties of his place.

STUDENTS IN DEFEAT

Student soldiers continued a determined fight, often with renewed vigor, as the possibility of defeat loomed large in 1865. In a letter to his mother, Charles Hutson exemplified the feelings of many fighting alumni.

March 29, 1865, camp near Cheraw, S.C.

We evacuated James Island on the 18th February and since that time have been marching up across the country through Monk's Corner, Kingstree, and Graham's Crossroads. But here we are at Cheraw and I know not where will we next move to as no one seems to have an idea where the enemy is. We are now in a battalion of artillery commanded by Major Burnet Rhett.

We have heard favorable accounts of the conduct of the enemy during their occupation of Orangeburg and trust that you have passed safely and comfortably through that ordeal. . . . This campaign is but begun, and nothing is to be foreseen; but I feel assured that it will result in brilliant success for us. We are at last having the sense to desert the seaboard and concentrate in the interior; and we have Joe Johnston as 1st in command.

In memoirs written several decades later, Hutson reflected on the final days of the war in his diary.

On April 18th the sad fact of the downfall of our cause seems to have forced itself upon my mind at last. Tom Huguenin, Bill Colcock, Keith Lanneau and one or two others [camped near Raleigh, N.C.] debated with me the prospect of our being able to dash away on the battery horses or teamsters' mules and cross the mountains and join some command still in the field, rather than surrender with this army. But the horses and mules were put under an infantry guard and our designs were frustrated.

On May 2nd, 1865, I was paroled on the surrender of Johnston's army. This ended my career as a soldier. To me the war brought physical health, self respect in regard to courage and endurance, a truer valuation of classes of my countrymen I had regarded as my inferiors, and a determination never to be discouraged.

The First "University" Students

South Carolina College escaped the worst of the burning of Columbia during the arrival of Union troops in February 1865 by virtue of its status as a hospital. Since 1862, college buildings had housed sick and wounded soldiers; and while nearly a third of Columbia burned to rubble, General Sherman's forces posted a guard to protect the campus from burning and pillaging.

By the summer of 1865, with South Carolina under military rule, the handful of remaining faculty members began working to reopen the college. Their ambitious plans soon produced the first University of South Carolina, opened in 1866 with an expanded and elective curriculum that included not only classical liberal arts subjects of earlier years but also modern languages and literature, military science, and civil engineering. The faculty soon added schools of law and medicine. Although chronically underfunded and dotted with refugee families whose homes were in ashes, the campus quickly became a beacon for students who had interrupted their education to fight for the Confederacy and for faculty who hoped to return to the classroom.

Charles Hutson, who returned from the war to attend as a resident graduate student in 1866 and 1867, recalled in his memoirs a campus that was socially lively and intellectually stimulating.

I took rooms in the university, at first in one of the tenements and later over the chapel, my expenses not being very heavy, even including the library fee. Old Tom cooked for me and served me meals in my room at the rate of $2.50 a week. This he was able to do in fine style, as he cooked for Dr. [James L.] Reynolds and could supply me with vegetables from the professor's garden. Coffee I bought myself. He parched and ground it for me.

. . . What I really did in my second and unofficial college life was to study modern languages. . . . I would read in the literature of the language extensively and aloud to gather as much vocabulary as possible. Then again I would translate for publication in a magazine some story. . . . In this way I studied German, French, Spanish, and Italian.

Most [undergraduate students] had been soldiers, and in one case my mediation prevented a duel and in another case my remonstrance kept a rash young madcap boarding in the same hotel with the Yankee general in command at this point from assassinating him.

I belonged to the dancing clubs of two sets, the older girls and the younger. We were very gay in an inexpensive way just after the war. It would be hard for me to give you an idea of how light hearted we were at this time. Both sexes had missed each other and were glad to be thrown together again. The men had had a rough experience and longed for the refining influence of the gentler sex. The girls were better educated than girls of their age before the war because, besides hospital work, they had had little to do during the war but study and read. All of us were so poor that no one thought of dress or of feasting. It was enough that we could meet and talk or dance.

. . . In the latter part of my life there as resident graduate I was employed by Dr. James Woodrow as book reviewer and proofreader for both the Southern Presbyterian Review and the paper of the same name. . . .

We had some fine lectures at the university during those years. They were largely attended and were full of interest, especially that given by Dr. Joe LeConte on the then recent discovery of the solar spectrum and the doctrine of spectrum analysis, a lecture he had lately delivered in Baltimore amid great applause.

The last sessions of white legislature before the crime of federal "reconstruction" was perpetrated were held during these years, and, as the Senate met in the University library and the House in the chapel, the University grounds were the scene of the political as well as the educational life of the State. It was one of our social recreations to make up parties to go into the gallery of the chapel and listen to the debates.

Besides the dances, plays, concerts, masked balls, charity banquets, and other entertainments gotten up by the young people and presided over by their elders, there was a select Shakespeare club that met at Dr. Joe LeConte's, of which I was a member, the meetings of which we greatly enjoyed. Many of us in later life looked back to that club as of high education value to us. Yet, there was lots of fun involved.

Not all South Carolina College alumni liked the idea of a University of South Carolina. James Wood Davidson, who received a bachelor degree from the College in 1852 and a master's degree in 1855, was particularly troubled by the range of courses that allowed students to select from several departments and create their own patterns toward degrees. He registered his complaint in the _Yorkville Enquirer._

May 21, 1866

The change from a college to a university has had, and must continue to have, two bad results. The natural and universally known principle in youth nature—that of evading unpleasant and laborious departments—will also operate to cripple the usefulness of the institution. Youths, if left to choose their own studies, will, by a law which every teacher perfectly understands, avoid those very departments they most need. We say nothing of the embarrassments that must beset the faculty in their efforts to systematise the recitations and studies of two or three hundred students (for we hope the number will reach these figures) with their unequal and heterogeneous attainments. Under the circumstances it becomes apparent that the institution, notwithstanding it has one of the ablest faculties in the South, will ere long become a respectable asylum to which genteel idlers may take refuge in their escapes from an education.

Despite his objections, Davidson enrolled in the University of South Carolina as a resident graduate student during the 1871–72 academic year.

John Calhoun Sellers of Marion attended the new University of South Carolina during 1867 and 1868. In 1912 he wrote to Prof. Edwin Green his recollections.

A large majority of us had been attending the severe school of the soldier on the hills of Virginia, the Western army or the coasts of Carolina from six months to four years, and we had learned a few things not found in the books by contact with the stirring and dangerous events through which we had recently passed. There were a number of the boys who had only one arm, some were on crutches with only one leg, while a large number had been seriously or slightly wounded, and some had languished for months in prison. The experiences through which many of us had passed gave us a decided advantage over the ordinary greenhorn we nowadays find at College.

You ask about our amusements. Why, we had a plenty and a variety. For instance, before they got trained not to come on campus, the dogs of Columbia afforded some amusement. A mischievous fellow like Will would coax a dog into his room, tie newspapers to his tail and give him a fright and start him running down the street, whereupon the whole student body would give the rebel yell and that dog would burn the wind.

We had a splendid base ball club of 60 members. In those days we all played ball; every man got to bat. It was not then as now a pitcher's and catcher's game, while the balance looked on and squalled; but every one of the nine had a share in the fun. On one occasion our club had a match game with a Columbia club. The whole city turned out. We played nearly all day and beat the Columbians out of their boots, the score standing 96 to 66 in our favor. . . .

The Yankee garrison was encamped on the green outside the wall south of campus, and they also had a club and played ball. After our "walk over" of the Columbia boys [a city team], the garrison club sent us a challenge. The challenge came to me a secretary of the club. I called a meeting of the club and laid the challenge before them. After several fiery speeches it was unanimously resolved to decline the challenge . . . , several spicy communications passed between us. The upshot of the matter was we were reported to the National Association of which all clubs were members, and that put an end to our base ball career, and our club was disbanded. It was near the close of the session of 1868 and things were beginning to look squally.

. . . The day after we left the University in 1868, at the close of the session, the negro House of Representatives met in the chapel and the Senate in the library and began the plunder of the prostrate State until they were driven out of power by Hampton in 1876.

For George Crosland, who wrote to his mother in Marlboro, S.C., student concerns at the new University changed little from those in the earliest days of the College.

February 9, 1868

Your last letter has come to hand and also the money Mr. Moury sent, amount being about seventy five dollars. . . . We will have to have one hundred and twenty seven and fifty cents here by the 15th of Feb. to pay for our tuition. . . . Tomorrow my examination comes on and I expect to come out as I always do, poor enough.

Please send me sixty dollars instead of fifty five as I forgot to add five for text books, making in all one hundred and thirty-two dollars.

While students enjoyed the liberalized educational and social advantages of the lively new University, many resented the political realities of Reconstruction. Edward Crosland, who entered in 1867 and left without a diploma in 1869, wrote to his brother George about activities on campus. His outrage at the meetings on campus of the Reconstruction legislature, with its many African American Republican representatives, demonstrated the reaches of anger within the all-white, all-male student body.

November 24, 1868

Miss Ella is looking very well. She inquired of you the other day. Nearly a dozen students are acquainted with her and all visit her.

[James J.] Frierson is back, spending money, drinking a great deal and studying very little. He begs to be remembered to you. He was engaged to a young lady, Miss Adams, about 20 miles from here, for some time. But she broke it off a few weeks ago. I do not know for what, but I suppose for his general triflingness and drinking.

Jim Thadwell has been round several times again this session. He is a great bore, sometimes coming in drunk, and sometimes going to other rooms and troubling them. He is looking well for a man that has been drinking for 5 years steady.

The "legislature" opens tomorrow I believe. I am very anxious to see the negro skunks making laws and will go down tomorrow to take a look at the "law-makers."

. . . Dr. John LeConte is going to leave this institution in July and take the professorship in the University of California with a salary of 300 in gold a month. Dr. Joe [LeConte] also expects the situation of a professorship in California, and perhaps [Gen. E. P.] Alexander. If these go, Dr. [J. L.] Reynolds will go to Kentucky.

February 27, 1869

The legislature is still in session in the campus, legislating with all their might and swearing and giving the lie direct to each other. It is the most degrading sight I ever witnessed to see the black imps in the college chapel, turned or bought from one side to the other by the most popular man. You can sit in the gallery and hear them say to each other, "If you do not vote for my bill I won't support your's." Among the sweepings of the hall you can see jot books and all the letters of the alphabet written on paper in the worst form and shape possible. They are written by those just learning to write.

Attending the Radical University

By 1873 Radical Republican forces in the South Carolina legislature fully controlled state politics and policies, including those regarding the University. Although Claflin College in Orangeburg was available to African American students, legislative leaders understood that it was very separate and not at all equal. To remedy the situation, they first established a state normal school to provide teacher training to all races on the University of South Carolina campus, located in Rutledge Chapel and the president's house. Next, the Board of Trustees, a racially integrated group, opened the University to African American students. On October 7, 1873, with the white faculty ranks depleted by forced and voluntary terminations, Henry E. Hayne registered in the medical school as the first student of color at the University of South Carolina.

Hayne, who was the secretary of state of South Carolina, was soon joined by a wide array of African American males, as well as white males, who comprised the small student body for the next four years. They were attracted by recruiting efforts of a determined new faculty and by scholarships made available by the radical legislature. Some were poorly prepared and needed to first enter the "preparatory department." Others, however, had benefited from good earlier schooling and were ready for the academic rigors of the University. Many were serious adult students who had waited a long time for an opportunity in higher education. The "radical university" that gave them their chance was a highly politicized entity. It closed in 1877 after a Democratic governor, Wade Hampton, and Democratic legislators took office.

Little remains of official records, memorabilia, letters, or diaries concerning the "radical" University of South Carolina. Undoubtedly, some records were destroyed by those wanting to eradicate the reality of African Americans on campus in the wake of the defeated Confederacy. Other evidence of the brief period of nineteenth-century integration may have been removed to individual collections. One student account that survived was a memoir by Cornelius Chapman Scott, an African American student who graduated in 1877. Excerpted here, it was published in the Columbia *State* newspaper, May 8, 1911, as "When Negroes Attended the University."

When Henry Hayne, secretary of state, matriculated, being the first colored student to do so, the record book was effaced. Great excitement followed. That afternoon a meeting of the faculty was held at which every professor, except Prof. [Fisk] Brewer, not yet arrived, was present. . . . The unanimous agreement was reached that the professors would acquiesce in the situation and enter on the work of educating all students placed under their charge in accordance with the recent law which prohibited discrimination on account of color. Following this action, some of the students quit the university. Outside pressure was brought to bear and some of the professors resigned. . . . Prof. [Maximilian] LaBorde denied positively and unequivocally that he had resigned because of his unwillingness to teach colored students, but said he was compelled to do so from pressure he could not resist, and he had been assured that his position on the faculty was not pleasing to those who were at the head of affairs. Prof. LaBorde, from what I learned about him belonged to that type of Southern Christian gentleman whose hearts went out in compassion to my people and who felt it no disgrace or dishonor to stoop down to the humblest of God's creatures, that they might lift them up to a higher level. They knew they were white, but they felt that the colored man was their brother in black. They never worried about social equality, but they were interested in humanity.

. . . When the University of South Carolina threw open its doors to colored students, I was a freshman at Howard University and learned of the changed conditions from Prof. F. L. Cardozo, who had come to Washington and had seen me and had me to acquaint the other college students from South Carolina of the change and to say to them he advised our returning to the State immediately and entering the university. He gave me $100 to defray the traveling and incidental expenses of William M. Dart, John M. Morris, Paul J. Mishow and myself. And we obtained honorable dismissal from Howard and left immediately. Each of us subsequently repaid Mr. Cardozo this loan. T. McCants Stewart and Alonzo G. Townsend soon followed, and later Joseph M. Morris. All of us were colored Charlestonians and all of us were in the college department at Howard University. Other South Carolina students from Howard followed and, I think, some from Lincoln [Philadelphia, Pa.] and other Northern colleges.

. . . The student body as a whole, I feel, was better than the average student body of either race at present. I believe they were awed by their changed condition and their surroundings. There were some bad men and some vicious ones. The discipline was not as strict as it ought to have been. The three ministers, Drs. [Benjamin B.] Babbitt, [Olin F.] Cummings and [Henry J.] Fox, preached at the city churches sometimes, but I do not recollect that aside from the regular chapel services, conducted in turn by most of the professors, any of them ever undertook publicly anything specially for our moral or spiritual uplift, except Profs. [Fisk] Brewer and [Mortimer Allanson] Warren. A student prayer meeting was held each Tuesday night under the direction of [students] Alonzo G. Townsend, Thaddeus Saltus and Cornelius C. Scott and Jacob J. Durham, each of whom afterwards became a minister of the gospel.

. . . Each Sunday afternoon, M. A. Warren [principal of the normal school] conducted on the campus religious services to which all were invited. He and his noble wife did more to influence the lives of the colored students of both the normal school and the university than any other two persons and will always be remembered with gratitude.

. . . During 1873–74, 57 students were admitted to scholarships. There were three juniors—C. J. Babbitt, H. J. Fox (white) and T. McCants

Stewart (colored); four sophomores—W. M. Dart, J. M. Morris, P. J. Mishow, A. G. Townsend (all colored); five freshmen—Olin F. Cummings, E. M. Babbitt, Lester D. Puckett (white); T. A. McLean, C. C. Scott (colored). Total college students proper, 12 [the remainder in the preparatory department]. Of these 12, the five whites were resident and native students, three of them having entered the university before the reorganization. Of the seven colored all were native Charlestonians; five were graduates from Avery Normal Institute, Charleston; one from Newburyport, Massachusetts, high school; six also graduated from the preparatory department of Howard University, Washington, D.C., the most notable institution in which a majority of students are colored. . . . Of the colored freshmen, one was a freshman at Amherst. . . . Prior to the opening to them of the university all had been compelled to leave the State because there was no institution in the State worthy of the name of a college or university open to them or capable of affording to them the facilities which they needed.

In 1874–75 there were 17 in law school, two of whom soon resigned; four in the school of medicine; two seniors; four juniors; five sophomores; 29 freshmen; [the remainder in the preparatory department]; total 166. Of the six graduates of 1875, T. McCants Stewart has been an eloquent preacher, a successful lawyer; has traveled extensively; is now I hear associate justice of the supreme court of Liberia. Joseph Henry Stuart became for a time principal of Sumter graded school. He is now practising law in Oklahoma. William Dart was elected principal of the Howard School of Columbia soon after his graduation.

. . . I do not believe the curriculum was in any particular inferior to that of the University of South Carolina before the admission of colored students or since. . . . Prof. Richard T. Greener was the only colored professor, a brilliant man and polished speaker. My impression was that the college library suffered from acts of vandalism committed by persons who were not in sympathy with the new regime, and that Professor Greener, more than any other member of the faculty, rendered valuable service in rearranging the books and restoring the library to its earlier condition. It was said there were 27,000 volumes.

Prof. Cummings was painstaking, exact, thorough, evidently a born mathematician and well earned the sobriquet "old mathematics." Dr. T. N. Roberts, professor of history, political philosophy and political economy was a marvel to most students. He made his subjects so interesting that many of them were sorry when the recitation period had expired. Prof. William Main, Jr., professor of chemistry, pharmacy, mineralogy and geology, was competent and thorough, allowed no shirking and was a martinet in discipline. I hear that he went to Wisconsin later, and made quite a reputation in that state and is prosperous. Prof. [of ancient languages and literature] Fisk Brewer was as perfect a Christian as I have ever met. His scholarship was country-wide. He had lived in Greece, he spoke and wrote Greek. . . . I think he was at one time a member of the Yale College faculty. His knowledge of Latin was almost equal to his knowledge of Greek, classical and modern, and he was a master of English.

Of C. D. Melton, professor of law, and of his successor, Chief Justice F. J. Moses, Sr., it is needless to say anything. I doubt if they have had many superiors or many equals in the State.

There were but three graduates of the class of '77, and these were from the college department—Olin Fisk Cummings (white), Thomas Alston McLean and Cornelius Chapman Scott (colored). Olin F. Cummings was of quiet demeanor and gentlemanly deportment, a close student and good scholar. Thomas Alston McLean was perhaps the best prepared scholar in the class, having graduated from Newburyport, Mass., high school and then entered Amherst college. When the University of South Carolina was opened to colored youth his parents had him return to the State and matriculate there. After his graduation in '77 he returned to Charleston, studied law and engaged in teaching and newspaper work. For a time he was employed out West by the United States government as instructor to the Indians.

I taught a country school for a few months [after graduation], and then became "head teacher" at Avery Normal Institute, Charleston, and later became principal of the Greenville graded school for 10 years, during which time I entered the Methodist ministry. Since then I have been pastor, school teacher, newspaper editor and publisher.

On the 25th of June, 1877, the final commencement exercises were held, and the class had the satisfaction of having the president commend us for the fact that during the four years of our student life we had not as a class or as individuals been disciplined or demerited by the faculty or any professor; and of receiving our diplomas signed by Gov. Wade Hampton. And the experiment had ended in a failure.

. . . Blessed be his [Hampton's] memory! It took a man—Southern man as he was, and an ex-slaveholder and Confederate general too—with strong nerve and a great heart to sign diplomas for negroes as graduates from the great University of South Carolina.

As president of the Clariosophic Society, it fell to my lot to turn over to Mr. [Perry P.] Butler—a perfect gentleman—nephew of Gen. M[atthew]

C. Butler—the records and other property of this society. We spent, I think, two days in taking an inventory in duplicate of the entire property of the society, each retaining one.

T. McCants Stewart, born in Charleston to free African American parents, transferred from Howard University to the University of South Carolina in 1873, his junior year, at age twenty-two. He became a noted orator and received bachelor of arts and law degrees from the "radical university." He described the integrated campus in letters to the editor of the _Washington, D.C., New National Era._

April 16, 1874

Both races are represented in the University classes. In the Professional and College Departments more than one-half of the students are white. Within the past week twelve new students applied for admission into the College Department. More than one-third of them were white.

The institution is calculated to do much good for South Carolina and the Negro race. If the time ever comes when the descendants of the Rutledges and the Marions shall believe in the unlimited brotherhood of man, the University of South Carolina will have a dwelling place in the breast of every Africo-American.

July 9, 1874

The University now numbers one hundred and ten students. I want it distinctly understood that the University of South Carolina is not in possession of any one race. Its advantages are being enjoyed by young men who want to make their State better by themselves having lived in it. The two races study together, visit each other's rooms, play ball together, walk into the city together, without the blacks feeling honored or the whites disgraced.

Being an old institution, we have almost every convenience for studying higher mathematics and the sciences. Our library contains thirty thousand volumes and an excellent collection of paintings and sculpture. The college literary society alone has a library of from twelve to fifteen thousand volumes. A student coming here has to look out mainly for books and board. There are no ordinary University fees.

Every Negro ought to be very much interested in this State. There is a bright future before it—bright for the friends of humanity and progress. With unshaken confidence, then, in a wise Providence, with faith in the possibilities of a Negro under a government that is democratic in deed and in truth, our efforts must be crowned with abundant success.

Many South Carolina citizens charged that the integrated University did not provide quality education. However, a group of students rebutted those claims in a letter to the *Columbia Daily Union-Herald*, February 10, 1875.

The university . . . is succeeding better than it did during the years of conservative rule. So far from being broken up, the university has more students now than it has had for the last eight years, when the State money was lavishly squandered to educate those who cursed the hand that gave it. . . . It was prophesied that the admission of colored students would never be endured—that it would break up the university, but white and colored students are now pursuing their studies amicably together, and there is no war of races nor other chimeras. . . .

As the final days of the Reconstruction University approached, faculty and students hoped they could somehow continue their education, as indicated by letters concerning a student, C. R. Bailey, seeking employment with the American Missionary Association, with the help of his professor, Fisk Brewer.

April 28, 1877, from Prof. Fisk Brewer to H. W. Hubbard

The enclosed letter from Bailey is its own explanation. I told him simply that you wished to give him information regarding the African work [of the American Missionary Association] and to bring him into connection with other young men who are looking forward to labors in that field.

Bailey has a great deal of good solid character, and a desire to make the best use of himself and his opportunities. He is somewhat slow in thought as well as in expressing himself, but has a pretty retentive mind.

I am glad that his wishes are so much fixed on Africa, and I think that he would be a good man for the A.M.A. to send. . . .

April 28, 1877, from C. R. Bailey to H. W. Hubbard

Professor Brewer informs me this morning that he has had a talk with you concerning me, after which you desired to see me and speak with me. I am very sorry indeed, sir, that I did not meet you.

I do not know what to write besides what Professor Brewer has already stated. My attention has been drawn towards Africa. I would rather work there than anywhere else. But I want to finish my education first. I believe when I have done that I can accomplish more good.

I am now, sir, twenty four years of age and will be twenty five on the eighth of July. Besides my English studies, including mathematics, algebra and geometry, I have studied Latin and French and I shall take up the study of German next year. I shall be very glad to hear from you.

The South Carolina Normal School had a brief, significant history. An integrated teacher training institution on the University of South Carolina campus, it counted only 8 graduates by the time it closed in 1877. However, many of its students—graduates and those attending only a year or two—became the teachers and school administrators who brought public and private education to several generations of African Americans in South Carolina.

During its first year, 1874–75, 39 students enrolled at the Normal School (33 female, 6 male) from ten South Carolina counties. The year-end report of principal Mortimer A. Warren chronicled an uphill battle against limited resources.

June 27, 1875

We have had no books, maps, charts or aids of any kind. The State is pledged to assist us to all these and has done nothing for us. We have had a little assistance however. The officers of Shaw School in Charleston, upon its surrender to the city, ordered two sets of encyclopedias sent us together with a few other books. I had a few dictionaries and devotional signing books which have been used and for which the State has paid me. Two maps have been borrowed from the University.

Yet, in spite of all this, we have prospered. A fair amount of work has been done. Arithmetic, geography, grammar, geometry, reading, writing, history, drawing, spelling, physiology, theory and practice of teaching, constitution of South Carolina have been taught. I think our pupils have become more independent than if they had books.

Only one of our students has roomed in the building and taken meals with the steward. There have been two causes for this: 1) the poorly furnished rooms; 2) the comparatively high price for board which the steward charges, viz money per month.

At the end of the second year of operation, principal Warren reported continuing scarcity, complicated by increased student enrollment (42 females, 25 males).

June 20, 1876

We have found it necessary to make two distinct divisions of the School, the Normal and the Training Departments. These departments are, however, more ideal than practical, the pupils in each meeting in a common study room. . . . The Normal Department is composed of pupils who have had some mental training and are able to do some little thinking on their own account. The Training Department contains such as have to be waked up to observe, to investigate, to think. They have principally, therefore, been taught from books; we give them no books (except a reading book), although we allow and require them to take notes of what we say.

. . . We cannot maintain our standards without a four years Normal course, I doubt; and yet there are but few of our pupils who can afford the time to complete the course. My conviction is that we can reduce the Normal course to three years (possibly, if good antecedent preparation be secured, to two) provided the Trustees give us apparatus and books. We have not got any books yet. We have finished two years of tolerable school without them. I do not claim that we have done as much as we could have done with them; I only claim that we have done something without them.

. . . Our plan of daily exercises varies somewhat during the year, of course, and yet it is possible to give an outline. . . . We separate Wednesday from all the other days as a sort of red-letter day. On that day occur our exercises in public reading, compositions are brought in, music is taught and drawing is taught. On other days, the principal, after the usual opening devotional exercises, gives a lecture on some general subject, taking up methods of teaching, giving an object lesson, speaking to some recent public events or giving some geographical, historical or other information. Following this comes a general exercise in spelling in which the whole school engages and then in succession the usual recitations. . . .

A year later the election of a largely Democratic Party state leadership, including a new Board of Trustees, signaled the end of integrated higher education at the State Normal School. Principal Warren dutifully filed his report.

May 31, 1877

This institution was closed today. Some three weeks ago I received written directions from the President of the Board of Regents, reciting that "In view of the fact that the legislature seems disposed to refuse to make the ordinary appropriations for the support of the State Normal School for the fiscal year commencing November 1, 1876, and inasmuch as our funds are entirely exhausted, I deem it my duty to direct the closing of the school at the earliest practicable moment."

On the 31st of May, we graduated a class of eight young ladies; their names are as follows: Fanny Stanley Harris, Verina Moore Harris, Maria Frances Avery, Celia Emma Dial, Laura Ann Grey, Clarissa Minnie Thompson, Eliza Jones Turner, Rosa Emma Wilder.

The exercises took place in the [Rutledge] chapel and were listened to by a large audience. There was a feeling of sorrow pervading the occasion impossible to describe. . . . And so closes my record of the proceedings, the history of the State Normal School while under my charge.

Prof. Fisk Brewer summarized the rationale for and contributions of the first University of South Carolina in a report written in 1876.

The admission of colored students for the first time in 1873 was too important a change to be overlooked in the development of the University. The indignation which was immediately expressed and has been often repeated since shows how offensive it was to a large part of the community. But most persons of intelligence will admit, and did admit, that sooner or later such an arrangement, or concession as some would call it, would be proper, if not necessary. . . .

The black boy who has solved all the knotty problems in arithmetic, who can explain the cube root and compute the value of partial payments, who has learned the long paradigms of Greek and Latin, and read in the original of Caesar's wars and of Xenophon's march, Cicero's patriotic orations and the poetry of Virgil and Homer, is no longer a cornfield negro. He has a platform of common knowledge and sentiment with his white classmate. Either there is no virtue in the humanities, or he has acquired something of true courtesy. He presses his society on no one who declines it. He regards the feelings of others with whom he has any relations. It is now true that most of the advanced students of color now in the University are gentlemen, and deserve to be treated as such. . . .

Young men here have the same feelings as young men elsewhere. The white neither occupy the same bedroom nor eat at the same table with the colored. But they do not see why, if a black man and a white man can ride on the same seat in the market wagon or in the railroad car for the sake of convenience or economy without impropriety, why they may not sit on the same seat to hear about medicine and law and science and literature.

3

Struggling to Survive
THE OLD COLLEGE FROM 1880 TO 1906

The University remained closed from 1877 to 1880. It reopened that year as The South Carolina Agricultural and Mechanical College, a name change designed to secure the federal funds provided by the Morrill Act, but one that lasted for only three years. During the last decades of the nineteenth century, the old College experienced extreme fluctuations in fortune as well as four name changes. That the institution would survive at all sometimes seemed doubtful.

Charles Coker Wilson, Class of 1886, recalled the state of his college in a paper he prepared for the Forum Club in 1926.

The South Carolina College reopened in 1880 with about 70 students, increasing to 175 by 1882, and in the next four years to 250. At this period it required a bitter fight in the General Assembly each year to secure an appropriation of $20,000. There was practically no standard for entrance, and all applicants were freely admitted and assigned to classes on probation until their proper grading could be ascertained by their work. The curriculum in most branches was scarcely more advanced or exacting than that of the high school of today. The students, however, were so ill prepared that, in spite of the elementary courses, not more than half of them were able to pass the final examinations. Yet scarcely any student ever left the institution without feeling an influence and an inspiration which made his stay there, whatever the sacrifice, well worth while. Dr. [Edmund L.] Patton used to say that anyone who would spend as much as a year on the campus and translate the inscription on the Maxcy Monument every day, though he did nothing else, would go away an educated man. Whatever truth there may be in that statement, certainly no one could live for a year in daily contact with that little band of devoted and able men who constituted the faculty at that time and not have his whole life influenced for good.

FOUR LOYAL SONS: THEIR LIVES TRANSFORMED

Four students who attended the University as it neared its centennial described the transformations that took place as they lived and learned on the Carolina campus.

Eugene Whitefield Dabbs came from a farm near Darlington. Though Dabbs's father died suddenly, and Eugene left after only one semester, his short stay positively influenced his entire life. From a frightened homesick boy, Dabbs turned into a sophisticated collegian, ready to join in the debate. He wrote often to his parents, sometimes twice a day.

October 7, 1880

While dressing this morning I saw a bed-bug on the sheet. I am sick of "grub." Maj [Benjamin] Sloan will not teach arithmetic. I am to commence in algebra. I am to study rhetoric and English history, Chemistry and geology or botany. I am very backward in everything I am afraid and too young to master the studies. I should go another year to school at home. I shall have to go to boarding tomorrow. I do not feel like eating though and am afraid I am going to be sick. I am in a room by myself so have no one but God to see me breake down every now and then. You and Pa must pray for me often and write a long and encouraging letter to me.

October 11, 1880

I came here a year too soon and so will have to study very hard to keep up. I wonder if you all miss me so much as I miss you. . . .

All work done on the farm and in the workshop is to pay for the instruction received. I will get no pay for such work so will not do much of it.

After School 1:20 P.M.

It may be possible for me to succeed in the studies before me, though it did not look much like getting along just now when I failed to reduce a fraction to its lowest terms on the blackboard. But as it is the first time I ever worked on a blackboard, I have hopes even if the sum was taken from my book. I am going to try to get full value for all money spent by succeeding by all hazzards God willing! . . . Oh! that I had not been in such a hurry to leave home and had stayed that I might help you all and get further advanced before coming to College. College studies are not school boy play. Forgive me, forgive me for ever saying I wanted to leave My Dear Darling Family. I pray that when I go back to you all I shall be a changed, better boy. . . .

October 21, 1880

I am feeling blue. So blue that I am in despair of learning algebra. Don't you think I had better go home and work and go to school for another year. I am feeling badly. It has been drizzling rain here all day up to now.

1:30 P.M.

Prof Miles did not ask me a question in rhetoric today, but I knew it all the same. . . . I hope you are getting the crop out fast now. I have got 41 examples in algebra for tomorrow's lesson. Multiplication. You must all pray for me. I feel that it is costing more than it is paying me from coming too soon. Love to all.

October 24, 1880

I was not questioned in history today and am sorry to say: did not know it very well. I had to study algebra more than common was the reason. Of 41 examples in Multiplication, I tried only 12 and worked only 8 of them. It discourages me. Maj. Sloan says he went 1200 miles from home at 16 years of age and that 250 of the worst boys imaginable ran him, a green country boy, down and almost tore the life out of him. I told him that he had studied algebra before and that I have not, but he only says "don't be discouraged. It will take you 6 months to get your mind in right training for study." Good consolation, is it not! for one situated like myself. If this is the case, I think I had better go home anyhow. Please enter my crop, at the Fair, for the most profitable crop, made by a boy under 18 years of age.

October 26, 1880

Today I think I deserve 100 in rhetoric and if I had not reminded Maj. Sloan of some mistakes in algebra which I made, I would have gotten 100 there too. Tell all to write about home. I like to hear about home.

October 28, 1880

Capt. O'Neale says he thinks I am improving and all that is necessary, is for me to fall in love with a pretty girl, then I will forget about home. I hope he is mistaken about the forgetting you all. Mr. Bomar says he is going to introduce me to some of the pretty girls soon. I know this College presents more and greater advantages to one who wants to learn than any other. The rules are that we come here with a desire to learn. That we come here as gentlemen, as South Carolina gentlemen. We are put on our honor and Prof. [William Porcher] Miles says he will resign before he will turn police and spy around to see that every one obeys a set of rules and regulations which no gentleman should ought think of breaking. By the way, Prof. Miles says he thinks honor is cut short enough without abbreviating the spelling, he spells it Honour. There is not a more polite set of gentlemen any where than I have found the faculty to be.

November 12, 1880

We have cause to rejoice at the decision of the Trustees to give me the room rent and $40.00 Dollars in money for ringing the bell. Mr. Boyd said last night, that he brought it up at their meeting night before last and they decided to give me the same that was given before the war, viz, the tuition $50.00. You see you were right. Trust in God and all will be well.

November 28, 1880

. . . "Well I have got the blankets," said I, now for the overcoat. I had been in several houses and the only one that suited was $12.00. I went to Kinards and found the one I was looking for: An Ulster no. 42 reaches to within 8 inches of my feet, very warm and a good looking one for $8.50. When buttoned up I cannot walk easily, it is like a frock. It is very near the color of my coat, weights about 10 lbs. I can never out grow it. Yesterday my wood gave out. I bought a one mule load, without lightwood, for $1.45. I have a balance of $5.05 on hand. I will get $5.00, more than enough to pay Mrs. O'Neale from the College. I will clear 75 cts. per month in the society. I will not have to buy anything but wood and oil and washing after this so I hope to be able not to call on you for any more money. . . . Yesterday I sweeped out the society hall and cut up and threw up my wood. Last night I joined the Society. The affirmative speakers tried to depreciate Washington and elevate Columbus. One made a glaringly false assertion about Columbus and the other about Washington. I took note of them and when I saw that the speakers on Washington's side did not notice them, I got up—I will not say what I said or how it was received by the audience, but the critic said I was the only one he could not criticize and the President (W. D. Simpson jr, son of the Ex Gov.) appointed me to head the debate 2 weeks hence. I do not know any thing about it, but by simply correcting two glaring errors I got myself appointed to a not very desirable position. Last night I was short, about one minute, but to the point. . . .

December 3, 1880

The last 3 days I have made zero in algebra; today by not being able to define a rule which I understood (Maj. Sloan tells us we never understand any thing we cannot explain or express).

. . . . Tell Pa to say something about nullification, I am on a debate for Saturday night week. My side is free trade. I have looked over Calhoun's works but cannot find much in my favour. Tell Uncle Stin. I jumped 14 feet yesterday. I do not think he ever beat that. It was on level ground. I ran about 15 yds. and then jumped. . . . .

On December 24 Dabbs's father was buried and his college career ended. The rhetorical skills he gained, however, served him well in courting Alice Maude McBride of Rip Raps Plantation near Mayesville. He wrote her letter after letter, some as long as thirteen pages, at last overcoming her family's objections to their marriage and taking charge of her thousands of acres of land. Their son, James McBride Dabbs, graduated in the Class of 1916 and became one of South Carolina's most distinguished men of letters.

In 1883 Andrew Charles Moore, another farm boy, came to South Carolina College from Spartanburg and graduated with what was later called "the brilliant class of 1887." Moore's first letter home revealed his confidence of success and reported on the renamed College's continuing commitment to a liberal arts education—it had embraced neither agriculture nor mechanics.

September 20, 1883

Your letter was received yesterday morning. I was extremely glad to get it, not because I was at all homesick, but because it was the first letter from home since I left. I thought I would get homesick in about a week after I got here, but now it is nearly three and I am all right yet. There is enough to keep my mind off of home, even if I wanted to get back. (There is a great deal in making up your mind and knowing what has to be done.) I knew that I had to stay away and resolved to do so without any grumbling, and with this determination I don't expect to get homesick much.

I suppose Paul saw a big time at the circus. Tell Paul that here goes a little fellow about his size on a bicycle, while I am writing. Just as he goes to turn a corner down he comes, but he gets up and tries it again. I see a big one now and then on the street. One of the college boys has one.

Everything is running along smoothly now. We have learned the different bells and when to go to the recitation rooms. I don't find any trouble with any of my studies except Mathematics. The Algebra was very hard at first, but now it is getting easier. We started in Ratio and struck some of the hardest problems in the book. There are about forty in the Fresh. Class and nearly all very ordinary looking fellows. John Coan and I will stand a good showing among them, unless they do a great deal better than they have been doing. I have only one recitation under a regular Prof (Prof. [R. Means] Davis). Mr. W. D. Simpson is tutor in Eng., J. L. Buchanan, in Math, and young Mr. [Edmund L.] Patton in Latin and Greek. Our class in Math. is divided into two sections—mine will recite to Prof. Sloan after Monday. They say that he is very strict, but I am glad of the change, for if I need to study anything it is Math. (I intend to know my lessons well and get on the good side of him.) I only wish I could recite Eng. to Prof. [Edward S.] Joynes—he knows so much and can talk so well. He knows exactly how to talk to boys to interest them and make them learn. Our board at the Stewards hall is still very good. Almost all of the boys board there and by order of Pres. [John M.] McBryde we elected officers to keep them straight.

Sorry to hear that the Jersey calf is showing symptoms of hydrophobia. Have you still got Pansy tied, and how is she?

You asked me to tell you with whom I was forming associations. (I have not formed any yet, I only know some of the boys. It will take a good while to find them out.) I don't know all in my building. The room opposite mine is occupied by three boys from Sumter. They are very good boys. Jesse knew one of them at the Citadel and says I will find him a nice fellow.

There is some danger of a boy being led astray here, if he does not make up his mind to the contrary, and absolutely stick to it. Sundays are spent very badly. Very nearly all do their studying for Monday and do not go to church, and if they go it is not for much good. John and I have been going to the Presbyterian Church, and expect to join the Sunday School. I think we will be able to conduct ourselves as we ought, both as gentlemen and Christians, or at least we have made up our minds not to be led astray by evil companions. When I know that those at home are praying for my welfare, it will not be so hard to keep in the right way.

August Kohn, a member of the Class of 1889, came from Orangeburg. After graduating, he wrote for the Charleston News and Courier and was active in University affairs all his life, serving as a member of the Board of Trustees. In one of his student journals, he captured the day-by-day content of a serious student's academic life—at least for the first month of 1888.

January 11, 1888

Called on in Physiology by Dr. [James] Woodrow, he gives me some German to translate—maxim—made good recitation. Had formulas in Chemistry to write.

January 12, 1888

Cold—Got to breakfast rather late—Dr. [William] Alexander goes over our work on syllogisms. Prof Davis gives us lecture on the Constitution of the U.S. Mr. [Phillip] Epstein away from city—court in Orbg—Acquittal of [Matt Grayson who accidentally shot James] Foy for murder. Had in Botany Cryptogamia—Dr. McBryde thinks [Alphonso] Wood so worthless on this that he does not hear class on it. Rainy and cloudy.

January 13, 1888

Rain. Recited on Progress of Poesy—Alexander "burst" good many in the hidden names of Shakespeare. Dr. [William B.] Burney gives about twenty boys formula at board to write. Dr. Woodrow comes a few minutes late and fails to meet class, but gives new lessons. [Charles] Arbuncle's breech of [marriage] promise case he pays [plaintiff Clara Campbell] 45,000. I believe Prof. Davis is temporarily acting as Editor of the Register. Big electioneering for the coming marshals for commencement exercises.

January 16, 1888

Rain. . . . Landrum, Means, Blease, Fairey are up in my room 'till 11.40, end up with a grand evolution controversey.

January 17, 1888

Rain and cold. F. H. McMaster seconded by J. S. Withers and P. H. Haskell have a free fight with A. O. Simpson seconded by P. H. Gadsden and Westfield. The former all S.A.E. latter all K.A. men, McMaster whips A.O.S. in 1½ rounds which rounds last 2 minutes each. The disturbance arises from the election of W. H. Hamer as president of the Senior Class, by F. H. Weston's vote. No injury in fight. J R Coan accepts the proposition of C. L. Blease to let matters drop as they stand. Alex [Alexander] gives lecture on Logic. Davis on Constitution.

January 31, 1888

Cramming up for Logic for tomorrow's examination. Sol [Solomon Kohn, August's brother, Class of 1889] has an examination today on III Math, which includes Calculus. The Board of Trustees of the college meets this evening, adopt the plan for the University as proposed by President McBryde. They elect Dr. McBryde as President. Dr. Burney as chemist for the agricultural department.

February 1, 1888

Stand examination today on Logic—under Dr. Alexander, he gives a pretty good one—values 5 syllogisms at 25—one had 8 sentences to state quantity, real, convert, quality etc—at 25. Give moods, give cardinal points, define denote and connote, why certain quantities <u>must</u> occur in certain figures. Define quantity, quality individual, single, general etc. I leave at about 2:45 with most other boys.

Some students kept track of their studies, others of their expenses. Laurens Watts Boyd from Laurens kept an account book documenting all of his expenditures—from tuition and books to bed slats and oysters— from 1886 to 1890. The first month of his sophomore year, October 1887, he listed the following expenses.

Oct 1st	Clothes	36.35
2	Church	.05
3	R.R. Ticket	2.75
	Hack	.35
4	Fees	45.00
11	Board for Oct.	11.25
12	Stamps	.25
14	Text book	.60
15	Society	1.50
15	Kindling	.05
17	Pocket book	.40
"	Blank-book	.45
"	Matches	.05
"	Wood	2.25
27	Stamps	.20
"	Oil	.20
"	Overshoes	.75
28	Apples	.10
"	Collar buttons	.05
"	Stationery	.25
"	Servants hire	.75
30	Washing	1.25
"	Apples	.15
"	Street Car	.05
31	Oil	.10

Four years later, by May of 1890, Boyd required different expenditures, including several entries for "cream," probably ice cream.

May 1	Board for May	12.50
"	Opera	1.00
"	Stamps	.20
"	Hack	.15
2	Milkshake	.10
3	Pictures	5.00
"	Pad	.15
4	Church	.10
5	Cream	.10
6	Watch- Chain	7.00
"	Belt & Tennis Cap	1.40
"	Fraternity	.35
8	Base Ball	.50
10	Cream	.30
12	Opera "Miss L.S."	1.50
"	Hack	.15
13	Base Ball	.30
"	Supper	.15
16	Base Ball	.35
"	Cream	.30
"	Haircut	.25
17	Camphor	.10
"	Flannel Shirt German,	
"	Miss LS"	1.50
22	Express	.40
23	Fraternity	.35
"	Medicine	.25
"	Cream "Miss LS"	.25
"	Cream "Miss LS"	.20
"	Hack	.10
24	Base Ball	.30
27	Opera	.50
"	Class Colors	.40
"	Cream	.20
29	Opera "Miss LS"	1.00
"	Note	.10
"	Cream	.35
30	Board for June	12.50

"	Drawers	1.50
"	Cream	.20
31	Oil	.50

His four-year final accounting reveals the inflationary nature of college expenses.

1886–87, Total expenditures: $236.35
1887–88, Total expenditures: $340.00
1888–89, Total expenditures: $353.25
Mch. 27 Stolen from me 3.00
April 30 Stolen from me 7.00
[Actual] Total expenditures: $343.25
 1889–90, Total expenditures: $445.00
 Total Expenditures for 1886–90: $1364.60

Evidently, Boyd's receipts had to equal his expenditures exactly. And so they did.

A DECADE OF DANCING

Whatever ups and downs affected the College in the 1880s, one constant remained: dancing. The *South Carolina Collegian*, begun in 1883 as the literary magazine of the Clariosophic and Euphradian Societies, included this typical description in 1885.

If you would see the beauty of South Carolina congregated, attend the State Ball, where every type of the beautiful woman—from the bewitching, vivacious brunette, to the fair and lovely blonde—is found, where the magnificent, self-possessed woman reigns supreme, and the youthful *débutante* shines the more brilliantly by reason of her innocence of the ways and wiles of the society world. . . .

About ten o'clock carriages began to arrive, and soon after Metz's German Band struck up "My Queen" Waltz, the inspiring strains of which soon had all devotees of Terpsichore engaged in the mazy waltz. Although we could readily see this band to be far superior to the one engaged at the last College Ball, in the performance of fine music, yet, for the purpose of dancing, it had not the power of inspiring as did the latter.

At two o'clock the doors of the Senate Chamber were thrown open, and a bountiful supper greeted the eye. Upon the table was all one could desire from the substantial fare of the laboring man to food fit for a king; everything to quench the thirst, from Adam's ale to princely champagne, was there. And in this connection I must mention an amusing incident.

One of the studious youths of the State College set aside a bottle of the sparkling beverage above mentioned, for his own particular use. Youth No. 2 happens by, and substitutes an empty bottle. Behold then the chagrin of youth No. 1, when after lugging the bottle down to his room, and inviting his friends to partake, he finds bottle empty, stopper gone.

After supper the German, under the leadership of Mr. M. C. Robertson, was kept up for some time, after which all left with their highest expectations realized.

ROMULUS ET REMUS

One of those youthful debutantes was Lil Butler, daughter of William Butler, librarian in the U.S. House of Representatives, and niece of Gen. Matthew C. Butler, Confederate war hero, state legislator, and U.S. senator. Her mother had died when Lil was ten, and in 1883 when she came to Columbia and lived at Miss E. S. Elmore's boardinghouse for women on Laurel Street, the invitations to South Carolina College social events began to arrive. They would keep coming—sometimes three for the same event—for more than a decade. Miss Lil was invited to Clariosophic and Euphradian Commencement Celebrations, Commencement Balls and balls on every occasion, fraternity parties, the fair and the circus, church and picnics, drives or walks, and always to the next "German" (short for German Cotillion)—a dance sequence for groups of four couples that required leaders and much changing of partners. Her collection of carefully saved invitations—there were no telephones—suggests that in the 1880s, at least for Miss Lil, the party never stopped.

October 12, 1885

Miss Butler:

    May I have the pleasure of taking you to the Circus on next Thursday Evening, Oct. 15th. Please answer in writing.

Yours Resp'y

Hutson Lee, Jr.

S.C. College

October 17, 1885

Miss Lillie,

    If you care to take the buggy ride we were speaking of sometime ago, I would recommend this aft. to be a very good time for it. If agreeable, please say at what time I may call.

Very truly,

E. Brooks Sligh

November 23, 1885

Dear Miss Lillie,

Our club (The Capital) will give a "German" at Stanley's Hall on Wed. evening, and if you have entirely recovered from your dissipation of "Fair week," I would be pleased to have you go with me.

Very truly,

E. Brooks Sligh

June 24, 1886

Dear Miss Lil:

I'm going to trouble you once more. The L'Arioso Club meets to night at Mrs. Barnwell's and if I'm not too late in asking can't I come up and go with you?

The walk to the German tomorrow night will be so short that I don't count it at all. Of course after we get there I'll not see but very little of you!

Very truly Yours

A. T. McCants

March 11, 1888

Dear Miss Butler:

I am dead: I committed "hari-kari" last Tuesday night immediately on receiving your note. I have been galvanized into a semblance of life and am going to make another break for liberty. There is said to be luck in odd numbers, and this is my third attempt. Can I see you tonight? Think well before replying, for another such a shock as I received last Tuesday would not only Kill one again but make me a raving lunatic.

Truly yours

G. W. Patterson

April 22, 1888

Dear Miss Lil,

If you can get the consent of your conscience to visit such a place, and in such company, it would give me great pleasure to escort you to our "Moot Court" tomorrow (Monday) night. I am going to hold forth with all the eloquence of a Webster. I merely throw that out as an additional inducement. Hope you are entirely recovered and that you will allow the above request to prevail.

Very Truly Yours

W. W. Johnson

June 25, 1889

Dear Miss Lil,

I have just heard that you fear you have the <u>measles</u>. I do certainly hope that this is not true for if it is it will be "simply awful!" And I shall feel like a lost sinner tomorrow and tonight. It was bad enough that you could not dance last night, but to miss all the dances of this week will be terrible. I don't see how you are to stand it, nor how the suffering community is going to put up with it if you have got the above-mentioned terror.

Yours,

W. T. Aycock

September 1, 1889

Dear Miss Lil:

I guess you have forgotten ere this that I once wrote a piece of poetry and dedicated it to you.

I have seen fit in my miserable loneliness to write another piece and will of course dedicate it to you, te volente (excuse this I couldn't help it). Please Miss Lil don't show it to anyone.

Very respectfully,

A. F. McKissick

Lil's brother William, president of Alpha Tau Omega, had to beg for a picture.

June 12, 1888

My dear sister:

As I won't be able to go to see you right soon and as I am afraid you will have disposed of all your photos by that time, I will drop you this note as a gentle reminder that I am still living and I want you to save me one. I have no doubt but that you will have a chance to give it away and will say you will give me one later. I saw the one you gave Bill Hamer, I don't think it is such a good one of you, yet it will do. Did you get your invitation: How do you like it? Something tony you know. Have an examination tomorrow in German by which time I shall be convinced that I am not much of a Dutchman as I was a Frenchman last week. Heard from Father yesterday. He says he sent your dress by express. Have you received it? and is it pretty?. . .

Save your photo.

Yr. affect. bro.

Wm Butler, Jr.

Lil's and William's father tried to control his lively children with letters from Washington, D.C.

November 22, 1888

Dear Lill

I do hope my dear child that you will have too much self respect to be frequenting all those dances, gotten up, by school, or college boys, and accompanied only, too, by one of them. A young lady cannot violate the conventionalities of society with impunity.

It is now very well settled that the democrats loose the next House, and I will of course loose my place. You can I suppose get along on $32 a month as that is all I can spare. I wish to keep the boys at school if I can.

Your affectionate father
W. Butler

Not everyone, however, fell under the spell—there were too few Miss Lil's to go around. Robert McMillan Kennedy, Class of 1885, remembered a different social scene.

In those days students had no outside diversions: the few parties we went to were, as a rule, in private homes. We visited the girls on the campus [daughters of faculty members] and in town but had no "dates." We walked to everything we went to. I remember parties out in Waverly at Mrs. Mary Preston Darby's, from one which old Bill Preston hung on my shoulder all the way walking home: he was a lazy but fascinating fellow and very smart.

Occasionally we boys in Eagle's Nest would brew a hot lemonade, getting the necessary spike from Mary who maintained a prosperous bar room one block from the campus at the corner of Main and College streets.

STUDENTS INTO PROFESSORS

South Carolina College survived repeated attempts at dismantling —even by as powerful a foe as Ben Tillman—because of the deep loyalty of her alums, many of whom became faculty members. R. Means Davis, Class of 1869; Andrew Charles Moore, Class of 1887; Herman L. Spahr, Class of 1895; George McCutcheon, Ashmead Courtenay Carson, and Henry Campbell Davis (son of R. Means Davis), Class of 1889; Elbert Daniel Easterling, Class of 1900—were but a few who made that ultimate academic transformation from student to professor.

When R. Means Davis sought an appointment to his alma mater, he asked for testimonials from his father's classmates. In a letter from Cheraw, March 22, 1882, William McIver's loyalty reverberates.

Your letter in behalf of your son came to hand last night, and I was very glad indeed to have my recollections of a very pleasant period of my life revived by a letter from an old College friend. It is against my rule to give any pledges to anyone, but I can say that, while I have not the pleasure of a personal acquaintance with your son, all that I have ever heard of him is of the most favorable character, and well calculated to incline anyone in his favor. My sole desire is to have the new professorships in the college filled with the most competent persons, for there is scarcely anything that I have more at heart than the success of the old College not simply because of the many pleasant recollections I have connected with it, but because I firmly believe that it is an Institution essential to the highest welfare of the State.

While scholarship and capacity for teaching (in which I understand your son has shown marked ability) are among the first requisites, I would also like to see the Chairs filled by graduates of the College, or at least natives of the State, not merely as a matter of State and College pride, but also because such persons would be more likely to understand the character of our young men, and feel a deep interest in the success of the College. It don't come natural for me to speak of it as a University therefore I unconsciously use the old and much more familiar title.

Andrew Charles Moore, Class of 1887, told his fiancée, Vivian May, of his "election" to a faculty position. Moore later edited the Alumni Record and served as dean and acting president.

July 22, 1900

Well, in the language of the classicist, I have crossed the Rubicon and have written a letter to Pres. [Frank C.] Woodward of the South Carolina College accepting the Associate Professorship of Biology, Geology, and Mineralogy. Just think of it! The developments in the case were so rapid that it has been difficult to follow them. Do you ask how it came about? After considering the matter for several days, discussing it with Dr. [John M.] Coulter and some friends, and after weighing the arguments you present, I decided that it would be best for me to apply for the place. Once decided, I set about vigorously to get it. The first move was to have Dr. Coulter telegraph Dr. [William Rainey] Harper who was in Charleston to see Dr. Woodward and Supt. [John J.] McMahan, members of the executive committee. I telegraphed Dr. [J. H.] Phillips to do the same and then went to work writing letters to my friends among the alumni of the college. Meanwhile, I received a letter from Dr. Woodward, asking me to send in my testimonials. I was unable to see several men from whom I desired to get letters on Saturday and it was Monday night before I mailed the testimonials. Tuesday afternoon a telegram came announcing my election, before the application even got in. Since then, letters have been pouring in from my friends with highest expressions of regard and promises to do all in their power for me. It is exceedingly gratifying to see how promptly and warmly they rally to my support. A letter from Dr. Woodward tells me that I was chosen by the unanimous voice of the Executive Committee and that they are all rejoiced to have an alumnus in the chair. All this is very flattering and I hope I have not lost my head. But it all means that a high standard is set for me and that to come up to the expectations of my friends, it will be necessary for me to do my very best. I cannot for my own sake afford to do less, and I trust I shall succeed.

I am delighted with the outlook. The old college is very dear to me and I go back with the old associations still alive in my breast. To go with such a strong backing and with the cordial support of so many warm personal friends is very delightful. If I am given a fair opportunity, and allowed sufficient equipment, I am confident that I can make the department felt in the college and the state.

Moore took the train from Spartanburg to Columbia to prepare for the fall term. The former student quickly adapted to the manners required of a faculty member as he wrote to his fiancée.

September 10, 1900

Upon my return to the President's house, I was warmly greeted by Mrs. President [Mary Leary Woodward] , and even ushered in to tea, where I was placed at a polished table with little napkins of every shape and size and texture scattered about over it and mingled with their little dishes, some of which I didn't know what to do with. One was intended for ice tea and when I didn't set my glass in it, I saw there was something wrong in the atmosphere and soon rectified the mistake. Both the Pres. and his wife were very pleasant and we chatted till nearly ten o'clock on various college topics. However, I was not very comfortable and would have left sooner, if I could have conveniently done so. Soon after supper Dr. W. handed me a letter [Moore had instructed his fiancée to write to him in care of the president], the handwriting of which I recognized in the moonlight on the piazza. I slipped it into my pocket, but wondered the whole time what it contained. Is it dignified for a professor in the S.C. College to stand on a street corner under an electric light and read a letter? That is what one did tonight. If you disapprove, I will see to it that he does not do so again. He was glad he read it and came on to his room smiling to read it again. . . .

Through all of the name changes—whether College or University—the dedication and public citizenship of loyal faculty members remained constant. R. Means Davis served his alma mater for more than twenty years, defending the institution, writing prolifically on historical and political topics, teaching prodigiously, and keeping in touch with former students as he wrote their testimonials, offered advice, and spoke at the ceremonies of their schools. Their letters back to him reveal the devotion he inspired.

John C. Buchanan, Class of 1884, wrote from Winnsboro, June 29, 1883.

I received your letter a few minutes ago. Much obliged to you for taking the trouble of writing. Yesterday I intended to thank you and your wife for the many kindnesses shown me, but I felt so sad at leaving that I feared if I spoke, I would commence crying. I thank you a thousand times for having aided me in obtaining an education. In some not so distant day I hope to pay you for boarding me as you have but I shall ever remember you with feelings of indebtedness and gratitude. I shall always owe you a debt which money can not satisfy.

William Haynsworth, Class of 1885, wrote from Sumter, July 13, 1885.

I was very much pleased at receiving your kind and friendly letter; I shall always look back upon my labors in your department, and especially my intercourse with yourself, as one of the brightest parts of my college life. I am perfectly satisfied with your recommendation—considering the subject, I don't think it ought to be made any stronger. I have just written my application for the school, and will forward it and the recommendations—yours and Pres. McBryde's. I intend to get that book on Pedagogics, which you taught in college, and study it, before commencing to teach.

I am glad to be able to relieve your fears as to my 'following my great ancestor's example,' for I have made up my mind that a wife is a luxury I will not be able to afford for several years yet; still I do not encase my heart in a coat of mail, and I entertain pleasant recollections of some brown and blue eyes in Columbia; but the picture you saw that evening, I had stolen, and I returned it.

Many students seeking graduate training, quite new in the 1890s, went to the University of Chicago and often found the experience shocking. C. E. Johnson, Class of 1895, wrote back to his old professor, July 20, 1898.

As to my "getting on" it is not very apparent. The work I am doing is extremely interesting, but I am left so entirely to my own devices that I never know what to do. I have a full course and I am recommended about 50 books. That is about all. I meet my professors four hours a week, and take notes to some extent, but so far as I can see, the theory is that a graduate student needs very little instruction. He is left pretty much to shift for himself. In English especially, I find it difficult to understand how I am to be examined.

As to Chicago, I am quite of the opinion that it is a sort of Sodom. I never go into the parks here without feeling that I may scare up a couple out of the bushes. The women generally ride wheels in skirts above their knees; some of them ride horses astride. In short, in public life, the people strike you as altogether shameless. I suppose we see only the lower classes, but I am simply disgusted by the coarseness of what I have seen. I looked at the legs at first; but now I never see any without sorrowing. . . .

Fathers wrote too. John J. Mikell of Edisto Island asked Davis to intercede on behalf of his freshman son, William, on April 1, 1900.

I received a letter from Pro. Woodward yesterday asking me to take my son William from College owing to his not being able to pass on his examinations. I write to you as a friend and friend of those who are interested in Willie, to do all you can to allow him to continue with his class; it would ruin Wm to bring him home now. I don't think he will ever get over the effects; he will never be willing to go back to his books, and all chance of his taking an education will be lost. I do not care about the expense attaching to his staying. I will give almost anything I have to keep him where he is. And I know that his Uncle Wm Hinson will feel it very much if he has to come home. I have written Pro. W. to see him, and use your influence with the Faculty to allow him to continue with his class. I hope to see you in person on Tuesday, but for fear something might happen to prevent my going I write this.

However, William did not return as a sophomore.

Years later Robert McMillan Kennedy, Class of 1885, remembered his professors.

February 10, 1938

The faculty was very small but I think very select. Dr. McBryde, I really believe, was the ideal president, better than any since with due respect. His home was always open cheerfully to well behaved students and it was a very delightful home. The students of that day were few enough to be on really friendly and intimate terms with the faculty.

Means Davis was very much loved. My recollection of him is his scarcely ever rising from his chair—I think it was laziness—in lecturing. He would whirl the chair round on its pivot and use a long pointer. I also remember his advice to me as a young teacher never to admit to my students that I didn't know a thing but to put them off and go look it up.

Dr. Patton was certainly one of the finest classical scholars we had. We used flattery with him to have him scan the whole lesson for us. He never seemed to catch on.

Major Sloan was the same soldierly gentleman that we knew for many years afterward as such. I always think of his classes by one funny incident. He called on Gilly McCutcheon to demonstrate a problem in geometry. Gilly wrote the theorem on the board and drew a magnificent figure. When Major Sloan said "Mr. McCutcheon will you demonstrate your problem," Gilly hemmed and hawed and made a few feeble gestures and then "Major, I can draw de figger but ah cawnt splain 'em."

[Edward S.] Joynes was much admired for his learning, but the students called him "Judas." They used to say that he weighed the papers when marking and that you could never tell just where you stood with him. One very funny incident in his classes I recall. When the Board of Visitors came during examinations to sit in his classroom, he called on old Bill McGowan to read some passages from say, Corneille, and then to translate. Bill performed wonderfully and the class, among whom were Miss Julia Bonham, Miss Nell Aldrich, Bill Preston and others were so convulsed with laughter that we nearly exploded. McGowan mispronounced every word and translated only two or three correctly. Dr. Joynes listened with rapt admiration saying encouragingly, "Yes, Mr. McGowan, yes, yes, Mr. McGowan." The Board expressed great pleasure in the recitation and congratulated Mr. McGowan. When they had left the room, Joynes looked over his spectacles and said, "Well, Mr. McGowan, you have made a spectacle of yourself. I thank God that Colonel Blanding was stone deaf and the rest did not know one word of French."

STUDENTS AS WRITERS

The literary magazine, the *South Carolina Collegian,* changed its name to the *University Carolinian* and then to the *Carolinian*—to match the institution's changes. Here students published papers they had written for classes. The October 1885 issue, for example, included articles titled "Dreams," "Medieval Latin Hymns," "Truth and Its Criterion," "Policy in Politics," "Grimm's Law," "On Flirting," and "Oleomargarine Butter." The student editors repeatedly lamented the declining interest in debate and begged professors for leniency. "A word to our Faculty: One complaint of our students is that they have not time for due attention to society work. Let us suggest that you can greatly relieve this difficulty by bearing the society in mind when you assign the lessons for Monday." But the student writer gradually replaced the orator.

The first yearbook, *Garnet and Black*, appeared in 1899. Now two publications provided student writers with opportunities to define themselves as well as to explain to student readers the constants of life on campus.

The October 1885 and November 1887 issues of the *South Carolina Collegian* included verses about freshman cheaters.

Pretty little fingers
On a little card,
Help the toiling student
Answer questions hard.
Dainty little ponies,
Glanced at on the sly,
Make the jolly Freshman
A sophomore by and by.

* * *

Freshman had a little "pony,"
With a greenish yellow hide,
And whenever Freshman studied Greek,
He also took a ride.
He rode it into class one day
Which was against the rule,
It made the fellows laugh and play,
To see a "horse" in school.
And so the 'fessor kicked him out,
But still he lingered near,
And graz'd contentedly outside,
Till Freshman did appear.
What makes the horse love Freshman so?
His classmates all did cry;
Because the *Fresh loves horse*, you know,
The 'fessor made reply.

Camping in the mountains to relieve the stress of studies is an old Carolina tradition. The *South Carolina Collegian*, November 1885, published
this narration, by an anonymous student author.

Summer Excursion

During the hot, sultry days of summer a few College boys, five in number, being wearied with the assiduous labors of the past session, determined to make a journey to the "Land of the Sky," in order to recuperate
for the labors of the coming session. These students, few in number but
excellent in quality, namely, D___, M___, G___, B___, and T___, all pre-
liminary preparations being made, mules, wagon, tent, cooking utensils,
and a respectable gentleman of color being provided, met in the large and
flourishing town of Easley, and from thence took their mountainward flight
at the rate of three miles an hour. Our first point was Table Rock, and there
we arrived the evening of the first day, having during the night the opportunity of testing the capacity of our tent to withstand a small-sized flood.
The rain descended and the wind blew, but our tent fell not, for it was well
tied down. Billy awoke during the night, and hearing the rain descending,
wanted to know what made the dew fall so heavily upon the mountains.
The next morning, however, dawned bright and clear, and fortifying ourselves with a substantial meal, we began the ascent. We were told that it
was only a mile and a half or two miles to the top, but by the time we
arrived there we concluded it was about ten. Notwithstanding the weari-
some ascent, we were amply repaid for our trouble by the magnificent view
to be obtained from its summit; description of mountain scenery not being
in my line, the imagination of the reader will have to supply the deficiency
in the narrative. Beginning our descent we arrived, after considerable
rolling and tumbling, at our palatial camping ground, where a sumptuous
repast was quickly prepared and more quickly consumed, our bill of fare
consisting of ham, corn-bread, stewed corn, and some very fine branch
water.

Having taken in Table Rock, we next directed ourselves towards the
celebrated summer resort, Caesar's Head. Camping the first night on the
beautiful banks of the limpid Saluda, feasting along the road on watermel-
ons and apples, traversing for awhile roads that would have tried the
patience of a Job, finally getting into the graded road, which wound around
one mountain after another, at one time passing along the edge of some
dark ravine, in whose depths could be heard the pleasant splashing of the
mountain streams, at another attaining some lofty elevation, from which a
grand stretch of mountain scenery would burst upon our view, we finally

arrived at Caesar's Head. After pitching our tent we proceeded to the Head, and from thence gazed upon one of the grandest sights in America, a sight which no pen can describe, no brush depict.

Blackening freshmen faces was a favorite hazing ritual (*Garnet and Black*, 1904).

The Soph
(With Apology to Poe.)

Once upon a midnight dreary, while he slumbered, weak
    and weary
From the knotty and perplexing volume of his classroom
    lore—
While he slumbered, soundly napping, suddenly there
    came a tapping,
As of some one gently rapping—rapping at his chamber
    door.
"'Tis some Sophomore," he muttered, "tapping at my
    chamber door—
Only this and nothing more.
Presently his soul grew stronger; hesitating then no
    longer,
"Boys," said he, "or strangers, truly your forgiveness I
    implore;
But the fact is, I was napping, and so gently you came
    rapping,
And so faintly you came tapping—tapping at my cham-
    ber door—
That I scarce was sure I heard you." Here he opened
    wide the door—
Darkness there and nothing more.
While he stood there in a shiver both his "limbs" began
    to quiver,
In there walked three dauber knights—the college
    knights of yore.
Not the least obeisance made they; but few minutes
    stopped or stayed they;
But with move of great and mighty, stepped within his
    chamber door.

Right upon his trunk they placed him, just within his
   chamber door—
Placed *him* there and nothing more(?).
Presently when this grim greeting had been given, they
   went fleeting,
And the Fresh. was left repeating maledictions loud
   galore,
Then betook himself to tubbing—till the daylight he was
   scrubbing—
Still berating Sophs. while rubbing off the color that he
   wore.
When the dark from daylight fleeted, when the blacking
   he'd unseated,
when to sunlight he was treated, this young Fresh.
   began to snore.
In his dreams, the sun o'er streaming, he could see the
   truth gleaming—
They had blacked him—nothing more.

J. Rion McKissick, Class of 1904 and president of the University from 1935 to 1944, wrote this account of the state fair when students were given time off to attend (*Carolinian*, 1903–4).

The Fair

The crashing music of the brass bands; the alluring speeches of the sideshow spieler; the merry crowds thronging the streets; the fun and the gleeful pleasure of the fair, have come and gone. Fair week is now only a pleasant memory, brightened and enlivened by the recollection of mirthful experience, and leaving many to regret that it comes but once a year. No one enjoys this glad time more than the Carolina man, who dresses in his best, decorates himself with a yard or two of garnet and black ribbon, swings his cane, and walks up and down the streets. He gets into the crowd at night and has all sorts of fun. He and his fellows yell and push through the jostling masses, ever going, never stopping. This year there were lots of pretty girls there, and most of them hooked on to Carolina men while the other college fellows looked on and smiled. Everybody was in a good humor. The two days' holiday at the College gave the boys ample opportunity to enjoy themselves and to see their visiting friends.

L.. J. [Lambert Jones] White recorded and bemoaned student slang (*Carolinian*, October 1891).

The Prevalence of Slang

No one will doubt that the use of slang is increasing. Our fathers and mothers used to fall in love with each other. We never fall in love but "get mashed on" some one. A student in college never makes a poor recitation, he "busts"; he never makes a good one, he "paralyzes" the professor—not much danger of some of our professors becoming paralytics. One person never has great influence over another, he has him "under hack." No one ever misbehaves in this enlightened age; but sometimes "gets on a tare," "paints the town red," "gets on a regular razee," and perhaps is finally "pulled by a cop."

Nearly every sentence we hear spoken is full of slang expressions. We hear them on all sides, from the slums of our cities to the palaces of our millionaires; they fall from the lips of the street gamin and the ball room beauty alike; the columns of our daily papers are filled with them; and, alas, too often we hear them from the pulpit itself—the place of all others where everything should be pure, whether it be thought, word, or deed.

The English language is a strong one, that no one will deny, and the use of plain, unvarnished Anglo-Saxon is an attribute of the careful student, and will have more effect on most minds than all the slang or vulgarism of Billingsgate or Bowery.

"The Diary of Charlie Classcutter, The Record of One Week, Loaned by His Friend B., Class of 1907," documented the life of a slack student (*Garnet and Black*, 1905).

Sunday.—Didn't go to church today. Sick with my foot. Ed. Croft accidentally stepped on it, but it isn't real serious.

Monday.—Went to chapel this morning, but had to leave. My foot throbbed. Went to two classes. 7 p.m. Am starting uptown for a little recreation.

Tuesday.—Took on a little Paul Jones [a brand of whiskey] for my foot last night and got it cured. Don't know just when I got back to the campus, but the electric lights were still burning. Saw Dyches waiting for me last night, or it was a tree, I don't know for certain. It was at the Marshal's office and I went around it, but didn't see the monument till I ran against it. Don't want no more hurt feet or Paul Jones in mine. It destroys the appetite.

Wednesday.—Went to classes today. Have that tired feeling, but hope I'll be alive tomorrow. Tried to outrun McKissick on the track this afternoon, but couldn't quite keep up. Called up the College over the phone.

Thursday.—Sick. Couldn't go to any classes after 10 o'clock. Got in an eating contest at breakfast, but don't think Scarborough got ahead of me. Potts gave up the race, but came near killing me before he did quit. I really wouldn't bet neither one of them that way any more for all the cigars or dopes, either, at Joe's.

Friday.—Went to *every* class today. Rested on the grass this afternoon a while and then walked round by the Colleges. She smiled at me from the upstairs window. Talked to her over the phone thirty-two minutes. Will call tonight.

8 p.m.—Worked at one problem thirteen minutes in succession since supper. Couldn't get it.

11 p.m.—As I write this part of my autobiography I am on the Belt Line, Columbia, S.C., on the back seat, riding my cares away. Had a killing good time at the College.

Saturday.—10 a.m. Missed breakfast and chapel this morning. Too tired to go to classes. Think I am going to be sick. This strenuous life is pretty strenuous—classes and chapel, and girls, and trouble and worry. Think I'll go to Ben David's and get some breakfast and to Abbott's, and then I hope I'll feel better.

4 p.m.—Dyches just brought me a special delivery letter from Major.

The *Carolinian* (December 1904) included a limerick for insiders.

Palmetto Limerick

A student whose name was Legare
Once got on a terrible spare;
He had to leave school—
For he'd broken the rhool—
And go home without his degare.

The tradition of oratory continued to inspire the reverence of alums. In 1943 Frank L. Dusenbury, Class of 1904, wrote to the Clariosophic and Euphradian Literary Societies, and his letter appeared in the *Gamecock* November 19, 1943.

My Dear Fellows:

About the turn of this century I matriculated in the South Carolina College. The first joining I did was the Clariosophic Literary Society because my brother James Saye Dusenbury and Parker Evan Conner were both rabid fans and were recruiting, just as were those enthusiastic rooters for the Euphradian society.

The jealousy at that time was keen as we did not have any fraternities and those two societies were the nearest we had to any secret societies—both did much to help green fellows like I was to get easy on their feet while talking or speaking.

I want to tell you that there is nothing you can do as a student that will be of any greater benefit to you than to be at ease as a debater, orator, reader, declaimer and to become familiar with the rules of Parliamentary law.

These halls were hallowed and revered in my time. Some of us never can be developed into those histrionic arts but even the dumbest should be given a chance, and how in the world can a striving lad ever get the polish he must have unless you Literary boys put him in the competition he should find in the practice you emulate!

WOMEN AT CAROLINA?

In the 1890s enrollment at South Carolina College declined to a frightening low; only 12 students graduated in 1894, and 6 of those were from the law school. The College was in trouble and the students knew it (*Carolinian*, January 1983).

What the South Carolina College needs just at this time is *life, vim, energy*. The reproach of her enemies that she is "dead," that she has fallen into a state of "inocuous desuetude" is, with regret be it said, not wholly unfounded.

Responding to state legislation in 1893, the Board of Trustees admitted women to the junior class, and then in June of 1895 to the College at all levels. Throughout the 1880s the *Carolinian* had noted women's accomplishments at other colleges around the country, but even those who believed that women had the right to be educated thought "separate but equal" was the best course, as J. R. F. [Jacob Risher Fairey] argued in 1889.

Let the State Educate Her Daughters

Do not understand me to advocate co-education. Nothing could be further from my thoughts; for I do not believe in any innovation that would tend to change the truly feminine character of our Southern women, and I firmly believe that co-education would bring that result. What I advocate is a female annex to the University, which annex shall be connected with the male institution only in so far that the two sexes shall be instructed by the same professors. Let the girls' college, including dormitories, recitation rooms, society halls, chapel, etc., be built on a campus away from the male part of the University. Let there be no intermingling in class rooms. No evils, such as are characteristic of co-educational institutions, could result from such an annex.

But they came—welcome or not—as an editorial in the *Carolinian* noted on October 1894.

The co-educational feature of the College does not seem to be very popular; no young lady has sought direct admission, but we have four fair guests from the city who attend the classes of English and Psychology.

Possibly, we are not much hurt by the fact that our female classmates are few indeed. We are proud, indeed, to think that our College has in theory made so decided an advance to the ideal plan; but now when the change is actually upon us, we flinch.

The December 1894 issue of the *Carolinian* reported—somewhat nervously —on Prof. J. W. Flinn's public lecture on co-education.

Dr. Flinn's plea for co-education throughout our Colleges, was full of logical reasoning and common sense. The young ladies of the audience were especially pleased by his gallant championship of their cause. We College boys smiled with secret pleasure, as we pictured to ourselves future scenes of blissful happiness, in which we mingled freely in the society of our fair friends.

Co-education is a mark of advancing civilization. Progress has done much to elevate women in many important particulars, but complete mental equality of the sexes is not yet universally recognized. When this stage in civilization is reached, man and woman will be mutually benefited.

Quoting from carefully gathered statistics, the lecturer showed that co-education is becoming more popular throughout Europe, as well as in this country. The presidents of the various institutions in which co-education is carried on, are pleased with the results of this change. Co-education is beneficial to both men and women. The increased cost of establishing co-educational institutions should not be considered; men and women are the jewels of a State, and opportunity for affording them the best education should not be lost.

The Clariosophic Society debated the Euphradian Society in January of 1895. Resolved: that woman should receive the same higher education as man. Decided in the negative. The "co-eds," not allowed in the men's debating clubs, founded their own debating group, the Parthenian Literary Society, and the "Minutes of Last Meeting of the Parthenian Society

as Read by the Secretary" appeared in the 1901 *Garnet and Black*—with parody for all.

President Bollinger in the chair. Minutes of the preceding meeting were read and adopted.

Miss Calvo moved—towards the table to get her fan. Miss Evans, in her usual practical way, moved that all boys be abolished from the South Carolina College, and further that a few men be induced to come. This was carried in a most satisfactory style. Miss Bateman was much moved and wept softly at intervals. Miss Nelson was completely overcome and promptly fainted but was revived later on. Regular order of business resumed. Miss Witherspoon read a very exhaustive and exhausting article on "The Benefits of Co-education." Miss Moore performed a very skillful treatise entitled "The Independence of Sense." After which Miss Bateman favored the assemblage with her latest poetic effusion, "The Waiting Man."

Debate: "Resolved, That woman's sphere is twice a hemisphere." The affirmative, consisting of Fickling and Lumpkin, began the argument, both speaking at one and the same time. The negative, Bookman and McDonald, retaliated in a most interesting style, but it was plain to see that the affirmatives had the sympathy of the entire gathering, including the negatives themselves, who fervently declared that "you all had lots the easiest side." A *viva voce* vote was taken without a dissenting chirp-note, showing the overwhelming victory of the affirmative.

The first article in the *Carolinian* by a woman appeared in October 1897, written by Beulah G. Calvo, Class of 1901 and the first woman on the editorial board of *Garnet and Black*.

Co-Education

We became restless, aggressive, iconoclastic, and the doors of South Carolina College opened to us, and we are here. Furthermore, we propose to stay, and to show the masculine portion of the students that Providence did not give the greater portion of mind to them. . . .

Mattie Jean Adams won the respect of peers and faculty and earned a feature story in the first volume of *Garnet and Black* (1899).

The First Woman Graduate of the South Carolina College

Her professors will learn only from her intimate friends, perhaps, how much enjoyment and inspiration she found in the two years' study within the walls of the old historic college; while, on the other hand, such is her innate modesty, she herself doubtless little suspects how greatly she is respected and admired by those who had the privilege of teaching her, and by all who knew her here. Although not well prepared for the Junior work, and having Sophomore studies, Miss Adams sustained herself well in her classes, and took her B.A. degree in 1898. In the words of one of the professors, we "predict for her a career of great usefulness and honor."

Some female students were not serious—not until later—like Katherine Hampton Manning, who entered in 1897, left in 1898 as a sophomore, and responded to President [William Davis] Melton's letter [to alumni] in 1926.

My dear Dr. Melton—

The University is good enough to claim me as one of the alumni. In doing so—someone has overlooked a record of which no one would boast—for during Dr. Woodward's regime, I was "shipped"! Co-education was then a tiny baby girl and instead of helping the child I was one of a group that did everything possible to hinder its development! I thought that when you were young and pretty, life was one endless good time. But Dr. Woodward didn't think as I did! And so—I learned from a righteously indignant Father that I had disgraced the name of "Manning" in the classic Halls where my Grandfather's portrait looked down and that the President in his letter had said I was "a demoralizing influence." When the shock of it all was over—(and our house was advertised for taxes)—the full realization of the seriousness of life, dawned upon me. Utterly unprepared, I had to go to work. And I dared to go back to the University, to the men of the Faculty who had been so annoyed by my lack of appreciation of all they were trying to do for me—and stating my case, asked them to give me letters that would help me to get a place in the Public Schools. They did—to a man! And I determined to make good. And did. I was elected and taught for years. Of course, marrying Ralph and having Buddy were the best things I've ever done in my life, but the years of service in the schools and the joy that went into that work—I do hope have in some measure proven my real appreciation of the kindly backing of the University—and that the University claims me, not on my record there, but because, in educational circles in our own little town, I hope and believe I conducted myself in a manner which would entitle me to be an Alumni of the University of South Carolina.

Sincerely,

Kate H. Manning Magoffin

While Manning was flunking out in 1898, Mary Anderson Leonard was earning a master's degree in history at South Carolina College. She then

taught history and political science at Winthrop College before completing her Ph.D. at the University of Chicago in 1904. Her letter to Prof. R. Means Davis (May 21, 1900) sounded the note of a new voice, a feminist academic.

I've enjoyed the work here [Winthrop College] more and more. To be sure, it has worked me you may imagine how hard. I've been very happy except when I've looked out to see more fortunate teachers here—those better salaried, much assisted, and of course, much leisured taking life as a very tame matter of course. But they are established and I'm not. As you predicted, I <u>have</u> earned my mush.

But I've got <u>work</u> out of these students: at first, because I was new, and they wished to please, and later because they were interested. Alas! for my short lived glory. For six hundred dollars and the hope of a better future, I've struggled along with 260 girls, doing twice as much actual work as any two other teachers here. Not a holiday have I had, not a half day's rest have I enjoyed, saving two thirds of the Sabbaths, for I tramp down street the other third—rain, hail, sleet, or snow—with girls to the Pres Ch, since here I've been. Why? Having been faithful in the much I expected to be rewarded in the little, at least.

Imagine my disgust, then, when a few weeks ago a certain Mr. Thompson, of great fame and learning in the land I call my own, approached me as the chair of the Com. on Courses of Study with: "The Srs. next year will have twenty-seven periods: twenty five is the maximum. Would you rather have Pol. Economy or Civics next yr?" Which interpreted into my language is, "the <u>men</u>, we high and mighty ones of great knowledge must take care of the standard of our respective depts.; our interests and self-respect demand that we sacrifice nothing, for in sacrificing, we lose the respect of the students for our depts. You are new, valued at $600, and are only a woman.

I've taken great pride in my work, especially as representing the old S.C.C. Shall all the snap be taken out of me by the selfish proceedings of a handful of men, some of them of not over great stature, merely that they may spread their wings and air their great learning?

I'm wondering if you cannot help me in some way. Couldn't you in <u>some</u> way give <u>some</u> other Columbia members of the Bd. <u>some</u> idea of the importance of the work I'm begging to be allowed to do? Let me plead with you to help me in these God forsaken parts to uphold the honor of the old S.C.C. in upholding myself? . . .

Decades would pass before J. Rion McKissick, Class of 1904 and president in 1935, began his speeches with the inclusive cry, "Men and Women of Carolina!"

TAINTED WATER AND PAINTED WOMEN

Charles Coker Wilson, Class of 1886, was city engineer for Columbia from 1896 to 1899 and later the University architect. He explained sanitation, or its lack, on the campus in "Fifty Years' Progress," a paper he prepared for the Forum Club in 1926.

The water supply of Columbia was taken unfiltered from the river and was supplemented by three heavily contaminated springs in Sydney Park. When the people complained too bitterly of the red mud, a change would be made to the greenish spring water, and it was pumped into the mains until its offensive odor forced a return to the river. Many of the people used open wells tapping a water bearing stratum underlying the whole city, and draining all of the cess pools and out houses.

There was city water on the college campus, but it was seldom used on account of its offensive character, and both students and faculty drew their supply from an open well in front of Harper College. Bathing was a Saturday night affair at most, as each student had to fill his tin tub with buckets from the well, heat the water in a kettle over an open fire, and finally pour the used water out of the window.

The sanitary arrangement on the campus consisted of four great pits about 12' x 50' x 10' deep with crude wooden houses over them. They had apparently not been cleaned out or disinfected since the founding of the college, and were swarming with great vile rats.

Conditions did not improve. No wonder then that Edward McKissick wrote from Asheville (October 3, 1901) to his brother, freshman J. Rion McKissick, with specific, sanitary instructions.

Now in reference to the cleaning of your room, I want, and hope, you will engage the service of a regular man (there is one in each building) to clean up your and Lee's rooms, the big room, to empty <u>slops</u> and to bring water to <u>wash</u> in. I want you to do this at once. Pay him every week and then you will get the best service.

My desire is that you go through College first in comfort, in health, in good appearance and with the best benefit to yourself, without losing your health in too much study or in too much confinement. Please join the "gym" and take walking exercise in the outdoor air as much as possible. <u>Eschew</u> <u>football</u>, pool rooms, and <u>Congaree</u> <u>water</u>. Do you get the spring water I ordered sent you twice per day?

Though bathing was an ordeal and the water too dirty to drink, vices were conveniently located. Charles Coker Wilson described them all in unvarnished prose.

There was a saloon on the corner of Main and College streets looking directly into the campus, another between Pendleton and Senate, and one or more on each block of Main Street up to Laurel, and on Gervais Street to the railway station. These were patronized by the college students with no restrictions, and by many of the leading men of the town, with the usual attendant evils; indeed there were several very distinguished lawyers noted as much for the periodic spectacle they made of themselves as for their brilliant oratory.

Gambling was widespread and unrestricted, and poker games could be found any night in the clubs, the hotels, the rear of the bars and the rooms of the students, while the State Fair brought every variety of gaming and swindling from horse races to shell games.

Every afternoon, when the weather was not too inclement, there emerged from this district a parade of all the barouches, landaus and victorias that the livery stables could muster, filled with gaily bedecked, painted and plumed women. It would move up Gervais Street, down Sumter, around the inside drive of the campus, back through the State House grounds (then open to vehicles), up Main and back to the starting points. On the campus there was exchange of badinage with the students on the green or in their windows, and on Main Street smirks and leers passed freely between the sidewalks and the carriages.

The Boys Play Ball

Baseball, the most popular sport of the 1880s, pitted South Carolina College athletes against city teams. At first the northern sport, football, seemed too brutal, but in the 1890s South Carolina teams played Furman, Georgia, and Clemson in a spirit of intercollegiate rivalry that sometimes exploded. The *University Carolinian,* later the *Carolinian,* documented the increasing popularity of football.

October 1888

Football is again getting to be very popular at the University. It has been well said, "It is good for the health of its votaries in more than one way; for those who play it never need to be bled by a physician, nor need their clothing ever be perforated for the sake of ventilation, because both these wants are inevitably supplied on the ball ground."

October 1890

If all the students were devoted to athletics, there would be less of the unfortunate division among the students of pale-faced brains and equally red-faced brawn; and the cause of studies and of health would alike be promoted. It is emphatically true that the standard of physical manhood is very low here. Listless, dyspeptic, inert, lazy, they groan at the effort to get up to the top of a tenement; they sprawl about over the Campus, like so many babies, kicking their weak little legs in the shade of the trees; they do not sit or walk erect and upright; and as for any active participation in outdoor sports, which require physical power and endurance, the vast majority exhaust themselves in discussing the abilities of the few energetic ball-players.

What must be done for athletics? Let the basement of Science Hall be turned into a gymnasium; let the adjoining field be fenced in, rolled off, a grand stand be put up, and all the appliances for simple, but interesting and beneficial, games be provided; and let it become recognized that "*mens sana in corpore sano*" is of practical import and value.

October 1891

The first game of football was played on the 5th. Much good material was brought out, and we hope before long to have a team that can successfully compete with any team in the State.

Rah! Rah! Rah!

Rah! Rah! Hoo!

Well done, 91, SCU

October 1892

It is doubtful if there is a college in the State that takes as little interest in athletics as we do, and yet our advantages in grounds, &c., are as good, if not better.

History of a Football Game

A Run

A Chase

A Tackle

A Fall

Three Faint

Two Stunned

Three Dead

That's all.

January 1893

Foot-ball

Of all sad words of tongue or pen,
The saddest are these: it might have been.
But the most consoling, and just as terse,
Are these few words: it might have been worse.

On Christmas Eve, two foot-ball teams faced each other at Charleston, South Carolina. One was the Furman university, champions of the State; the other was the eleven of the South Carolina College. . . . The game was well contested, but the Greenville men's superior skill, training and weight told greatly in their favor. The score at the end was: Furman 44; S.C. College 0. After cheering for their conquerors, for the referee and the umpire, our boys boarded the train for home, where they arrived, slightly "disfigured, but still in the ring."

November 1894

Georgia 40   Carolina 0

Football seems to be the thing. The late defeat has had on our team the usual effect of defeat on all forcible men—the breeding of a new determination.

November 1896

Carolina 12   Clemson 6

November 1897

We were glad to note that the rivalry between Clemson and the South Carolina College is apparently quite friendly, and for the most part devoid of those elements of jealousy and spitefulness, so often common to athletic rivalry. We are sure that the two colleges, as well as the two teams, bear each other nothing but good will, and we say, with pardonable pride, we think, that we, as well as Clemson, are to be congratulated upon the clean, gentlemanly game of ball that took place on the gridiron Wednesday of Fair week. And we further venture that if all foot-ball games were of the same character, we would not hear the great cry that is now filling the newspapers against it.

November 1899

Clemson 34   Carolina 0

> Zero, Zero,
> Rip, Rap, Ree,
> Nineteen Hundred,
> S.C.C.!

November 1900

Clemson 51   Carolina 0

Spring 1901

The Legislature has seen fit to replace the old wooden mess-hall, which has served its purpose for the last half-century, by a more modern and improved one. One can hardly estimate the value that this improvement will add to our athletic interests. There will no longer be any trouble about a training table as the "mess" is to be fitted up with the latest culinary apparatus. Besides the improvement in the cooking of the food, a greater number of boys will board together, and hereafter we shall look for that longed for state in college when each and every one will pull together and make our athletics more successful.

November 1902

Carolina 12   Clemson 6

> The tiger tail was truly twisted and at last tied in a hard knot.
> Carolina won! old Clemson fell!
> In future years our kids shall tell,
> For we did give those tigers—well,
> Three cheers for Carolina!

The Faculty Minutes (November 25, 1902) carried a complete account of the first tiger burn. Then the faculty banned the Carolina-Clemson game until 1909.

The Faculty Athletic Committee who were instructed to look into the recent trouble between the students of this college and Clemson College submit the following report for the consideration of the Faculty.

Some days before the Fair the Clemson foot ball team decorated one window of Solomon's tobacco store and the other window was decorated with emblems and colors of the South Carolina Athletic Association, by Mr. Solomon's clerk, Mr. Wyse, and some of the students.

The Clemson window contained a lithograph of a tiger, the emblem of Clemson with a plug of tobacco in his mouth, on which had been painted S.C.C.

After the game in which Carolina defeated Clemson, the Carolina Team on entering Solomon's store, took out the lithograph and tore it off. They carried it to the house of a gentleman who gave them a lunch, and left it there where it still remains.

The students of the S.C. College displayed that night a transparency as an emblem of victory. This transparency showed a game-cock crowing over a crouching tiger. They marched with it down Main St. and a number of Clemson students attempted to take it from the Carolina students. This effort on Clemson's part resulted in a scrimmage in which it is said knives and swords and knucks were used and some little blood was spilled. No one was seriously hurt. The transparency was so badly injured as to be useless for further display.

Clemson students then made threats that if the Carolina students attempted to take the transparency into the Elk's parade the next night they would take it away from the Carolina students and not permit it to be carried in the parade.

Carolina students assuming this to be a threat presented themselves in line that night with a facsimile of the transparency held aloft. All this was unknown to members of the Faculty.

Col. Sirmyer, the Commandant of the Clemson Cadets, asked the parties in authority to have the transparency removed, as he could not be responsible for his men if it was carried.

Col. Jones and the chief of Police said they would use their influence to have the Carolina students abandon their purpose to carry the transparency, but they could see nothing objectionable in it.

They did then ask Mr. Benet, who commanded the Carolina students in the parade, to abandon the idea of carrying it. Mr. Benet informed these gentlemen that he could not consent to do so under the Clemson students' threat, and these gentlemen then said they would have nothing more to do with the matter, whereupon, one of the Clemson students turned to Col. Sirmyer and said, "We will get it," and Col. Sirmyer replied, "I know you will."

After the parade Col. Sirmyer dismissed the Clemson cadets in the State house grounds, and retired on horse-back down Main St.

The Clemson cadets then put up their guns and retaining their bayonets and swords marched in a body to the S.C. College campus and drew up in front of the brick wall on Sumter Street.

The S.C. students had immediately after the parade returned to the campus with the transparency and dispersed.

On seeing the Clemson cadets line up in battle array in front of the College, such of the students as were on the grounds and in their rooms, armed themselves as best they could and drew up on the Campus and prepared to resist the attack of the cadets.

Mr. Benet asked the Clemson cadets what they wanted and they replied they must have that transparency. Not wishing to see a bloody battle between young men of the same State and blood, and wishing to avoid death and disaster to any, Mr. Benet offered to meet in single combat any one they might select from their ranks and thus settle the issue. This offer was not accepted.

Mr. Benet, still actuated by high minded and humane motives then suggested that a committee of three be appointed from each side to confer, and settle the issue. This was accepted and the two committees were selected.

In the meantime many of the Professors and one of the Trustees had arrived on the pending riot field. These gentlemen attempted in vain to find the President of Clemson College or the Commandant among the crowd of cadets.

Failing to find any one in authority, they appealed to the Clemson cadets as S.C. gentlemen to go quietly back to their barracks. But at this time, as the Committees were already conferring, the cadets preferred to await their decision.

Some time later the Committees reported they had agreed, and the Chairman of each asked their respective student body if they would abide by their decision. Each student body replied, "Yes."

They then announced, that as the transparency bore an emblem of each athletic team, they had agreed that it should be produced and fired by the joint committees.

The Clemson cadets accepted these terms, and the S.C. students also accepted with great reluctance.

The emblem was then burned by the joint committees, and each body of students gave three cheers for the other, and the Clemson cadets retired.

This report was unanimously adopted and ordered to be spread upon the minutes.

Frank H. Wardlaw in his introduction to *"Men and Women of Carolina"*: *Selected Addresses and Papers* by J. Rion McKissick (USC Press, 1948) told the story from a participant's viewpoint.

But while the Carolina student body was "dug in" behind the Sumter Street wall awaiting the onslaught of the cadets who were drawn up in battle array in the street, Sophomore McKissick occupied a spot in the front line.

The Colonel later related that a senior, a country lad from the "Independent Republic of Horry" came up to him and asked solemnly, "McKissick, are you armed?"

The sophomore showed him his revolver.

"How many bullets do you have?"

"Five."

"McKissick!" The senior's hand grasped his shoulder in fervent appeal. "Make every shot count!"

In 1905 the faculty eliminated intercollegiate football, inspiring this lament in *Garnet and Black* (1906).

Resolved, by B. Brown

WHEREAS, the Trustees in their might
Have said that football and a fight
Are real synonymous, and quite
        De trop at our college;
Adjudged and ordered and decreed
That in this thing they'll take the lead
And quell our *inter*-(so forth) greed,
And give us naught by knowledge:
NOW, THEREFORE, it's by us resolved:
We think the game is too involved
A problem to be quickly solved
        By tearing out the pages;
And hope you'll take it like it's meant,
That, doubting not your good intent,
We feel, in zeal for good, you've bent
        Your judgment into rages.

4

A Whole of Many University Parts

CONFRONTING THE TWENTIETH CENTURY

Students at South Carolina College in 1906 witnessed yet another institutional name change when legislators passed into law an "Act to Convert South Carolina College into a University, Under the Name of University of South Carolina."

Prof. Edward S. Joynes described the rationale and anticipated meaning of the change in the 1907 *Garnet and Black*, noting, "The institution had outgrown its collegiate organization. The increase of its departments and especially of its elective courses had rendered its administration under the collegiate system increasingly difficult. The successful incorporation of the Law School and the Teachers' School had already opened the way for the development of professional study. . . . In a commonwealth so fully supplied with excellent colleges, it was felt that one central institution was needed which should offer larger and more liberal courses of study than seemed to be practicable under collegiate forms—an institution distinct yet comprehensive, which might serve the development of an harmonious and well-articulated system of higher education."

The new University was poised for expanded extracurricular offerings and increased student numbers. It quickly got both. Enrollment surged from 285 students in 1908 to 551 in 1913 and over 2,000 in 1940. Campus changes included the first women's dormitory and first student activities center (the converted Flinn Hall) as well as new classroom buildings. Carolina students added basketball to their intercollegiate sports teams and brought a Y.M.C.A. and a Y.W.C.A. to campus. They held their first "homecoming" celebration in 1919. The women, a steadily growing force on campus, founded two female literary societies and their own dance club. Students fought in World War I, marched for women's suffrage, and worked part-time jobs to get through the Depression. They grasped the university ideal of many routes to learning.

FRESHMAN YEAR EXPERIENCES

Growth was a common theme of the early-twentieth-century university—in South Carolina and elsewhere. In 1910 freshmen confronted Carolina growing pains most dramatically as a housing crisis. One student wrote an unsigned letter, September (n.d.), 1910, to his parents describing the machinations of finding a suitable place to live, with only limited assistance from University officials.

My dear Mother and Father:

I arrived here yesterday afternoon about six o'clock. The train I came on was awfully dirty and when I reached Columbia I was filthy.

I came up to the College and saw Dr. [Pres. Samuel Chiles] Mitchell. It was too late to see to getting a room so I had to wait till this morning: but in the meanwhile I met some boys among who one was a senior, and I slept in his room last night as there was no other place to stay. The College is over crowded so that there is more than they can accommodate. They are putting three and four in a room.

Dr. Mitchell said he did not get my application card saying to reserve a room; and so far I have been unable to get one. This is Tuesday night and I guess I will have to sleep on a lounge in the boy's room again. I guess I might get in a room by making four or five to the room, but you know that won't do, will it?

Well, after so long a time finding that I could not get a room without being in the same room with four or five, I went up and had a talk with Dr. Mitchell, and asked him if it would be all right to get a room out somewhere and still eat in the mess hall, and he said yes and referred me to some private families who had a room to rent.

I went to one and asked about the room, and she said that the room with a private bath was $15 per month. That was a little high so I went to Mrs. Dozier's and she had a very nice room, completely furnished and just as neat as a pin, and said she furnished the linen and in fact everything except fuel for $11 per month. That is about as cheap as I can find a room for with nice people.

Upperclassmen singled out freshmen for special treatment that ranged from wearing "rat caps" or "freshman beanies" to enduring practical jokes. Although physical hazing was discouraged by policy and, in 1914, prohibited by state law, students did not entirely discontinue the practice.

The freshmen of 1910 related such an experience in their class history section of the *Garnet and Black.*

We held in chapel our first class meeting on the afternoon of October the fifth. These meetings each year are always well attended and ours was no exception to the rule. The gallery was filled with visitors, well supplied with pails of water, which were emptied at short intervals, upon our inno- cent heads. Notwithstanding this, we transacted all business and, though soggy, retired in good order.

A poet using the pseudonym Chicken penned a warning to freshmen in the *Gamecock,* September 29, 1910.

Oh You Fresh

Into the campus parading in state
Comes now the Fresh all prepared for their fate
Ties all of green and with bows on their shoes,
Bands on their hats all of various hues;
Eyes of all open with mouths all agape,
Pompadours brushed into latest of shape,
Shouting with laughter and raising a roar,
Threatening to break in the Sophomore's door.
But! When the 'morrow had come, it is said,
Half of these Fresh were found under the bed.
Pompadours ruined and ties out of shape,
Bands on their hats are replaced with some crepe;
Eyes are downcast, and mouths are all dumb,
Some of them wish they never had come.

John Erskine Hankins, B.A. 1924 and M.A. 1925, recalled in an unpub- lished memoir the treatment of a freshman who was a state legislator.

During my tenure as a graduate assistant, I had in class a freshman named Dewey Foster from one of the upstate counties. I found out he was a member of the legislature, elected before he had entered college. We had several student legislators, but it was unusual to find a freshman in that capacity.

Foster was older than the other freshmen, but he was a model student, quiet, efficient, and always careful to wear his freshman cap. One evening I had gone to his room to ask about a theme, when two sophomores entered. One said, "Rat, bend over that table; I'm going to paddle you." Foster bent over and was paddled, first by one and then by the other, after which he quietly went out. One of his upper class roommates asked the boys, "Do you know who that was you paddled? That was a member of the Legislature. He can kick you out of here and put you away in the state's prison for what you have done, so you'd better hide out for a while." The two boys were terrified that Foster might do just that, for hazing was against university rules, though they were not usually enforced. Their paddles enjoyed a vacation for a time.

Freshmen sometimes collectively resisted their treatment, as indicated in this letter from Olin D. Johnston, then studying for a master's degree, to his fiancée, Gladys Atkinson.

May 8, 1923

Our freshman class last night had a big celebration by making a bonfire out of their caps. I fear they will have to buy new caps or suffer the results. We had a student body meeting this morning and it was resolved that all freshmen must have caps by the end of the week or they would be reported to the discipline committee. Much may come from the action the freshman class has taken. Wholesale hair clipping may follow.

In 1929 the editors of the *Gamecock* supported hazing and chided freshmen for ignoring long-standing rules of decorum.

Editorial: The Freshmen Untrammeled

October 14, 1929

There has been hazing on the University campus, the paddle has swung and fallen and rat caps are everywhere perched on the heads of freshmen. Yet, the two highest laws of the sophomore and upper classes are trampled in the mire daily.

Not many years ago, the mustachioed freshman was treated to an improvised shave. . . . Today "rat whiskers," curly, straggly, barely visible, or thick with a hirsute heaviness, trail beneath many freshman caps.

But the crime of crimes lies not even therein. In the past, freshmen have been counseled not to smoke. . . . Now the traditions of the past are violated, succumbed before huge billows of cigar and pipe smoke. One freshman even invades the monopoly of Dean J. Rion McKissick and uses a cigar holder, of imitation ivory at that.

In 1926 members of the Y.M.C.A. began three-day orientation camps to acclimate incoming freshmen. Academic deans, coaches, and student

leaders attended to help new students navigate the University. Currie McArthur, Class of 1938, compiled a handbook for the 1937 camp that included a list of tips for the first year on campus.

—Wear your freshman cap, especially while out in Columbia. It distinguishes you as a Carolina man.
—Bare your head during the singing or playing of Alma Mater.
—Carolina is no country club. Try studying and spend four years on campus.
—Take the Honor Pledge seriously and remember it. Carolina has no greater tradition.
—You should attend chapel. The programs are interesting and instructive.
—Learn all you can and keep quiet.

HIGHER HUMOR

Shortly after the *Gamecock* was founded in 1908 as a joint venture of the Clariosophic and Euphradian Literary Societies, an anonymous student contributed a humorous account published in the March 7, 1908, issue.

The Story of a Chicken Raid: A True Account of the Memorable Fowl Foray of One Night in January, 1908

We were desperate; we desired to let the college know that there were unsuspected Raffleses [*sic*] in its midst; we wanted to do something early at night, when there would be an element of danger to quicken our blood and set our pulses to throbbing; we were daredevils, inflamed by no beverage save the effervescent cup of youth whose champagne is our daily draught. At 10:30 pm, the campus is deserted, save for a few straggling lights in Rutledge. Our dark forms noiselessly vault Dr. M___'s [probably Pres. Samuel Chiles Mitchell's] back fence, and glide spectrally in the underbrush of the yard. S' death—there are no chickens in the coop! What to do? "Try Dr. [Edward S.] J[oynes]'s coop," suggests D___. But the Doctor has been wise in his generation; his coop is a sepulchral vault, tenantless, and there is nothing in his refrigerator, which you may find on his upper back piazza.

In despair, we proceed to the neighboring roostery. There is a discordant squawking within that tells of fat hens. Success crowns our efforts, for in ten minutes we are back in our room with six fine Dominicas littering the floor of the bedroom. Not satisfied with this, we visit an adjacent hen resort, poke a stick through the bars thereof, and six more fowls calmly strut into our hands.

The next night there are beer, cheese, crackers and chickens galore.

Garnet and Black humor included lists of spurious student groups. The 1908 edition included a drinking club and a gaming club.

Order of the Sons of Schlitz

Object: To beer up under our numerous college duties
Place of meeting: Under the Anheuser-Busch
Sign: Blue Ribbon
Favorite Plant: Hops
Motto: With few equals in the art—no limit.

Carolina Matchers' Club: In Luck We Trust

Motto: Heads I win; tails you lose.
By-word: Call it
Time and place of meeting: Any hour, anywhere

A Semester in the Life of a Law Student

James Henry Hammond, a law student in the Class of 1910 and a grandson of Gov. James Henry Hammond, kept a sparse, anecdotal diary of his experiences at the University of South Carolina during spring semester 1910. It is a telling account of student extracurricular and, occasionally, academic life.

February 19

Was installed in [Euphradian] Society as president. Made a little address. [Irvine Furman] Belser and [Clinton Tompkins] Graydon are pushing a scheme in joint assembly to establish a third society in college. Our enrollments in the two societies is too large, and we really need one more; but I seriously doubt the advisability of letting two such schemers lead the movement. All they think of is pushing themselves into prominence. . . .

Went to see final session of House and Senate this afternoon. The Senate gave $5000 to build us a pool.

Took McNair to see Janie Marshall. I think a lot of Miss Janie.

February 22

Wrote to papa, Smith, Miss Hane and Miss Kenson. Called on Miss Catherine Moore for the first time. She is very smart, but not so attractive.

February 23

Got Finches Cases on Real Property, $5.50. Called on Susie Fitzsimons. Saw Mrs. Fitzsimons. She is just up from an operation for appendicitis.

February 24

Examined for hook worm with [Randolph] Murdough, [Charles Alfred] Ashley, McNair and Shears. All of us but Ashley have it. I have wondered why I was so dull at times. Will take treatment this week.

February 25

Went to party at Miss Sue Flynn's.

February 26

Went to hospital to get treated for hook worm, but as Dr. Watson was to have charge, I decide to wait until Weston came on.

Matter of third Society was launched again by Belser and Graydon. Graydon especially tried to run everything with a big hand and his movement was finally killed by a small majority. I believe we need the Society, but do not like these ones to be at its head, for they can't be trusted.

February 27

Slept late and missed breakfast. Josh, Kid and I called on Buster and Bob. Then we went to walk down by the river and stopped in the penitentiary to see Percy Sweat. I feel sorry for him and gave him $1.00, although pretty broke.

Called on Miss Marshall tonight. Really enjoyed my visit very much. Have got to study tonight to make up for last time.

February 28

Read a little book Miss Marshall lent me called, "When a Man Marries."

March 1

Professor Herndon Moore died this afternoon late. He has been Dean of Law Faculty for four years. He was the most polite, most courteous, and most respected gentleman I have ever seen.

Ashley drunk today.

March 2

Moore's funeral. No classes on account of Professor Moore's funeral. Buster and I sat up from 1 to 4 with the body. Funeral at Trinity [Episcopal Church]. Nearly all of us Law students went to the cemetery. I have felt pretty blue all day about it.

Went to the Little Grand tonight to revive my spirits. Wrote to Misses Byrd, Simons, Bostick, Middleton and to Sligh. Thinking about Miss Marshall lots.

March 3

Randall Kelley stopped by to see me for a few minutes. Poor fellow married too soon.

Wrote mama. Seems long time since I've heard from home. Tried to steal some chickens with Cooper tonight, but failed.

March 4

Played in the senior-junior baseball game. Juniors beat us 11 to 4.

Had about 15 fellows up here to help me eat the fare of geese I swiped Tuesday. Had a splendid time. Quitman Marshall spent the night with me.

March 8

Went to Courthouse with half the class to look up records.

It sure is discouraging. Called on Miss Susie Fitzsimons tonight.

March 14

Went to Columbia College reception. Enjoyed it very much. Talked to Miss Ford and Miss Ruth Byrd.

March 18

Took tea with the Marshalls. Had a pleasant time.

Hard at work on records. We are all at sea in the Clerk's office.

March 20

Went to Trinity. Walked home with Miss Marshall and Miss Fitzsimons. . . . Went to see Miss Marshall at night.

April 4

Went to a party at the Flynns'. Met the misses Cheves of Charleston. Had a splendid time.

April 5

Carried Miss Janie Marshall to our Easter German. Had a fine time. She sure was the sweetest and most aristocratic girl on the floor. It was through her that I enjoyed myself so much. I am afraid I am in love once more.

We beat Davidson 10 to 5 this afternoon. Good game. Harper pitched splendid.

April 6

Met Miss Elise Simons. She goes to cotillion with Mr. Seibles tonight. Slept all afternoon. Sent Miss Janie a season ticket.

April 7

Took Miss Elise to ball game. College of Charleston 5, Carolina 10. Carried Miss Elise to Shandon dance. Had a fine time. Miss Elise sure out-shined them all. I am afraid all of my old regard for her has not entirely vanished.

April 8

Went out with Miss Elise, George Orr and Miss Wilkins in Orr's machine. Had a fine time. Went to Columbia College reception. Drank a little boose up here and felt so sick, I had to leave abruptly. Orr, Bob and Kid drinking. John drunk. Buster nearly so.

April 9

Felt bad all day. . . .

April 10

Saw Miss Elise off at 4:45 pm. Walked with Miss Susie Fitzsimons and tea there. Called on Marshalls.

April 12

Miss Byrd got in on 1:45 train. I met her. Called again tonight. She loves me yet. Well, I am sick of love affairs. Think it best for me to get down to work instead of all this foolishness.

April 14

Caught ball a little. . . . Went to cheap show with Quitman Marshall. I am not studying as I should.

April 15

Had a fine time in the game against the Juniors. They beat us 11 to 6. Most of the fellows were drunk before the end of the game.

April 18

Took tea at the Marshalls'. Carried Miss Janie to Shandon Dance. Had a fine time. . . . Miss Janie is quite popular for a debutante.

Miss Sue Flynn asked me to tea for Sunday and Miss Fitzsimons for Friday.

April 24

Called on Emma Beth. Sligh called on Dickie. Took tea at Flynn's. Large crowd. Miss Sue is just the sweetest lady I ever met.

April 28

Moot court and beer. Had a time. Nearly everybody drunk. Serenaded both colleges.

April 29

Have something wrong with my kidneys.

May 2

Felt bad all day. Presided over the Southern Oratorical Contest. Carter won it, although he broke down in his delivery. He sure recovered himself though.

Went home with Miss Marshall. Wrote to Mama. Worn out. I have got to do more studying.

May 3

Did little all day. Went to reception at Miss Annie Lowry's. Had a fine time. Strong punch.

May 17

Studied a little. . . . Appeared before the faculty as chairman of the committee from the student body in behalf of Brandenburg, who was expelled for being drunk. After working for the last few days, we got him reinstated.

May 21

Saw Haley's Comet.

After graduation Hammond became a well-regarded lawyer and a senator in the South Carolina General Assembly.

SCHOOL SPORTS AND SCHOOL SPIRIT

The ban imposed on football in 1905 was lifted by the trustees halfway through the 1907 season, and the return of the sport sparked heightened enthusiasm for cheerleaders and cheers, songs, parades, pep rallies, bonfires, and spontaneous outpourings of school spirit.

The 1909 *Garnet and Black* printed a "Carolina Song Book" section with a number of school "yells" and songs. Of course, delivery by a spirited crowd of students was everything.

Cheer: Rah! Rah!

Rah! Rah! Rah! Rah!
South Carolina!
Carolina, Rah! Rah!
Carolina, Rah! Rah!
Hurrah! Hurrah!
South Carolina!
Hika! Hika! Hika!
Sis! Boom! Bah!
Carolina! Carolina!
Rah! Rah! Rah!
Hulla, Balloo, Canec, Canec!
Hulla, Balloo, Canec, Canec!
Wah, Hee, Wah, Hee!
Look at the man,
The college man—of U.S.C.!

Song: Never Defeated

Carolina hike her,
There's no one like her;
We will forever play football,
Never defeated,
Except when cheated,
Then by no team at all.

Faculty Song

In Heaven above
Where all is love,
The Faculty won't be there;
But down below,
Where all is woe,
The Faculty will be there, singing:

Rah! Rah! Rah!
For Carolina, cheer for victory today
Ere the sun is sunk to rest,
In the cradle of the West,
Oh, we'll proudly, proudly float our banners gay.

Apparently the content of some cheers could be quite spicy, as noted in a *Gamecock* editorial, "Our Yells," February 25, 1911.

Among our college songs and yells, we have one or two that are rather objectionable. There is nothing that helps a team along more than good yells and songs, but it seems to us that we might dispense with the ones which are not fit for ladies to hear. . . . We are not endeavoring to begin a campaign against the use of profanity in general, but only in our public places. Many complaints have been made about the careless way to which our fellows make use of their unique, though thorough, vocabulary of adjectives. Dr. [William W.] Daniel, [president] of Columbia College, has repeatedly had us give him our assurance that the objectionable yells would be dispensed with before giving the girls permission to attend the games. The College for Women girls have often been placed in the same position, many of the girls remaining away on account of their previous experiences on the grandstand. Mr. Cheer Leader, it is up to you and your assistants to see that nothing objectionable is allowed to reach the ears of those in the grandstand.

An editorial, "Respect to Theatres," in the September 24, 1929, *Gamecock* suggested the consequences of school spirit beyond campus boundaries.

During the football seasons heretofore, when a shirt tail parade was staged by the students after winning a football game, they most invariably marched through the various theatres situated on Main Street. The Gamecock feels that this is not right and especially it is not showing the operators of the theatres due respect nor the patrons patronizing them, for everyone knows how it interrupts the entertainment going on when 600 or 700 gayly attired college youths, who are making much "whoopee," march in and out of theatres.

Now the managers of these theatres were very hesitant in advertising in *The Gamecock* and all other college publications on account of this reason, and only after much persuading did they advertise.

"Beat Clemson" was the consistent rallying cry. In 1929 an anonymous student poet invented a hopeful Henry Wadsworth Longfellow parody just before the Carolina v. Clemson football game.

"Tiger's Fall"

Listen my children and you shall hear
Of a famous event in this very year,
It happened in old Columbia town
At a football game of great renown.
Clemson had licked the Lutherans,
Davidson, Auburn and N.C.S.
They came to play the gamecocks
The tigers sure were dressed.
With their trappings all so shiny
And their cheers (they knew so well)
But when the roosters lit upon them
They got licked plumb to—well—
The victors had to celebrate
They split the town in twain
They moved Main Street to the river
And laid it down again.
They took the dome of the Capitol
And turned it upside down.
Filled it full of water,
And the poor old Tiger drowned.
The Angels up in heaven
And the devil down in hell
Were afraid for the good old U.S.
When proud Clemson fell.

The poem soon became wishful thinking. Clemson won the 1929 football game.

By the close of the first decade of the twentieth century, baseball was in full swing each spring and the *Gamecock* editors called for basketball (December 17, 1908).

There is a need to be filled—the need of a strong, clean sport, the need of something to try the nerve, to test the muscle, to develop the body, to satisfy the American craving for strenuousness, excitement, skill and uncertainty. This want has been long felt and there have been many efforts made to supply it. The most satisfactory results have probably been accomplished by basketball. It is primarily associated with the Y.M.C.A., but all of the Northern colleges and high schools have adopted it to fill the winter interim. . . . At present, however, there are very few colleges in the South at which basketball does not hold a firm place in the front rank of athletics, and among these is the University of South Carolina. There are several reasons why we should have a team—not the least of which is that Charleston College and Furman and Wofford have already adopted the sport. . . . Our ultimate aim is to rank among the largest universities in the country in athletics. But can we ever hope to achieve it, when we refuse to take advantage of a means by which these institutions keep their men in training during the long period of winter rust?

Let's Party

As the student body grew in size and diversity, adding various professional schools, graduate schools, summer school, and part-time students, the campus and surrounding area created expanded opportunities for social life. Dances occurred on weekday, as well as weekend, nights. Intercollegiate sports, movies, swimming parties, and picnics were frequent diversions; and road trips became options for at least some fortunate students with access to cars. Of course, gambling and drinking persisted, regardless of state laws and national prohibition.

When various classes wrote their yearly histories for the *Garnet and Black,* they typically included discussions of male-female relationships, as demonstrated by a "History of the Junior Law Class" in the 1907 annual.

The law class of 1908 contains several luscious ladies' men. There is Cunningham, the Kentucky Colonel, who puts up a line of talk to the blessed "damozels" that stretches from the "Immortality of the Soul" to Anarchy. It is said that he has successfully demonstrated the truth of the Nebular Hypothesis, and is the rival of Lumpkin for the walking advertiser of "Cook with Gas."

Clarkson, the swell swain from Wateree, is the original Fast Male after a certain fairy around these parts; he has lost four hats this year in his mad pursuit—not to mention his head.

Then there is also McDonald—the real "Buster Brown," as foxy "as they make 'em." But the "Tige" that follows him at times belongs to "the Lady fair," and from what we can gather, the dog is a consolation prize.

The women also enjoyed their active social lives, as indicated in this letter from Agnes Stone to her mother, Lil Butler Stone, in Greenville.

April 15, 1926

Last night a crowd of girls went to stunt night on campus. It was perfectly darling. Saw Carlisle and Jimmie on the campus yesterday afternoon. Saw lots of darling boys and afterwards they had a shirt tail parade. Lillie phoned up and asked me to go to the pictures so we went to "Mare Nostrum" this morning. Tonight we are going to a picnic about nine miles from here at Adams Pond.

Did you think Tunney would win the fight? I didn't, so I bet on Jack and lost. I've got another bet on the Furman-Carolina football game so maybe I'll win it back.

Students could, of course, get into trouble—including suspension or expulsion—if their social pastimes became too notorious. Such was the fate of J. S. Hoey of New Jersey, who appealed for reinstatement to Pres. Samuel Chiles Mitchell.

August 17, 1916

I am very glad to be able to tell you that I have been reading law all summer in this office and that I like it very much. The last couple of weeks I have not been very regular as their [*sic*] has been a horse show and aviation meet here, but outside of that I think that I have been doing pretty well.

I am also extremely glad to tell you that I haven't touched a card to play poker since I left Columbia, although I have had many chances to do so. I believe that I have finally conquered that weakness. I have been very much better for it and I can see now what a fool I was last winter.

You remember that you told me that if I behaved myself this summer that I could come back in September and I think I can tell you absolutely that I have. I also want a chance to redeem myself with you and the other members of the faculty if possible. I want to make a try to graduate if I can get the exams that I missed in June when I go back. I want to go to law school somewhere and would like to either graduate or get enough credits to enter one next year. . . . I would be much obliged if you would send one of the new catalogues as I have not seen one.

The editors of the *Gamecock* favored more social activities on campus, as indicated in an editorial titled "Face the Facts," published in the April 21, 1933, issue.

Recently, President [Leonard T.] Baker officially announced that beer would not be sold in the canteen. He gave as his reason fear of criticism from outside the University. Is the purpose of the University administration to gain the approval of a small outside minority or to achieve the well-being of the students attending the University? Any sane person can see that among college students the best possible solution for the liquor problem is beer. Beer should be made as accessible to the students as possible if it is to be a real agency of temperance.

The problem of student drinking is too important to be lightly disposed of. This is no time for a holier than thou attitude; this is a time for action and straight square thinking without fear or favor.

James Fant, whose family lived in Lockhart and who attended USC from 1938 to 1940, recalled that students took their social lives very seriously.

When you came to Carolina, you had to have a tuxedo for the formal dances, even during the Depression. There were a lot of dances, most of them held at the gym, now Longstreet Theatre. The big annual event was the June Ball. It started late and went all night—until about 6 o'clock in the morning. There was a place on Gervais, the Toddle House, where you could go late and have a piece of pie and cup of coffee. And there was the Metropolitan Café—the Metro—where everybody went after a dance. And we used to dress for football games—you wore a coat and tie. And if you could afford it, you sent your date for the football game a corsage, which was a chrysanthemum with garnet and black streamers. That cost about $1.50.

Helen Anderson Waring-Tovey of Summerville, who attended the two-year School of Commerce secretarial program in 1939 and 1940, recalled the reaches of a busy social life in an interview sixty years later.

Not many girls got to college those days. We were just barely out of the Depression. My father came down here [Summerville] as an accountant. . . . After I finished high school, I begged and cried. My parents saw how much it meant to me [to go to Carolina]. Only two girls in my high school class of 39 students graduated from college. I cried and I got there.

I did not pledge [any sorority]. My father had read it was a situation where a lot of girls were so hurt if they didn't get in with their friends and such. And he was such a kind man, he said, "I don't want you to go into that and go into a sorority." But my friends said, "Come on just for the rushing, because you'll meet a lot of people." And it turned out to be a good thing. I met people and got into "Damas," the girls' dance club.

They had junior and senior Damas. The boys' dance club was the "German." Each club had two formals a year. . . . There were maybe 15 informal dances a year. And the fraternities and sororities had their formals each year. There were so many, they had to get it down to where the fraternities and sororities could give their formals every other year.

. . . We dated every night. But we had to be in by 11 p.m. Every night. But for dances you could come in at 1 a.m. Every single night. We went to a movie, maybe a hayride. It was really the age of innocence, and we girls were on a pedestal. . . . It was like Gone With the Wind before the war [World War II]. The girls were supreme. Remember Scarlet O'Hara with the Tarleton boys, sitting on the porch?

. . . The most important thing in a girl's life was the number of breaks you'd get at a dance, especially at a formal dance. They'd have stag lines lining up. You'd take one little step and then a person would tap the boy dancing with you on the shoulder and step in—a cut in. Maybe they'd have four "no-break" dances during a ball where nobody could cut in.

. . . The atmosphere and the friendliness. I don't know whether there were 1,800 students or what, but everybody knew everybody. Maybe my education wasn't as academic as it should have been, but it was a wonderful memory. . . . And the students were close to the professors. They would invite the students over. We dated different boys. Then you chose, when you became engaged. . . . We didn't have a lot of money, but we didn't know it, because everybody else was poor. We didn't know we were poor.

There were many more girls than boys. We had a lot of boys, but the war had not started. We lost a lot of boys in World War II. . . . I was socializing too much. But when you think about it, those days went and they never came back after the war. . . . And I couldn't tell you how wonderful they were. They were memories that would keep you going today.

Not all students were involved in whirlwind social lives, according to a memoir by John Erskine Hankins about his undergraduate years (1920–1924).

At the time the student body might be considered as two groups: the sophisticates, who belonged to the German Club (a dance organization), drove cars, and had money to spend; and the others, mostly small-town boys who had never danced and vaguely thought it might be sinful, who had little money and in many instances worked to pay their way through college.

THE CONTINUING SAGA: WOMEN ON CAMPUS

Although legislation to admit female students had passed in 1894, and a few women attended and graduated during the next dozen years, the college that reformed as a university in 1906 still was not committed to the education of women on its campus.

The Organization Committee of the Faculty drafted a report to the legislature of 1907 favoring restricted numbers of women students. In

1913 the Board of Trustees began negotiations with the College for Women, a small female postsecondary school in Columbia that was under consideration as a separate, but coordinate, college for women seeking admission to the University of South Carolina—similar to the relationship of Sophie Newcombe College to Tulane University or Radcliffe College to Harvard University.

Women, however, continued to arrive and to succeed in the face of little support and much skepticism. The 1906 Garnet and Black echoed common feelings about their presence on campus.

Sentiments of a Sophomore

A co-ed is a funny thing
That cannot talk, that cannot sing.
It never has a thing to say,
When spoken to in the proper way;
But it knows how to giggle,
Or to make a pass,
And in silly questions, leads its class.

The editors of the *Gamecock* noticed that the women on campus did not have the same extracurricular opportunities as the men, in a 1917 editorial, "Coed Athletics."

What has become of the coed's physical training? Why should the boys have a monopoly on athletic teams representing the University? With two girls' colleges right here in Columbia, and scores within easy reach in the state, the plea certainly cannot be no opponents. The trouble lies with the University authorities and with the coeds themselves. Some one of you fair sex take the lead and start something moving. Let the boys know you are on the campus in some other way besides forcing them to dodge into tenement doors on a hot afternoon, or waiting to blush under some of the rasher professors. Wake up! There is something more to college life than attending classes!

An anonymous coed responded the following week.

We are severely criticized because we have not loyalty enough to get up a basketball team. Now Mr. Critic, have you ever stopped to think where we would practice if we did attempt this? There is not a brick or a chunk of wood on the University campus that the girls may call their own. . . . The boys have their gymnasium, athletic field and special coaches. The coeds have never had one word of encouragement from trustees, faculty or alumni, and only an amused interest from the student body.

We are often asked why we do not stay for student body meetings. To answer frankly, because there are some few who seem to forget we are ladies and that they are gentlemen, or supposed to be. We have our own meetings on Saturdays, but at other times most of us would gladly stay if we could feel sure that our presence would be respected. We are fair minded enough to acknowledge that we do not take as active a part in college life as we should, but we will not take all the blame for this. . . .

Little had changed fourteen years later, as noted in a *Gamecock* editorial in 1931, "Basketball for Girls."

Carolina is coeducational in name—why not in activities? Is it fair for the girls at Carolina not to have a single inter-collegiate team of their own while the boys have seven? It isn't that there is no material, for last season a wealth of material was brought to light by the interclass games, and a makeshift varsity with a week's practice behind it lost after a stiff fight to the Columbia College varsity with a season's practice and four years of varsity basketball behind it.

The Woman's Athletic Association is willing and desirous of staking its total resources to back the team. Any girl honored by being on the team would be willing to help pay the expenses of any trip. It would be hard, but possible, for the association and the girls to bear the total expenses. So the university treasury would be taxed to no degree to support the team. Nothing is lacking but permission from the authorities.

Several months later the appeal for an intercollegiate sport for women was denied by the University administration.

In her valedictory address in 1932, Sarah N. Cassels described a hopeful future for women in higher education.

Classmates, as we are about to go forth from these halls of learning hallowed by a thousand sacred traditions and memories, we are faced squarely by the present situation. Have women in the college in general shown the advisability of such education? In view of the radical onslaughts being made on all kinds of education, what shall be the policy of the friends of this institution?

Does not the history of the past women graduates show that they have been an asset to the University? Does not the fact that in some schools the women surpass the men in scholastic achievements show their ability? Does not the fact, for example, that each year a larger per cent of women are elected to Phi Beta Kappa than men prove their mental ability? Does not common sense after all dictate that the distinction of sex is an artificial one in the halls of learning of our state? Whatever has been the history of woman's education in the past, whatever have been the achievements of women in the past, whatever have been their accomplishments up to the present time, one thing is certain: that the women yield to none as devoted daughters and as loyal supporters of this their beloved Alma Mater.

ORATORY UP AND DOWN

Literary societies, oratorical contests, and debates continued into the twentieth century as popular extracurricular activities. The women students founded two new societies of their own—the Hypatian in 1915 and the Euphrosynean in 1924. However, the expansion of higher education beyond preparation for professions requiring oratorical skill and the popularity of other campus clubs and groups eventually contributed to the slow demise of oratorical interest.

In 1912, when oratory was still a popular endeavor, a Carolina law student from Charleston won the regional oratorical contest, and the *Gamecock* reported a celebration evoking the energy and emotion of a major football victory.

James Allan, Jr., Wins Southern Contest

James Allan, Jr., representing the University of South Carolina, won first place in the Southern Intercollegiate Oratorical Contest held at the University of Alabama. This is the second time Carolina has won first place in this contest.

When notice was received the campus reverberated with the glad shouts of four hundred and fifty students. Classes were suspended for an hour after chapel and every student joined in one of the most enthusiastic parades held this year. Marching up Main Street the cheering students proclaimed to the citizens of Columbia that they had won the Southern. The line of march continued down Blanding Street to the College for Women. Arrangements are being made for a great parade as soon as Mr. Allan returns.

Editors of the *Gamecock* gave a front-page story to the debating team in 1921 when it announced a meet with Harvard debaters.

University Will Debate Harvard

The University of South Carolina has accepted a challenge from Harvard University for a debate to be held between the dates of April 27 and April 28 in Columbia.

The Harvard Debating Council substituted a Southern trip for its debating teams in place of a trip to the West, and included the University of South Carolina among "the three leading universities of the South."

. . . Carolina's debating schedule for this year calls for debates with New York University and Harvard, in addition to the annual triangle debate with Tennessee and Florida and with Clemson and the Citadel. There will also be a freshman debate with Wofford college freshmen.

A sampling of questions debated in the Clariosophic Society shows changing student attitudes during the early twentieth century, as well as a tendency to debate local, including campus, issues.

1909:

Resolved: "That Abraham Lincoln was a friend of the South" (decided in the affirmative)

1911:

Resolved: "That the literary society should give its books to the University library" (decided in the negative)

Resolved: "That foreign immigration to the United States should be further restricted by the imposition of an educational test" (decided in the affirmative)

1912:

Resolved: "That the women of South Carolina should have the ballot if they want it" (decided in the affirmative)

1913:

Resolved: "That Carolina should have a holiday to entertain the Winthrop girls" (decided in the affirmative)

Resolved: "That women exert a greater moral influence over men than men over women" (decided in the affirmative)

Resolved: "That the action of President Wilson in refusing to recognize the Huerta government in Mexico was for the best interest of that country" (decided in the affirmative)

1914:

Resolved: "That the United States should intercede to bring about cessation of the hostilities in the European crisis" (decided in the negative)

1918:

Resolved: "That South Carolina should grant the right of suffrage to the women of the state on the same basis as that of the men" (decided in the affirmative)

Resolved: "That football is a better sport than baseball" (decided in the negative)

1919:

Resolved: "That the State of South Carolina should have an illiteracy test as a requirement for voting" (decided in the affirmative)

Resolved: "That the government should provide farms for soldiers returning from war" (decided in the affirmative)

Resolved: "That all immigration to the United States should be excluded for the period of five years after the signing of the peace treaty" (decided in the affirmative)

1920:

Resolved: "That it is better to marry a homely woman with a sweet voice than to marry a beautiful woman with a harsh voice" (decided in the negative)

Resolved: "That the entrance of women into politics will decrease the welfare and happiness of the home" (decided in the affirmative)

1924:

Resolved: "That instead of having holidays scattered all over the year, we should have spring holidays" (decided in the negative)

1925:

Resolved: "That the United States should legalize the sale of light wines and beer" (decided in the affirmative)

Resolved: "That it is better for girls to wear dresses that are short and stockings that are rolled than for the men to wear the big legged trousers" (unrecorded)

1926:

Resolved: "That examinations should be abolished at the University of South Carolina" (decided in the negative)

1928:

Resolved: "That the University should abolish student instructors and replace them with faculty instructors" (decided in the negative)

Resolved: "That suspenders are of more use than a belt" (decided in the affirmative)

1932:

Resolved: "That the prohibition law should be abolished" (decided in the negative)

Resolved: "Laws restricting birth control are detrimental to the welfare of society and should be repealed" (a draw)

In his inaugural address as president of the Clariosophic Society, John Bolt Culbertson was candid about the waning popularity of literary societies on campus in 1931.

In all fairness, it must be admitted that the literary societies have retrograded. Even in my own career as a student, they have lost in prestige, in membership and in intrinsic worth. Little by little they have deteriorated until literary pursuits are at a minimum, and politics at a maximum. This has been due largely to the invasion of fraternity groups. Journalistic and literary fraternities have both cut into the membership of, and weakened the position of, literary societies.

The literary societies have become more mere political machines for the distribution of their rich plums, publication editorships and the like, than capable and functioning literary groups in their own right. It must be admitted that the greater part of our literary activities consists of dry forensics which only too frequently are degraded into arguments and general confusion of little value and of less inspiration. . . .

The creative artists on campus view us only too often as a boring necessity, to be endured solely for the sake of a desirable position on the publications.

STUDENTS AT WAR

Some students left campus in 1916 to fight against Pancho Villa at the Mexican border; and when the United States entered World War I in April 1917, most students and many faculty began training in earnest to participate on the European front. An unofficial training unit formed immediately, involving 240 of the University's 340 male enrollment. By August 1917 these men were installed in an official Army ROTC unit on campus. The women on campus, still fewer than 50, organized a Red Cross unit and a detachment of the National League for Women's Service. A total of 531 alumni and students served in the armed forces between 1916 and 1918, 28 of whom died in action, in training, or from disease.

Gadsden Shand attended an ROTC training camp in 1918 but could not immediately get a commission because he was only nineteen years old. Instead, he was sent back to campus to train students. He later recalled students' earliest notions of their involvement in the war.

It was, of course, quite a subject of conversation. Because we all knew we were going to get into it one way or another. . . . I don't think any of them were rarin' to go, but they were willing to go, and they were ready.

Training soon became complicated by the outbreak of the worldwide influenza epidemic of 1918. Gadsden Shand turned a dormitory into an infirmary.

There were no hospital beds available, so the University gave me a dormitory to house the men in my company. I was in charge of them. I couldn't even find a doctor, they were all so busy. So I looked after the whole company. Had to feed them and clothe them and everything else. I managed to get by with it somehow. They all lived.

One alumnus, Cornelius Kollock, Class of 1915, had already fought on the Mexican border when he left for training camp in Tennessee to prepare for action in Europe. He described his experiences in letters home to his mother in Cheraw, S.C.

May 15, 1917

We got here [Chattanooga, Tenn.] about nine thirty Monday morning and were assigned to our companies. Not a single one of us got in the same company. We are all scattered about. There certainly are a fine bunch of men here. Everywhere you turn you see somebody you know. The pick of South Carolina is certainly here. All my old college mates and a good many that were on the Border. . . . The camp is right in the hills, about six miles from Chattanooga and right on the battlefield. The monuments are all around us.

We have three long houses holding about 50 men each and we all sleep in the one big room. It is not as nice as our tents but it has its advantages. We have electric lights and water and we really have sheets and pillows.

I certainly was sorry not to see Papa in Columbia. I suppose he did not get my telegram. But there was such a crowd at the station that I could have very well missed him.

June 21, 1917

I think a good many would like to get out now. We start digging trenches this week. We are going to build the kind used in Europe so we have some work ahead of us. We are going on the rifle range sometime soon. I am looking forward to that. We are not working as hard now as at first.

October 11, 1918

I know it must be fine at home now. I think this is the best time of the year there and Aunt Nettie's place must be awful pretty.

Well, I am at last in the front line trenches [in France] and enjoying myself very much. I have been up before but only in support. But now we are right in front. I am writing this in one of the German "Pill Boxes," as they held this for a long time. I don't know how long I can make this letter as the candle looks as if it might quit and it is the last until our supplies come again.

I didn't know whether I would like this or not, but really it is great fun, a lot like bird hunting, but more mice. Of course we are not where the great work is being done, but we will be soon I suppose.

I sure hope Oliver will have a chance to stay at the Citadel for some time anyway. I think we will end it before he can get here. I sure wish I could send you some pictures of this country, as it is beautiful even if the villages are in ruins.

October 18, 1918

Only a line because I can't write any more right now. We have moved again and are really in the midst of some things, although it is very quiet and peaceful. We are in a beautiful country in the mountains, and I am enjoying myself to the fullest extent. The guns open up every morning and evening. We call them the morning and evening guns. Have seen several air battles and we all stand out like a bunch of sight seers with our eyes on the sky. I wish I could tell you what has happened and the things I have seen, but not now.

This life reminds me of Saluda [S.C.], and if it was not for the guns every now and then, I would hardly know the difference.

October 25, 1918

I have come softly out of the trenches, but we have been marching every day up to a few days ago, so I have not had time to write. We did not have a bad time in the trenches. All the men enjoyed themselves very much and some of the things that happened were great. We had just enough action not to become tired but enough to lend excitement. The boys say now that we have seen the side show and are going into the big show.

We are getting out of the mountains and into farming country. It is great, very beautiful. All the leaves are turning and the woods are wonderful. . . . I certainly hope the influenza is over by now. They are having a lot of it over here also. I have been feeling fine ever since I came over, except for a light cold that I got in the trenches, which is better now.

November 14, 1918

Well, the great fight is over and has ended about as I thought it would, all at once. Our outfit was in at the death and were making a drive up to the last minute, but I didn't see it. I got a little souvenir at 4 P.M., November 10, a bullet in the fleshy part of the left leg above the knee, and am now in a base hospital near Bordeaux, France. I'm feeling fine and think that I will be up and around soon. I certainly consider myself lucky to have come out with only this wound when I look back on what we went through the day I got it. I will be able to tell you about it soon I think.

I know you are all glad the war is over. I sure am, and I am glad that Oliver did not have to come, although I hope they will still continue the military training for young boys. The French people have gone wild with joy here. They closed up all the stores for two or three days and everybody celebrated, and they sure know how to do it.

Another alumnus, John Schreiner Reynolds, Jr., first lieutenant in the Thirtieth Infantry, did not survive to witness the war's end. A month before he died on the battlefield near Nantilles, France, he wrote to his wife in Columbia of his hopes for their future together.

September 1, 1918

Darling: I am hungry for you—so hungry that I can feel the smoothness of your face against mine, the sweet roundness of you in my arms, can sense the fragrance of you and taste the kisses as of old. And the intensity of the longing for the reality is only enhanced by the vividness of the fantasy. On this Sunday the sense of needing you has been especially strong. My mind has over and over run back through the wonderful happiness of our married life, has gone back to the days of our engagement, when Sunday was the only day of the week for me—Sunday afternoon and a bright little bit of Monday morning. How different this Sunday, when you so wholly belong to me and yet are so very far away from me! If only I could have you—the real you—just for a little while, how sweet it would be!

This war is the only thing that could tear me away from you—there is nothing else that we would let come between us. And when the war is over, there need be no more separations; there won't be, for we'll have such a long time to make up.

Yours, John

Speaking of Faculty

Carolina students openly and frequently shared their views of the University, the administration, and the faculty. A brief essay, "A Chapel Scene," by "Flip" appeared in the November 1916 *Carolinian*.

Some of the professors come rushing in in a disjointed procession and with the utmost coolness take their unaccustomed places in the Holy

Row—late. Please notice, thereby setting a horrible exemplum of non-punctuality. And above all things, Mein Herren Doctoren, you should be consistent. But speaking of consistency calls to mind how one member of this reprehensible crew stands with his hand on the door knob of his class-room, eye on watch, counting the fatal seconds of the grudgingly allotted five minutes. "And woe unto ye that thereafter knock, for it shall not be opened unto you."

A 1915 editorial in the *Gamecock* appealed for greater respect for the faculty.

The custom of students tipping their hats to professors is becoming dusty and we wish to register our feeble protest against this indecorous degeneration. The practice of hat tipping is a good one and we hope that no Carolina man will in the future neglect to show to the faculty the respect that is their due. Not all the professors are thieves, nor are they all bad men. No, some of the faculty are very amiable gentlemen.

Students flexed their collective muscle in a rare mass communication to the Board of Trustees in 1919, signed by 166 students who demanded the removal of Pres. William S. Currell.

We feel that the students who are thrown in daily contact with Dr. Currell and who see him at closer range than members of the Board of Trustees may form a more correct estimate than members of your body. Out of our association with him has come a firm conviction that the university will not catch step with the other educational institutions as long as he continues as its president. . . .

Personal qualities of Dr. Currell for which perhaps he is not responsible, but which nevertheless hamper his work are:

• A lack of inspirational power
• A lack of tactfulness in dealing with men
• A coldness in association with students which has resulted in his form-ing few, if any, student friendships
• A lack of qualities of imagination and idealism to such a degree that few have received from him an impulse to better living

He is thoroughly incompetent to preside over chapel services. A stiff and stilted manner and the lack of poise make his efforts to maintain order, to say nothing of impressing one with the dignity of the exercise, futile. . . . He is incapable of energizing any organization in which he serves. He takes only a purely academic interest in the Y.M.C.A., the literary societies, the student publications, and the Debating Council. He is incapable of impressing the value of the university's services on the people of the state and thus of drawing to it proper support from the state. . . . He is reactionary, as seen by the university's narrowing scope of influence and activity. . . .

We respectfully submit that the university's future with Dr. Currell as its head is well nigh hopeless.

President Currell resigned in 1921. As a professor in the ensuing years, however, he fared better with students. Two anonymous coeds included him in their review of various faculty in the *Carolinian*, February 1933.

Dr. Currell is surprisingly and quaintly witty—puns unexpectedly—is one of the most interesting professors on the campus . . . not as well-known as he should be among students.

In 1928 Fenelon DeVere Smith, a student from Greenville, assessed the University and its faculty in a notebook he kept for Prof. George Wauchope's English class.

I thought that personal contact of teachers and pupils in an institution the size of University of South Carolina would be almost impossible. Experiences on the campus of the institution have convinced me otherwise, and I am very glad to find that my opinion was a fallacy.

The institution appears to be a great, vague, many sided, and inefficient institution made up of individuals who have common interests. The word "inefficient" is not intended to be offensive. . . . I believe in the idea of a university, but I am averse to the degree system, the system which stamps a man with a label, which is often meaningless, makes the steps in advancement seem greater, and discourages an individual's effort for gradual progress by giving him no intermediate goal.

The Reverend Dr. George Elias Meetze, Class of 1930, later recalled several of his professors with fondness and amusement.

Dr. Havilah Babcock was a young professor at that time. I believe he came to the University in 1926. A very popular young man. He was one of my favorite professors. Back in those days, we wrote a theme nearly every week. In one theme, I was sort of carried away with adjectives. I wrote it and flourished it all up. Babcock folded the paper and on the outside he wrote, "Words, words, words, words. Try sending a few telegrams." My other very favorite was Dr. Josiah Morse, who was professor of philosophy and psychology. . . .

Yates Snowden was in History. But I understand he was not very good in mathematics. He came into his history class one day, and this girl had her math book on top of her other books. As the story goes (now I didn't see this), Snowden walked over and picked up this math book and dropped it out of the window to indicate his disdain for mathematics.

Ruth Hunt Woodruff, Class of 1933, also mentioned Snowden among the professors she remembered.

[Yates Snowden] was a colorful character. I can see him now, coming to class. He had all that white hair, a cape, and a little black boy carried his books in a basket; and a little dog, a little fox terrier, walked along with the little boy. That was the little procession that they made.

I was an English major with a double minor in French and Art, so most of my memories are about English professors. And, of course, the most entertaining one was Dr. Babcock. He was a marvelous storyteller. He told us once, "My digressions are going to be a lot more interesting in this class than anything else."

Benjamin W. Woodruff, Class of 1933, recalled his chemistry professors.

I had Dr. [Guy F.] Lipscomb for freshman chemistry. . . . He made his family wealthy, developed stuff there in that laboratory. Professor [William B.] Burney had studied under [Robert W.] Bunsen in Germany. Dr. Lipscomb was sloppy. He'd be smoking that cigar and mixing up stuff [in his laboratory], and ashes would fall in and he'd just stir them on in. Dr. Burney would say, "My God, man! Bunsen wouldn't have you in his laboratory for 15 minutes!"

THE DEPRESSION HITS CAMPUS

The Depression ushered in numerous changes for students. Many were forced to drop out of college; others begged forgiveness on late tuition payments, worked the few night and weekend jobs that could be found, and scrambled to find summer work. Those who managed to graduate found that employment for the college educated was scarce or unavailable.

Typical of letters to the University in these hard times were those to Pres. Leonard T. Baker in October 1932.

Dear Dr. Baker:

We have a son, A. Z. Butler, at Carolina and are hoping to keep him there the full term, but fear it's going to be hard to do under present conditions.

I teach in Loris High School and you know how teachers fared the past term. I want to know if it is possible for me to pay any of A. Z.'s expenses with school vouchers. I asked him to find out and let me know, but he hasn't looked after it yet. I wish so much his meals could be settled for that way or partly so at least.

Dear Dr. Baker:
Because my father, M. F. Bush, has been physically unable to see you as he had planned, I am asking you to allow me to pay my fees later in the semester. Please write Daddy if I may register before October 8.

Hard times continued for a decade, as letters in August 1941, to Pres. J. Rion McKissick, indicate.

Dear Dr. McKissick:
My brother, James Ousley Bryant, plans to return to the university as a junior student this fall. I have $50 cash of the first payment and would like to know if it will be all right to send you a post-dated check, October 20, 1941, for the balance of payment.

My only source of income is from teaching school; therefore, it is a very inconvenient time for me to get hold of cash money.

Dear Dr. McKissick:
I shall be a senior in civil engineering at the university this coming term. . . . I would like to borrow about $200 from someone to carry me through my last year. If you know of any bank or individuals who you think I might be able to borrow from, I would appreciate it if you would let me have their names so I might contact them. I have a good scholastic record at the University and can furnish good character references.

Some South Carolina students with plans for college out of state found they needed to save money by staying closer to home. Marshall Williams, who later served in the state Senate and House of Representatives, recalled a familiar story.

I was going to law school at Harvard, but I didn't have the money in 1933 when I finished college [B.S. at USC]. So I thought I was going to have to work. . . . Burroughs Adding Machine Company offered me a job for $120 a month. And I told them if I couldn't make any more than that, I thought I'd better go to law school. He said, "We could make you a vice president, but a lot of people would object."

. . . So I went to Carolina. . . . best thing that ever happened to me, but I didn't know it at the time. I mean, they thought, you know, if you went to Harvard, why you were a cut above anything else. I ran into some Harvard graduates during my years in practice, and I thought maybe I was as well educated or better than they were. You take what you want to. I was a good student and I learned a lot about politics at Carolina. I don't recollect ever losing a race that I ran where people voted.

James Franklin Miles, who attended one of Wil Lou Gray's "opportunity schools" and graduated from the two-year Textile Industrial Institute in 1936, was determined to attend the University of South Carolina although his family had no source of income. In a letter dated July 11, 1935, his friend Katie Lou Craft, Class of 1936, warned him about working too much when he came to Carolina.

Dearest James,

. . . If you can avoid textile work, extracurricular activities shall play a much larger part towards molding your life, God's wonderful gift, into an integrated whole. It's going to be a problem, but you can and will make the best of it. I feel as if I've missed very much, indeed, by working at night.

Sixty years later Miles recalled his Depression-era student experiences.

I would have gone out for debate team—my best friend, Coley Craft, was on the debate team—except for my working. That interfered with some of the extra-curricular activities. I spent so much time working to earn money because I didn't have any other source of income. Of course, you could attend then for $300 a year, including room and board. But having to work both night and day in order to earn my way, I was not able to participate as much in athletics or social activities as I would have liked. . . . I didn't engage in social things. I didn't go to dances; I didn't go to athletics. My social development was somewhat handicapped by having to spend so much time working instead of courting. . . .

I did take an over burdensome load of courses, some of which I had no need for or interest in, because I was required to take an advanced course at U.S.C. for every course which I transferred in for credit from Textile Industrial Institute. I had to take an extra full year of Bible and an extra full year of French . . . to demonstrate that although I attended a non-accredited school my training was as good or better than other Carolina students.

I studied bookkeeping, but I soon decided I didn't want to spend the rest of my life in a small cubicle keeping books for somebody. It was more cramped and confining than a textile mill. It was just not a healthful situation, so I became interested in economics.

But my primary interest was to study law. But, because of validating all these courses, I found I could get a Ph.D. in economics quicker than I could get a law degree.

In 1951 Miles received a Ph.D. in economics from Cornell University.

The Depression employment situation was particularly gloomy, as indicated in a 1931 _Gamecock_ editorial, "College Bred Bums?"

Will the graduates of 1931–32 find jobs? Will they come back for M.A. degrees? Or will they join the army of the unemployed and march in single file up to the gates of soup kitchens?

Thousands of people will go out from the universities to try to find jobs this February, and yet other thousands in June. And judging from present conditions, we cannot say that the outlook will be bright for them.

Specialization has been The Big Idea in modern education; the old traditional education is fast becoming a luxury, or, for those without means, a foolish extravagance and waste of time. And to what avail? A few days ago a brilliant graduate of one of the University's special schools was seen walking up and down Main Street looking for employment; a former well-to-do industrial chemist, with a wife and child, is now peddling candy on the streets of Richmond, Virginia. Nor are these unusual stories.

Mr. Hoover and the big guns are still waiting with folded hands for prosperity to turn an imaginary corner. We guess and fear.

James Fant described inventive student socializing in 1938 and 1939.

A big date was to rent tandem bicycles from Mr. Bond, who had a place on Hampton Street. The date would hop on and off we would go. That was a lot of fun. A few times my close friend Jack Davis was visited by his aunt and uncle from New York who owned the Ambassador Hotel. Jack would pick me up in their limousine, and we'd be in back with a glass partition and a telephone. Then we'd pick up our dates, and they were really impressed.

. . . In general, transportation was scarce in those days. My brothers and I would put our rat caps on our heads and hitch hike home [to Lockhart, S.C.] for vacations. You could take a bus, but it stopped at every cow path and took forever.

The editors of the _Carolinian_ offered their suggestions for "How to Relieve the Financial Situation" in January 1933.

1. Cut the University's appropriation.
2. Send the co-eds to Winthrop.
3. Merge Clemson and the University.
4. Do away with the Law School.
5. Do away with the School of Pharmacy.
6. Go back to high school.
7. Quit going to school and become a legislator.

A RESONATING VOICE: JAMES MCBRIDE DABBS

James McBride Dabbs, of Mayesville, S.C., made his name at the University as president of the Class of 1916, president of the Euphradian Society, president of the Y.M.C.A., and editor-in-chief of the *Garnet and Black*. His senior classmates voted him "hardest student," "best debater," "best writer," "brainiest man," and "man with most executive ability."

In the following years Dabbs confirmed his classmates' estimations by gaining national prominence as an award-winning author, a distinguished interpreter of southern social and cultural realities, an effective ally of the Civil Rights movement, and president of the racially progressive Southern Regional Council.

During his university years, however, Dabbs wrote letters to his father, Eugene W. Dabbs, that simply portray the life of an earnest young man learning to live away from home.

September 19, 1912

It is now about 3 pm. We have dinner at 2, and I have all my classes before dinner, and so I have some time to spare now. I have three hours a day in class which makes 18 a week [including Saturdays]. . . . I don't deny that I get homesick, but the more I have to do the less I think about it. I wouldn't miss the talks at chapel for anything. They make me feel so much more at home.

I got hazed pretty good last night. The fellows were asking me to sing, and one made me give him my name saying I ought to belong to the glee club.

The money that you sent me won't last until the first of October. I have only $3.99 left now, and it will take about $2.00 to finish buying books. . . . By next Wednesday, I've got to have a gym suit, which will cost $1.75. I have got to get a pitcher and basin. I don't know what I'll do about a wash stand and table yet. I think my laundry is going to cost me about 30 cents a week, but I will try to make expenses as low as possible.

October 20, 1912

You say that Dr. [Pres. Samuel Chiles] Mitchell wants to run the University to suit everyone. Well there is one thing I wish he would do and that is: abolish most of the classes on Saturday. The way it is now, we have just as many classes on Saturday as any other day. If a man really intends to know his lessons, he can't study them all before supper Saturday. A few minutes after supper the [literary] societies meet; and last night the Euphradian Society was in session until 11:20.

January 11, 1913

I guess you saw in the <u>State</u> that one of the students of the University died a few days ago with typhoid fever. A strict investigation has been made, and everything goes to show that he took the typhoid fever by eating at a Greek restaurant up town. . . . To be on the safe side I went over to one of the state health offices in LeConte College this afternoon and was vaccinated with typhoid serum. My arm is beginning to hurt me a little, but they say it will all be over in the morning. Of course, I have to take two more injections, ten days apart.

May 3, 1913

What is the matter at home that everyone has quit writing? But I am not writing tonight to get after you, but to ask about some money. It is time to buy the May meal ticket now, and I have only $1 in the Bank of Sumter. . . . It will take $20 to do me. If it is all right you can send me a check for this amount. Please write me at once for I must get the ticket before May 10.

. . . I saw my report today, and saw seven A's. That course in public speaking is good, especially second term. . . . There are so many good courses here that I scarcely know which to select.

I saw a demonstration of aluminum ware last Monday night. It was given in Davenport's room by one of the head agents of the company. He cooked batter cakes on a griddle without using a particle of grease. Then he made coffee in the percolating pot . . . the best I've ever tasted.

May 25, 1913

The two classes in public speaking had a debate in chapel last Thursday. I was one of the representatives of the lower class. The query was: Resolved: That the next General Assembly of South Carolina should pass a uniform statewide compulsory education law. . . . We took the affirmative. We won the debate.

November 23, 1913

I am boarding out in town now. [Theodore] Jones said he did not feel like he could stand the mess hall this month, so I am boarding out with him. We have a very good place at $13.50 a month. It beats the mess hall all to pieces, and is but very little farther from the campus. We get a plenty to eat, and it is better prepared. We will probably go back to the mess hall after Christmas, though. Even if the fare is not as good there, I would rather be with the fellows.

. . . We are certain to get a half-day holiday on Thanksgiving, and we may get a whole holiday. I hope our boarding place will be able to scare up some kind of a turkey. The big football game with the Citadel is played here that day.

February 27, 1914

This letter tonight, I'll not deny it, is primarily to ask you to send me some money. We will have to buy meal tickets in a few days. And I owe some money for coal. Besides this, I have been absolutely broke since Feb. 10 or 11. I wouldn't get any money from you the other day because I had made up my mind to go till the end of the month on what I had, or rather didn't have. . . . If you can do so, I wish you would let me have about $30. There are so many things which have to be gotten here, and really I don't think I waste my money in any way.

I suppose you have had snow? I have had just about a plenty myself. Every time you go out on the campus you are liable to run into a crowd who will snowball you. Of course, I have my share of the fun. A good many of us went out to Columbia College yesterday afternoon, and had a snow fight with the girls.

September 27, 1915

I am starting a letter now, but will have to go to class within a few minutes. However, I will finish it this afternoon or tonight. The class I am going to now is Greek. We have begun to read St. Matthew. It is very interesting in the Greek, and very easy; easier than most of the Greek that we have to read. . . .

It is now 3 o'clock, and I am just back from French IV. Which same is some class. We have read 30 pages of poetry in two days, and have had 150 pages of French parallel assigned to us to read by Oct. 4. And there are two of us in the class. There were four when the class first met; two smelt a rat and got out. I guess the other two will wish that they had smelt a rat before they finish. However, the poetry is beautiful: that much can be said for it.

January 11, 1916

It is five o'clock now; I have just finished my classes for today; my last was philosophy under [Josiah] Morse. We are studying mysticism at present. . . . None of us know very well what mysticism is, Morse not excepted.

March 6, 1916

I went over and met Dr. [Edward S.] Joynes today. About the first thing he said was, "Mr. Dabbs, you are improving." "How's that, Doctor?" says I. "Well," he replied, "you have a poem in The Carolinian this month entitled 'Your Hand in Mine.' That is doing better, much better."

. . . By the way, I will probably have a sonnet in this month's Carolinian entitled "To M. W." Go to guessing, ye who love to guess; and I warrant me the sun will go down upon your guessing many times, and the moon traverse many a weary league of sky before you solve the riddle. Sometime I shall tell you who she is—some day. Till then, the secret is mine!

By the way, I need about $35, if you can let me have it. I meant to ask you about this Saturday, but the matter slipped my mind.

The pictures came from Annie Lamar today, and were especially well done, one of them in particular.

Regardless of financial worries, difficult studies, Saturday classes, and the usual food complaints, Dabbs recalled a much more poetic side of campus life in his 1960 autobiography, *The Road Home*.

I shall never forget [English professor] Reed Smith, walking back and forth from window to door, talking in a quiet voice, pausing now and then to read a poem and saying afterward, in a tone of mock condescension, "Well, that's not so bad is it?" I shall never forget the newly awakened rapture with which my friend [Harrington C.] Brearley and I—and perhaps others—heard him. . . . I have never experienced again the expanding wonder of those days.

. . . Those were the days when, watching the sunsets burn on the hills beyond Columbia, I longed for words to match their matchless beauty. Those were the nights—how dream-like it seems now—when Brearley and I sat in his room and talked till three in the morning, occasionally reading a poem from "The Shropshire Lad" or the then new "Spoon River Anthology." And then I walked home across the dewy campus, through silvery grass and black tree shadows, the moon riding high above the oaks and the white dormitories that, like prisons by day, were now touched with some unearthly charm.

By the time he wrote his autobiography, with a forty-year perspective on undergraduate life, Dabbs also was ready to explain more about female friends he had alluded to in his student letters home.

I found then, during my college days, a kind of friendship in nature. . . . Nature had now become significant, both for its own sake, with its colors, shapes, and surprises, and as an appropriate setting for human friendliness. Much of this friendliness was with girls, my own age or a little older. The most important of these was Annie Lamar. It was during May, in my senior year, that the dean excused me for several days to go to Atlanta to read proof on the college annual. . . . Several hours after reaching Atlanta, I was on my way to Anniston, where Annie Lamar lived. It was May—everywhere—and I didn't know whether I was in love or not.

I hoped I was. I had thought a good deal about falling in love. Perhaps everybody does. But I had considered it seriously, and with a faint fear that I might not. . . .

"Well," I said to myself, "if she drops her eyelids when I tell her good-bye, then I shall know." (I had read that in a book.) She did drop her eyelids when I said goodbye. Perhaps I lost my courage. Perhaps I thought it was the sunlight that blinded her. Perhaps I thought I should write her—I knew I was better at writing. But though we kept up a correspondence for a long time, I never wrote her what I had intended, and I did not see her again for thirty-eight years. I was twenty, and she was the friendly spirit of May, and both have gone forever.

Student Statesman: Olin D. Johnston

Olin DeWitt Talmadge Johnston (1896–1965), a master of arts graduate (1923) and a law graduate (1924) of the University of South Carolina, served the state for many years as a governor and a U.S. senator. A World War I veteran who arrived on campus in 1922, he quickly compiled an exhaustive list of extracurricular activities. He also found time to win election from his hometown of Anderson to the South Carolina House of Representatives, where he served while completing his graduate studies.

Johnston added to his busy schedule a long-distance courtship with his future wife, Anderson College student Gladys Atkinson. His letters offer a rare glimpse into the life of the student who would be illustrious statesman and devoted husband.

October 30, 1922

I have always been honest in everything I have written you, and to be frank I have hesitated putting many things in my letters that I would like very much to tell you. You write that you want me to be frank with you, so I am going to do as you say. Gladys, I have had a girl in Columbia up until recently, but for some reason we have decided to break off our friendship for good. I am now all yours, if you will permit me so to be. I have thought I loved you from the time we first met, and for some reason my love for the girl down here has been constantly on the decline or decrease ever since I met you. . . . From now and forever I want you to know that I am yours, if you see fit for me to be. I fear that I have expressed my feeling to [sic] strongly and that you may take them as hot air. But if you do I assure you you will be taking the wrong view.

Gladys, I am going to ask you to do me one favor and I will return it in the same way. Please write to me a little oftener.

January 29, 1923

I feel relieved somewhat for I have just finished an examination, but at the same time I feel like I have been relieved of part of the small amount of my "brains" that I have. I am just in the midst of my examinations, having stood exactly one-half until noon today.

You may think I am not a good correspondent, which is about correct, but you must remember I have more work on hand than I can possibly do the next month. . . .

I hope you will be able to come to Columbia, for I have a new "Ford." Oh! I mean my roommate has and it is the same as if I owned one, for I can use it anytime I care to do so. Therefore, I hereby promise you if you come down here I will carry you to ride in a "New Ford."

February 16, 1923

I have been so awful busy that I have not had time to answer any of the many letters that I get daily. Gladys, I had a wonderful time down in Charleston last weekend. Next Friday I think I will go over to Nashville, Tenn., to represent the University Y.M.C.A.

Everything in the House [of Representatives] is moving along to suit me.

September 17, 1923

I received your letter today, which thrills my heart to its very depths, for in it you told me some things that I like to hear you say. . . . Dear, I don't see how we can continue to live the single life much longer.

Well, I guess the best way to live it is to try to not let marrying stay on our minds to [sic] long at one time. . . .

I am still playing football, play from three in the afternoon until seven. I am also working in the Library every morning, and tomorrow and the next day I will be busy meeting the Freshmen at the trains.

I have the same roommate this year that I had last year, but it looks like they are going to pile in several more with us this year, for our student body is going to be much larger.

September 30, 1923

There are many things that will keep me from studying during the next two months. First, football will continue for about two more months; second, we will have many receptions during the next two months for the Freshmen and Rats. The reason we give many receptions for the Freshmen is that we try to make them feel at home and not be home-sick. . . . All the churches cooperate with the college in giving these receptions. Every First Church in town gives or bears the expenses of a reception. . . .

I sometimes sit and wonder how it is that I have stayed away from you so long, realizing at the same time how I love you. But then I think of the thing that has kept me from you—money, money—oh, if I only had enough to finish this year like I would like to have. No one but myself knows how I am up against it for money this year, and the biggest handicap is I am so tied up with different things that I have practically no time to make any money on the side.

Gladys, I played my first game of football at Carolina yesterday. We beat Erskine College 35 to 0. I play a tackle. . . . Our team has made up its mind to win the State Championship this year. Watch us do it.

December 12, 1923

I stood one final examination one day this week on suretyship and made 100. There were only three in a class of 60 that made 100.

Still, I am looking forward to my mid-year examinations with much fear, for I realize I know very little about the subjects. I have been planning to do a <u>little</u> reviewing during my Christmas holidays. While school is going on I don't have time to keep up with my daily assignments, let alone doing any reviewing.

February 10, 1924

I am living a dog's life every day for I am all the time on the run, and it seems like those around me seem to think, or else they leave the impression, that I have nothing to do but listen to their needs and likes and dislikes. Such is the life of a politician.

From what I can learn I passed all my examinations, but this is not official for I have not heard from four of them. But the four that I have not heard from is [*sic*] under professors that are <u>good</u> friends of mine, and should I fall down I believe they would help me <u>just a little</u> in making a pass.

June 2, 1924

I am in my room all alone, both of my roommates having gone out to Adam's Lake to take a swim. I am thinking of the one dearest to me, and wishing with all my heart that I were with you this evening.

Dear, I passed my last examination today, and I can say I believe I made 100 on my last examination. I am now marking time until I get through with the commencement.

Listen, I did not write that letter last Friday to make you lose faith in me or to cause you any grief, but I just wanted you to understand my position. I did not want you to be counting on September and at the very last minute something to turn up to prevent our marriage. One reason I wrote as I did is I have been offered a government position in Washington, D.C., in the Legal Department, by Senator N. B. Dial, where I can work and take a course at the same time in Georgetown University. Don't take anything I might write to [*sic*] seriously, for all I say concerning the future is subject to change—except we are to be married.

5

Nothing the Same Again
WORLD WAR II AND BEYOND

Students entered the 1940s still greatly influenced by the Depression. Summer work and part-time jobs were increasingly frequent. Cars and telephone calls were almost unknown. A date was a walk to the Toddle House to get a Coke. Making ends meet had become a way of life.

Financial problems suddenly lost their prominence on December 7, 1941, the day of the bombing of Pearl Harbor. Over the next several years, the campus transformed as students left for service at points around the world. Some would never return. New kinds of students arrived when the University became a site for several navy training programs. Even when the war finally ended in victory, students and faculty seemed to understand that a new campus had evolved.

The postwar students were of two kinds: the older veterans and the younger collegians. Each type may have influenced the other for the better. Certainly, the veterans served as a buffer against isolationism, and the young collegians offered welcome respite from the heavy undercurrents of remembrance. A few years into the 1950s, only the collegians were left. Their interests were familiar territory—social events, athletic events, final exam jitters, grades, and the job market. But they also found themselves at the leading edge of the issue that would define the next great campus evolution: racial integration.

WHERE WERE YOU DECEMBER 7, 1941?

When the USC Alumni Association held a War Years Reunion in 1995, former students shared their recollections about the news of an attack on Pearl Harbor.

Dick Anderson, Class of 1942

On Sunday, December 7, 1941, when the news of the bombing of Pearl Harbor came over the radio, I was working in the University canteen.

My first thoughts were of my friends with whom I had served in Company C of the 121st Infantry of the Georgia National Guard, who were already on active duty. I knew that I could not stay at Carolina while they were fighting for our country. As a senior, lacking only nine physical education credits to graduate, and a member of the varsity basketball and track teams, I found myself facing a difficult decision. My need to defend my country had to take precedence. The next day, after talking with coaches Frank Johnson, Rex Enright, Whitely Rawl for whom I worked in the canteen, and Dr. Francis Bradley, I enlisted in the United States Army.

Mary Crow Anderson, Class of 1942

I was at the Columbia Hotel when I heard the news about Pearl Harbor. I was visiting with friends from New Jersey, whose sons, as members of the Essex Troop, were to participate that afternoon in an equestrian demonstration at Fort Jackson. Immediately thereafter, the parade and activities were canceled. My first thoughts were of my father, Dr. Orin F. Crow, Dean of the School of Education who was on leave from the University to serve with the 378th Field Artillery. Soon he would be involved in another war, having already served with General John J. Pershing in 1916 on the [Mexican] border and in World War I in France.

Fred H. Bremer, Class of 1943

On December 7, 1941, I was working as an usher at the Palmetto Theater. My first reaction was that many of us would soon be in the service of our country and that our lives would be changed forever.

Albert S. Eggerton, Jr., Class of 1943

I was napping after Sunday dinner when my parents woke me to hear what was coming over the radio. My first thoughts were: How could we get caught like this? And, this is the war I am probably going to lose my life in. . . . While mulling over the uncertain future, I got a phone call from a classmate, Ernie Lent, who suggested that we might earn a little pocket money by going out and selling the "extra" papers that were rolling off the presses of the local newspaper. We did and with very profitable results. So you might call us the first war profiteers. Interestingly enough, the last of our supply was sold to Robert H. Wienefeld, our professor of European history, who invited us in for coffee and a discussion of what all this was likely to mean.

Samuel T. Roach, Class of 1944

On December 7, 1941, I was in a Columbia movie theater watching a Glen Miller movie when a painful message moved along the bottom of the screen: "Pearl Harbor was bombed by the Japanese." I turned to Sam Beacham (class of 1944) and asked, "Where is Pearl Harbor?" When we walked out of the movie, "extras" were being sold all over. We bought one, read it, and both realized nothing would ever be the same. One year and one day later, at the age of 18, I enlisted along with my cousin in the Army Air Corps.

Maude Byrnes Chisholm Grenfell, Class of 1941

I was in Estill, SC, with my parents. We had attended "Streak" Lawton's wedding on Saturday evening. We were en route back to Columbia when we heard the news. I had a date on Sunday evening with a Captain from Fort Jackson. Needless to say, he never showed. He was put on duty guarding the dam at Lake Murray. In one day, Columbia had become a guarded city. We were stopped before we crossed the Broad River coming into Columbia for identification. Columbia had blackouts for months prior to December 7, but that night even street lights did not come on.

Jane Brooks Mays, Class of 1945

On December 7, I was with several classmates at Dorothy Johnson's house for a Sunday afternoon. The group was shocked and thrilled at the news. Amazingly our attitude was, "Well, at last we are really in this." The boys were already in the Naval ROTC and perhaps they felt differently, but I doubt it. Most of America was ready to go. I guess we had little idea of what war would really mean for all of us.

Edward K. Turnbull, Class of 1941

December 7, 1941, found me filling prescriptions at Breedin's Drugstore on North Main. The store was across from the Jefferson Hotel in the building that used to be the bus depot. Men from Fort Jackson came in to tell me they would soon be on their way to the war zones. I knew I would not be far behind.

James H. Watson, Class of 1942

December 7, 1941, found me on duty running the master control room of radio station WIS. We were feeding the NBC program "Sammy Kaye's Sunday Serenade" to our South Carolina audience when the network abruptly cut the program to announce the Japanese attack on Pearl Harbor. My reaction was pretty much shock and anger. It was much the same as those of our listening audience who immediately jammed my phone lines. I needed to be able to call the telephone company because when the network returned to the program, I was getting CBS instead of NBC. . . . I graduated on a Saturday evening in May, 1942, and the draft board furnished me with a letter the following Monday morning. Ten days later I was inducted into the Army, and approximately six months later I was loaded down with field pack, belts of ammunition and a machine gun and was charging across the beach of Morocco in northwest Africa. My thoughts after this were in the form of a question: Did I really need a B.S. in Business Administration for this?

OVER THERE

As U.S. involvement in World War II expanded, hundreds of students and alumni left for training camps and on to Europe and the Pacific.

One of the youngest to enlist was Frank Williams, a student at University High School (located in the current College of Education building) whose service in the U.S. Navy, 1942 to 1946, predated his student days at USC. He later recalled his years in the Pacific.

I was 15, and I raised cane at home to go into the service. It was such a huge patriotic movement. People were standing in line to enlist. We'd just been through the Depression, and now this seemed to so many of us like a big thrill. I just lied about my age. If they found out you were underage, they sent you packing immediately.

I went to boot camp in Newport, RI. I even enjoyed boot camp. I was scared, but I was also thrilled. I had my 16th birthday in the Solomon Islands. By that time, I felt like I was 40. Action was a rude awakening. And I had dengue fever twice. The whole thing was a lot of sheer boredom interrupted by short bursts of sheer terror.

J. B. Woodson, Jr., who reported for the *Gamecock* as part of a journalism course assignment, captured the sense of sudden departure from campus in a note to Pres. J. Rion McKissick, March 29, 1943.

H'lo Colonel:

Any news on the Navy as far as USC is concerned? What about future use of Maxcy College by the Navy? Will be around Wednesday for any news stories that you may have.

Uncle Sam has called and I must go! Selective Service, April 15. Am withdrawing from school the latter part of this week. Would like to finish up my journalism laboratory course by turning in as much material as possible this time. Therefore, all the news items you have will be greatly appreciated.

My withdrawal will leave only coeds in this course, so it's a cinch a member of the fairer sex will be around to see you next week.

Yours for Victory,

J. B. Woodson, Jr.

Alumni editor of the *Gamecock*, Ralph Lewis, Class of 1929 mailed hundreds of copies of the student newspaper to servicemen and women and encouraged their reports back to campus. Letters and oral histories of alumni in service offer a glimpse into the years spent "over there."

Wallace Elliott Crum, Class of 1937, an Orangeburg native, sent a letter to Lewis, published in the *Gamecock*, February 26, 1943.

Well here I am down in the South Pacific. I saw the Tennessee game the day I left for active duty and was satisfied with the Gamecocks considering the condition, though I hear the rest of the season wasn't so good. But I know where most of the boys are for I run into them often down in this wild country. I left the states in December, spent Christmas in the Panama Canal and shipped over the hump [the equator] on New Years Day.

. . . Please send me The Gamecock and any newsletters or anything about the old university. I guess you heard I had a new daughter just before I left the states. We are all looking forward to having the Japs cleared up and being back for football season next year. Regards to everybody and tell the boys down here to look out for me.

A group of letters from alumni was published in the *Gamecock*, April 8, 1943.

From R. David in North Africa

I have intended writing you for some time, but this African campaign has kept me as busy as a one armed paper hanger with the seven year itch. And speaking of "paper hangers," I think I know of one who will soon be back at his old job.

You don't know how much I appreciate The Gamecock. Words can't express. Sincere thanks to the Alumni Association and all persons responsible for delivery of it to my foxhole. I was reading Tina's "Cannon Fodder" column when I was suddenly disturbed by a hail of enemy artillery shells bursting all around me. From then on, I read the column from the bottom of my deepest foxhole. I had the pleasure a few days ago of watching our boys enter Tunis from my mountaintop observation post. I could also enjoy a nice cool breeze from the Mediterranean from there.

From Lt. Alex Sawyer, Class of 1942, in the South Pacific

I am now stationed on an island in the South Pacific. My first day on the island was a very pleasant one. I bumped into Ensign Carl Hartness and Captain Ralph Darth. Later I attended jungle school with Ralph. I understand Jerry Hughes is also on the island, but I haven't seen him.

It is inspiring to see how well represented Carolina is. After five months in "tropical paradise," I would give a year's pay to see Columbia.

Army Capt. Fred C. Craft, Class of 1937, wrote a letter of appreciation published in the *Gamecock*, May 13, 1943.

I have been receiving The Gamecock for the past few months, and I am afraid I have not the words to express how much it has meant to me. I am able to follow all the doings at Carolina, and also of most of my classmates who are now serving with the armed forces in foreign countries. A country not your own is truly a lonely place. You never know what the right thing is to do and you never have time to find out what is right, so you stay behind the proverbial eight ball just as homesick as Hell. This where The Gamecock finds its best service—it helps you to forget where you are and what you are doing and to relax, turn the pages and see Carolina grow.

Lt. James B. (Ben Joe) Williams, Jr., Class of 1939, was a marine fighter pilot when his letter to Ralph Lewis appeared in the *Gamecock*, February 4, 1944. In it he recounted a chance meeting with his brother, Harry S. Williams, Class of 1943, a marine private.

I am enclosing a picture of my brother, Harry S. Williams, and myself, which was taken on Bougainville, where we met for the first time since we have been in the service. Harry joined the Marines after completing his junior year at the University in 1942. Since then we barely missed each other on several occasions. He is with a Marine Raider Division and made the initial landing on Bougainville. He has seen some interesting and rough action. When I first saw him they were still sleeping in foxholes. To make the bed soft they loosen the sand before laying the blanket on it. I am with a Marine Fighting Squadron, and we were one of the first to land on Bougainville after completion of a strip for operations. I have several Jap planes to my credit, and Harry and I had quite a time discussing our experiences. It was really good to see him, and the rather unique circumstances of our meeting added to the pleasure.

We are both receiving copies of The Gamecock, and although they are somewhat delayed in reaching us in this area it is very interesting to read news about our friends and the University.

The Naval ROTC newsletter of October 1944, *The Salvo,* printed a letter from Ens. McIver Leppard, Class of 1944, written to his parents immediately after the allied invasion of France about experiences on the Normandy beachheads.

I have really seen the hell of war. The Germans really play for keeps and they haven't lost any of their fighting spirit. Unless they run out of supplies, I believe it will be quite some time before they quit.

Prior to the invasion, we were located at what had once been a great city but it had been completely wrecked and there was nothing but the ruins of the once beautiful city. There had been thirty-two churches there but thirty of them had been completely destroyed and the others damaged and disfigured.

We were on the beach for about a week while we were waiting to go on board our ship. While we were there we manned an anti-aircraft gun. Things were pretty quiet except for occasional German air raids. We had several close "misses" from German aerial bombs, but they were more of a nuisance than anything else. After we got our ship into commission again, it was a day and night job, but it was really great to be out on the good old waters once more.

It is impossible for me to describe the invasion. The magnitude of it staggered the imagination. One day I saw thousands of Allied planes, mostly bombers, passing over in a continuous and never ending stream. It was the most beautiful sight I have ever seen.

. . . I am with the greatest bunch of men in the world and the best fighters in the world. If they can't win this war, no man can. We are all bound together in our thoughts and dreams of home. We all work day and night for only two things: To defeat the enemy and go home to live in peace for the remainder of our lives. . . . I shall always remember what I have seen on the beaches where we landed. I had a "not so good" opinion of our Army until I saw them on the battlefields. They are really a great fighting machine. I shall always take my hat off to the boys who had to run off our ramps into pure hell (excuse the language, but it is the only expression I have for it). The sad part of it was that if they lived through the fight for the beach heads, their battles had only begun.

. . . I haven't seen any of the boys who were in my class in the Naval Unit at the University and, so far as I know, I am the only one in my class that was in the invasion. I have seen some of the 84 ensigns who left the Solomons with me. Several of them were killed and a number of them injured.

Commencement still took place on the Horseshoe in 1947.

Registration bottleneck, 1935

In 1955 the Miss Venus title did not consider contestants' faces, hidden behind paper bags.

Frisbee on the Horseshoe, 1978

Antiwar demonstrators take to the campus to protest the war in Vietnam.

Pope John Paul II addresses a crowd on the Horseshoe, September 1987.

Officers of the ROTC association, Compass and Chart, 1942 (*left to right:* Thomas Stevenson, Bill MacMillan, Othniel Wienges, unknown). Photo courtesy Othniel Wienges.

Remembering Gamecock football. Photo memorabilia courtesy Michael Safran.

Remembering Gamecock basketball. Photo memorabilia courtesy Michael Safran.

An Army v. Marine ROTC water battle on the Horseshoe, 1999. Courtesy Sean Rayford, photographer.

USC Women's Club lacrosse scrimmage, 1999. Courtesy Sean Rayford, photographer.

Students in Preston Residential College, 1996. Courtesy University Publications.

Theater production, Department of Theatre and Speech, 1998. Courtesy University Publications.

Men's soccer team, USC v. Davidson, 1997. Courtesy University Publications.

Music laboratory, School of Music, 1996.
Courtesy University Publications.

Women's softball team, 1998. Courtesy University Publications.

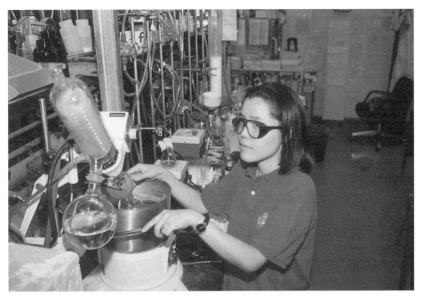

Student researcher in chemistry laboratory. Courtesy University Publications.

Cocky on parade. Courtesy University Publications.

Pres. John Palms helps a student move into Preston Residential College, 1997. Courtesy University Publications.

James Fant, a Carolina student from 1938 to 1940 before he join joined the army and left for Europe, recalled that sometimes academic preparation came in handy.

One day in Paris I ran into a student I'd known at Carolina. After greeting each other and conversing a bit about our service experiences, he asked, "Did you take French?" I said, "Yes, I had Madame [Grace] Sweeny." He was carrying a French newspaper, and he had been trying to read a column about music. He asked me about a particular phrase. I looked at it and was able to tell him right away it said, "Americans are singing, 'It must be jelly because jam don't shake like that.'" Well I guess Madame Sweeny really did teach me some French. I remember she was something—used to come to class with a big picture hat on.

Rhett Jackson, who was on campus for navy officer training in 1943 and 1944, literally bumped into one of his USC classmates, Robert Chapman, when they were both serving in the Pacific.

We were anchored off Bikini during the preparations for the nuclear testing there, and I was officer of the day. I got a call from our captain saying our water was very low and instructing me to call on shore for a barge to bring some water out. . . . It was blowing like the devil, and we were rolling around, but here comes this water barge. I said, "Whoever's the captain of that vessel is coming too fast for these conditions." Then he hit our ship, bumped off it a few times, took off a whole lot of paint, circled around, and hit us three of four more times before we were finally tied up. Then my phone rang, and it was the captain saying, "Tell whoever is the captain of that water barge to report to my quarters immediately." I knew he wanted to talk to him about taking all that paint off our ship. Then I saw this guy coming up from his ship to ours; and, to my complete surprise, it was Bob Chapman. So I called out, "Hey Bob, how'd you get to be captain of that?" He said, "I don't know, but I'm sure taking paint off all these ships." I told him, "Well the captain would like to see you for a minute." He said, "Every captain out here wants to see me!"

Judge Robert Chapman retired from his noted career as a federal judge in 1999.

Alumnus Dom Fusci was stationed in the Pacific when he wrote Dean Francis Bradley on May 13, 1945, a letter soon after published in the *Gamecock* (May 25, 1945).

The war with Germany is finally over. Everyone in the world had a big celebration except the boys out here. We went about doing our daily tasks. Of course we were glad because we knew the boys from Europe would be out here soon helping us finish these monkeys. . . . This war with Japan should last, at most, another year.

I believe I told you I'm on a P.T. tender. That's about all I can tell you about the ship. On one of the torpedoes I have a note, "From the Game-cocks to Tojo." That's one gift from Carolina they're going to get a "bang" out of. I'll try and get a picture of it before the gift is delivered.

Othniel H. Wienges, Jr., who spent two years on campus as a naval trainee in the V-12 program, Class of 1944, was a navy ensign in the Philippines when he wrote an optimistic letter to his parents on July 27, 1945.

Today has been like many others. The hot sun, lazy breeze, stifling heat below, and always a thunderhead in part of the sky.

Tomorrow's length will outdo tonight's brevity, I promise you. Did too much playing today. Visited several ships.

You know I would appreciate it very much if you would buy two extra seats for the Carolina-Clemson game this fall. You never can tell.

Much love,
Othniel

The Home Front

Many students did not feel the effects of the U.S. involvement in World War II immediately. Mary King Butler, Class of 1942, a busy coed and the first USC homecoming queen, recalled life on campus during the first months after Pearl Harbor.

At that time, late 1941 and 1942, very few professors and not many students talked about or seemed to realize the seriousness of the world situation. The war seemed so far away!

For most students, life on campus continued as usual—daily classes, science labs, clubs, sorority and fraternity meetings, dances, athletic events, intramurals, and many other activities. But then, many of our friends and loved ones began leaving campus to go to training camps. Too soon, many of these young men were sent overseas. This made a definite change in our attitudes toward the war.

Carolina co-eds became busy participating in wartime activities: USO dances, "home dinners" for Fort Jackson soldiers, war bond rallies, band-

age rolling in Red Cross classes, and even knitting scarves for the RAF—
"knittin' for Britain."

**An editorial in the _Gamecock_ (May 13, 1943) called for more war effort
on campus.**

There is still no move on this campus, as there has been on other campuses, to start a scholarship through the purchase of war bonds, the money
to be used in the post-war days to help returning soldiers to finish their
education.

There is still no extra-curricular group discussing regularly, intelli-
gently, the issues of the war and the questions we must answer at its termination.

There are still dances costing $5 a throw, with none of it to go to war
helping aids. There are still discussions at literary society meetings on
insane subjects. There are still girls who think nothing of using the telephone for unimportant long distance calls and the trains and buses for
trips home, although they have been told repeatedly how much both these
mediums are needed for necessary use of soldiers.

**Sometimes the impact of war on the home front occurred in subtle ways.
One anonymous coed authored an editorial in the _Gamecock_ (November
20, 1942) to highlight inflationary pressures on scarce, seemingly essential, goods.**

The canteen situation in Sims dormitory, the building for upper class
girls, is rapidly becoming unbearable. . . . Most objectionable among the
high prices charged in Sims canteen, is the 8 cents demanded for Coca-
Cola. The 2 cents extra is for the bottles, and is returned when the bottles
are returned. But all too frequently, the coeds say, they never get this
refund because they carry the Coca-Cola to their rooms to drink, and the
maids who clean the rooms remove the bottles and collect the 2 cents
themselves. . . . Coeds also are not given straws to sip their Coca-Cola and
milks after they've paid for them. Formerly straws were furnished free of
charge, but now they cost 1 cent each.

The manager of the Sims canteen claims that the war is advancing
prices on everything, and that they have to charge more for goods sold. But
coeds yowl that the war is being financed by the canteen alone. . . .

**Students in the tenement dormitories had a different set of complaints,
according to a letter to the _Gamecock_ (March 26, 1943) from students
Dwight Holder and Charlie Baber.**

We are writing this letter with the hopes of improving the hot water system in the tenements at the University. We do not know where the blame lies, but we would like for the proper authorities to remedy the situation as soon as possible.

Shaving and taking showers in cold water day after day makes a man want to turn into a hermit. We admit cold showers come in handy after dances and celebrations, but we would like to have hot showers before attending these affairs.

With many college-age men in training or at war, female students discovered some new options for equal opportunity. University band director George Olson pressed their cause in a letter to President McKissick, September 15, 1942.

I should like to ask your advice and direction in handling the following problem:

There are a good many young ladies on the campus who are very proficient in playing band instruments. Some of them came from schools where girls were used in band. . . . They want to play in our band. Personally I do not object to it. I talked to Dean [of Women Arney] Childs about it and she favors allowing them to play.

If these young ladies are allowed to play I shall require them to use the same uniforms as are used by the boys, replacing the trousers with skirt of like material. I do not think they will be conspicuous in the band. I have already informed the applicants for drum majorettes that their costumes must be conservative and inoffensive if they are to be considered this year.

The student profile changed as World War II continued. USC hosted two Navy College training programs—V-5 and V-12—that brought new men to campus, many older than traditional undergraduates and already alumni from other colleges.

Rhett Jackson, who had spent his freshman year at Clemson, explained his participation in the V-12 program at USC.

The government realized in 1942 they were going to need a lot more Naval officers than the Naval Academy could provide. A lot of universities already had Naval ROTC, and the Navy decided they could supplement that with officer trainees who would generally take two semesters, maybe a bit more, with courses like Naval history, math, engineering, and others in the regular curriculum. Then, these individuals would be sent to midshipman school for about 4 months for navigation, seamanship, ordnance, etc. . . .

I was at Clemson when the Navy came around and explained these programs. If you were interested they gave you a written test, then you went to Columbia to take a physical. . . . Eventually, I was in the first V-12 group at USC, starting July 1943. . . . Clemson was all male and still a full military school, very disciplined. As a freshman, I could only even leave campus three times a year. I hadn't picked up any loyalty to it, and I liked Carolina immediately. There were women there, and you had more freedom. I kind of fell in love with the place right off.

I stayed longer than most, because they needed engineering officers and that took longer than line officer training. V-12 students were out of their rooms by 5:30 am for calisthenics. Then we went to class, then to drill practice, then back in our rooms by about 6 pm. But you could still enter a lot of university activities if you had time. The students were very welcoming, and we were incorporated right into their classes and clubs. There were very few men on campus by then, but there were a lot of women, so we did just fine. The president of the student body was a V-12 trainee. [Former governor] Bob McNair was also V-12, and he encouraged me to join Kappa Sigma. Then I was elected head cheerleader. Winning head cheerleader was the only political thing I ever accomplished in my life.

You did summer semester too, so pretty quickly I had five semesters. But I didn't have the general requirements in English and some others. Professor Frank Herty, a wonderful and amazing guy, took a look at my record just before I left for midshipman school and said, "You know, when you come back, we need you to be a university graduate. I think I'll take your case to the trustees and see if I can get you through. After all, it's wartime." And that's what he did. I didn't have some of those requirements, but I got my B.S. in electrical engineering.

Wartime rationing and general shortages touched everyone but did not prevent many student social activities, according to Rhett Jackson.

You couldn't have a car if you were in V-12, although my roommate, who was president of the student body, hid a car at a friend's house. I did most of my traveling hitch hiking; with a uniform on, someone would pick you up immediately. We'd walk with our dates to movies or places to eat. There was a restaurant where the Town Theatre is located, and my roommate and I used to get together and walk there with our dates for a hot roast beef sandwich. The V-12 program paid us $50 a month, but some went to the required war bond and the insurance. So we got about $30 at the beginning of the month, and by the end of the month, the women would have to pay for our sandwiches.

A Postwar Student Boom

By 1945 the campus was beginning to feel the presence of a new kind of student—the veteran. Older, wiser, and eager to reestablish normalcy in their lives, their numbers swelled as they applied G.I. Bill funding to college educations that many had never dreamed they could afford.

For U.S. senator Fritz Hollings, the timing of returning from service as a U.S. Army officer in Europe and North Africa was crucial to his decision to attend USC School of Law. He described the circumstances in a 1991 interview with John Duffy for the University's Modern Political Collections.

I came back [from service overseas] at the end of 1945. It was in November, after Thanksgiving. I had applied to the University of Virginia Law School, and they had accepted me. But by the time I got back, it was too late to start there. So then the question was whether I was going to miss a whole year. USC said for me to come by to see [dean of the law school] Nelson Frierson, so my uncle met me at Ft. Bragg and we went to Columbia. Frierson told me he didn't see how I could catch up, but I could come and audit the courses. If I could pass, I could work on cases. Everyone was very considerate and wanted to help veterans. I was still in uniform.

I went home that night and the next morning I came back to Columbia and got a closet on Marion Street. . . . When you opened the door, you nearly fell out the front window. It was just a window and a bed, but I was glad to get it. I audited the courses, worked in the library, and by January 17, I had passed first semester.

. . . We marched on the legislature to keep the law school open in the summer. So by May, I had finished a year, and by August, I had finished a year and a half. . . . We started with about 122 students in our class, and 22 graduated. We really cleaned them out of that law class of ours. Everybody was coming back from the war and they all thought they wanted to be lawyers.

We had Marcellus Whaley for torts and Coleman Karesh for everything. I had Coleman for contracts, wills, trusts, mortgages. I went through all the courses I could get from Coleman Karesh.

For many G.I. Bill veterans the reality of college life was both frightening and fascinating. Frank Williams entered college in 1946 after four years in the Pacific and later described his reactions.

A lot of us never thought we'd go to college at all, so the academic side was a big feat. For vets, they waived language and math on the entrance examinations, but you had to take high school courses in these once you were in. My first year, I took freshman algebra and high school algebra at the same time. I passed the college version, but flunked the high school course!

I remember being amazed by Professor [Guy F.] Lipscomb, who I had for chemistry. He wrote notes on the board with one hand and followed behind with an eraser in the other. You had to write incredibly fast to get those notes before they disappeared. I had an economics professor from somewhere in the Middle East. The entire class flunked. We couldn't understand a word he said.

There was social life, but a lot of vets were working at least part time. I was an usher at the Palmetto Theater. On campus, I used to park my car on the Horseshoe, get out and go to classes. All the action was on the Horseshoe and Gibbes Green. I'd meet a date at what is now the president's house. It was a sorority house. But to a certain degree, the regular students were somewhat in awe of us vets. We'd been everywhere, seen everything. They were a bit shy of us. But that was okay, because I'd become somewhat anti-social. I'd lost a lot of friends in the war, and I didn't want new ones.

Dan I. Ross, from Blackville, S.C., attended USC for two years before serving in the war and reenrolled in 1947 to complete his degree. In recollections he wrote for the USC Reunions program, he, like many others, found he had changed when he returned.

I was a very poor student before World War II and a somewhat improved student after the war. When I arrived at USC in January, 1947, I was determined to do better [than in 1941 to 1943]. When I made the Dean's list for the first time, it was a great personal thrill and even more so when I later learned my father went around showing my report card to anyone who would listen. . . . From that moment forward, studies meant more than football. . . .

After making 13 straight hundreds on chemistry tests given by Dr. Lipscomb, he suggested I might wish to major in chemistry. I turned him down because I was scared all the time when in the chemistry laboratories. Yet, for 34 years I worked as a health physicist, measuring radiation and contamination. . . .

In the summer of 1950, Dr. L. L. Smith called me and asked if I would like to teach in the Department of Geology and Geography. I told him that I lacked one course toward completing my [bachelor's] degree. He told me that was no problem; that he and the staff knew what I could do. Thus, I went to work teaching 16 hours per week for nine months, for $1,800.

It was only after I enrolled in graduate school at the University of Texas (Austin) that I realized how well I was prepared and how much I owed to many professors.

STUDENTS BEING STUDENTS AGAIN

As the 1940s drew to a close, the campus began to return to its prewar look and feel. *Gamecock* editor Joe Molony described the transformation in an editorial titled "College Goes Collegiate" (September 23, 1949).

That long awaited day, anticipated for years by many of us, has come at last. We are now living in a collegiate atmosphere. Take a look around you. Rat caps, shaven heads, scared expressions and everything that typifies a college "rat" is there. Our enrollment is gradually dropping to the pre-war level according to the latest figures from the Registrar's office—it's 3,800 compared to 4,200 a year ago.

After close contact with some 75 of these freshmen at the university YMCA camp two weeks ago we can't help but feel optimistic over the future for Carolina. . . . So let's get off our high-horses, admit to ourselves that the veteran has had his day, and give way to the young, high school graduate who'll be building the Carolina of tomorrow.

With their renewed collegiate attitude, students became more concerned and outspoken about their surroundings, their professors, and their peers. A group of editorials and letters in the *Gamecock* demonstrated the reaches of their criticism.

On the actions and decisions of faculty and administration, the student writers were particularly candid. Columnist Al Bahret provided such an example (May 7, 1949).

In general there are three kinds of professors: first, those you respect but don't like; second, those you like but don't respect; and the, third, those you neither respect nor like. The predominant latter gained ascendancy with the advent of the inevitably coupled nemeses of dull lectures and, alas, low marks.

They differ in one respect from high school teachers—they can smoke in public. They live apart from the thundering herds. Their heads are often in new clouds and their feet upon old desks. Their comings and goings are shrouded in vague mutterings. . . .

They are the core of the university. There is no real need for students—the professors would talk to themselves if there were none; there is a little need for an administration—some one has to take care of the incidentals also and hire and fire janitors. In order to make coin professors are forced to work in a mill for long hours and very little pay processing diplomas by instructing students. . . . Like other mill hands they suffer from occupation diseases. Dry rot and mildew take the heaviest toll.

Editorial, November 2, 1951.

An administration founded in insecurity finally gave way to outside pressure last week. . . . Rear Admiral Norman M. Smith, U.S.N. (ret.), announced his resignation as president of the University of South Carolina. Since he was rushed in under the wings of shifty state politicians, Smith and his administration have been the acme of failure. In all fairness to this man, he tried in his inadequate way to do his job. He has spent up to fourteen hours a day working at being a college president. For various reasons these 14-hour days have resulted in monumental bungles and a continuous loss of prestige for the university.

In retrospect, the Admiral's term of office can serve as a criterion for selecting Carolina's next president. . . . 1. The presidency of a state university is a career, not a retirement. 2. The president of a state university should be young. 3. He should be a man of sound intelligence, which has been tried and accepted elsewhere. 4. He should be well-spoken. In short, he should look and sound his office.

Student writers were equally annoyed at the legislative commitment to USC.

Column by Carroll Gilliam, May 13, 1949

The state appropriated less for maintenance of the University in 1947–48 for 4,497 students than in 1924 for 909 students. The state also contributed less per capita to the University for maintenance last year than at any time within the past 30 years. Now if you wonder why your rent is going up while the plaster is falling down, remember that the dollar in 1949 has to spread over more buildings and more students than in 1924. When your wardrobe collapses or you have to wait in line for a shower, thank your legislature.

From 1918 to 1948, the percentage which the student has paid for maintenance of the University has increased from 10 percent to 83 percent! Correspondingly, the state's contribution has declined from 90 percent to 17 percent. This part of the game has not been too harsh on South Carolina while Uncle Sam was the party being soaked, but those days are ending and Mr. and Mrs. Parent will be paying through the nose. The General Assembly has evaded the responsibility of the state for maintaining an adequate state university.

One anonymous student parodied Edgar Allan Poe to expound on meager legislative appropriations for the University in the *Gamecock*, May 13, 1949.

The Raving

As I lie with heavy eyes, in my mind I visualize,
Chunks of plaster of great size,
Joining me in bed.
As I toss on sweat-soaked sheet,
My mind turns to that civic leech,
Who in his legislative speech,
Said we were all bar-flies.
Plastered yes, that is true,
From the ceilings falling through,
Not each one, just a few,
He did not mention that.
I could blame no man for drinking,
When he knows that death is slinking,
For lack of legislative thinking,
Through his dear fire trap.
Which kind of death more filled with splendor,
To be burned into a cinder—or to alcohol surrender?
It doesn't matter much.
Here a choice that appeals to few,
Have the plaster bury you,
Nay rather death from drinking brew,
You have a choice you see.
Inside of me a voice is calling,
(Heard above the plaster's falling),
Senators, quit your stalling,
The sand is running out.
Spend some money on these slums,
That we may be normal chums,
Instead of alcoholic bums,
To quote you more or less. . . .

The postwar extracurriculum was perhaps as important as academics. Isadore E. Lourie, Class of 1954, found that his experiences as president

of the student body and in other activities prepared him for later election campaigns and service in the South Carolina House of Representatives and Senate. In a 1998 interview with Herbert Hartsook, he explained the connection.

I ran for student body treasurer and got beat by several votes in 1952. Then in 1953, I ran for president of the student body and won by several votes. Both elections were close. . . . Being president of the student body was the first really big position I ever had. [I learned] how important it is for a leader to be a leader, even at that young age. You must try to listen to other people's opinions, consider them, but you have to be a catalyst to get things done if you're going to be a leader. It was also formative in those years because the racial crisis was beginning to develop. There were some people wanting the University of South Carolina to pull out of the national council of student bodies because they had integrated and so forth. I was opposing all that and trying to ensure that we stayed in it. In fact, I even got active in the college YMCA. So, it was wonderful. . . .

You also learn there's nothing like the personal touch. I remember a week before the elections for president of the student body, I went door to door, campus dormitory to campus dormitory. If you understand being Jewish at that time, I was not involved in the real social life of the university student body. I didn't get invited to the big formals of the Tri-Delts and K.D.s. I had a lot of friends there, but fraternities were along religious lines considerably, so I didn't have exposure to a great deal of social life in that sense of the word. I had a lot of social life in my fraternity and some at large on the campus, but I had to go at it doubly hard to make contacts and meet people.

Josef Euringer, a German student, wrote a farewell letter summarizing his experience in the *Gamecock*, May 16, 1952.

On September 22, at one o'clock pm, I arrived in Columbia. A few minutes later I was in McBryde. You can't imagine how I felt! Five thousand miles away from home, in a foreign country, nobody whom I knew, everything new to me. This one wanted to help with that, the other explained to me this, everybody was helpful in an unobtrusive manner.

During these months I have been called at least a thousand times "Kraut" ("damned Kraut" only by my better friends), I've been taught how to play poker, I have acquired noteworthy patience in studying while exploding firecrackers made the seat beneath me shake and tremble, I've become convinced that the proper moment for enduring a water fight is only after midnight, I've become aware of the fact that a dormitory is a place where you can do anything except sleep. . . .

I've met friendliness, that genuine helpfulness and downright honesty that are the main characteristics of the Americans. And, I'll tell you, I've been exposed in these nine months in McBryde to more noise than I've been the 24 years of my previous existence in Europe. I've been forced to listen to four radios at one time, each one tuned in to a different station, at the same time another boy practiced trumpet in the bathroom, while two other guys were singing for at least five consecutive times the song "Tell Me Why."

Through the war the Clemson-USC football rivalry never waned. By 1954 student Landis Perry, Class of 1956, looked to William Blake for poetic inspiration (*Gamecock*, October 20, 1954).

The Tiger

Tiger, tiger, burning bright
By the Statehouse late at night.
Why did Howard's foolish hand
Bring thee from thy Guernsey Land?
When the tiger under Columbia skies
Gazes around with two black eyes,
He'll wish forever he did not aspire
To try and dampen the gamecock's fire.
Watch that rooster's fighting heart
Rip the yellow beast apart.
When the beast seeks his retreat
We'll clap our hands and stomp our feet.
What no hammer? What no chain?
Then why this figment of a tortured brain?
Watch the gamecock's disastrous grasp
Bring the tiger's dying gasp.
Tiger, tiger burning bright
By the Statehouse late at night.
Coach Frank Howard, that foolish man
Should've left thee in thy Guernsey Land.

TOWARD AN INTEGRATED CAMPUS: THE FIRST VOICES

The struggle to integrate the campus initially was marked by silenced voices—those of the African Americans who would be University students. Their letters of inquiry and applications for admissions were rebuffed for more than two decades before the force of court rulings at other institutions would announce inevitable change.

To the Board of Trustees, June 27, 1938

Gentlemen:

I am enclosing copies of two letters that I have written, one to Dean Frierson of the School of Law and the other to the President of the University of South Carolina. To date I have received no reply from either and am now appealing to you to help me in this matter.

As the letters are self explanatory, I need not repeat their contents here. I will appreciate your giving this matter your personal attention and your forwarding me such application blanks as may be necessary to complete my application to the School of Law and a copy of the latest catalogue of the University of South Carolina.

Very Truly Yours,

Charles B. Bailey

To the registrar, School of Law, July 29, 1946:

Dear Sir:

I wish to apply to the Law School of the University of South Carolina for fall term. I graduated from Morehouse College, Atlanta, Georgia, with the A.B. degree in 1939, and from Atlanta University, Atlanta, Georgia, with the A.M. degree in 1941. My major field of interest in college and graduate school was economics, and my minor interests included sociology and history.

For the 1937–38 and 1938–39 school years, I was a member of the varsity debating team and participated in engagements with many of the leading schools of the country. In 1938 I was editor of the college Year Book, and in 1939 I was managing editor of the "Maroon Tiger," a monthly student publication of news and stories of current interest.

I am a veteran of World War II with three and a half years of service in the Army of the United States. My service was spent both in the Zone of Interior and in the Pacific theater of operation. My highest rank was Staff Sergeant, attained both in the Air Corps and the Quartermasters Corps of the Air Forces. I was honorably discharged in January, 1946.

I shall be happy to supply any additional information. With your request I shall have sent my college and graduate transcripts. Thank you very much.

Yours sincerely,

Daniel George Sampson

To the Board of Trustees, August 17, 1946

Dear Sirs:

On the 30th day of June, 1946, I made application to enter the School of Law at the University of South Carolina.

I possess all of the qualifications for admission. I am a citizen and resident of the State of South Carolina. I am a graduate of Avery Institute, Charleston, South Carolina, and am now a senior at South Carolina A & M College at Orangeburg, South Carolina.

On or about the 6th day of July, 1946, I received a letter from President Norman M. Smith of the University of South Carolina informing me that the University was unable to act favorably upon my application and has refused me admission solely on account of my race and color. There is no available school of law in the State of South Carolina which I can attend, other than the School of Law at the University of South Carolina.

I request that the Board of Trustees overrule the decision of the President of the University of South Carolina and grant me permission to enter.

Respectfully submitted,

John H. Wrighten

To Pres. Norman Smith, February 25, 1950

Dear Sir:

As a Negro citizen of the State of South Carolina, I wish to pursue graduate study leading to the Ph.D. degree in Speech. The State A & M College at Orangeburg does not offer such a curriculum. This letter comes to inquire if the University admits qualified Negro students in the graduate school. This, I know, is true of many southern states.

To prevent law suits, many southern universities through their state legislatures have set up graduate work in the Negro state colleges, or provided out-of-state aid for the colored students who wish to attend the northern universities since they are denied this privilege in their own state.

Since the State College at Orangeburg does not offer the courses I want, I would like to attend the University of Wisconsin at Madison for the eight-week 1950 summer session. Please advise me as to how I should go about applying for out-of-state aid, in the event I cannot attend the University of South Carolina.

I hold the M.A. degree in Speech and general Linguistics from the University of Michigan (1936).

Yours truly,

Marcus H. Boulware

Gamecock columnist Carroll Gilliam reflected the progressive view of the student press (February 14, 1948).

Now the United States Supreme Court is making rulings with teeth in them. Oklahoma, like South Carolina, met the Waterloo of no law school for Negro citizens and was ordered to set up one immediately. The University of Arkansas threw tradition aside, beat the NAACP to the punch and opened the gates to Negro legal trainees in the face of this rising tide of dissatisfaction. . . .

South Carolina, using that peculiar talent to find legal loopholes through which to pump oxygen to antiquated tradition, set up a facsimile of a law school at the State A & M College at Orangeburg. . . . To continue dual education is to continue throwing tax money into too many needless drains. Duplicity is the law of the day, based on prejudice and pure political expediency.

We are 100 years behind the time. The Negro who wants to absorb the law of torts or advanced zoology is not the same man who was flung upon our shores, ignorant and in chains. . . . The two races laugh at Bob Hope in the same theatres, worship the same God in the same churches, and could acquire learning in the same educational institutions without destroying that inborn desire to be with one's own kind.

Columnist Ken Powell enjoyed baiting segregationists with the news that at least one African American student already was attending USC (*Gamecock*, September 18, 1951).

It's amazing that we still have a goodly number of students enrolled in our university this semester, what with all the reports that students would drop out of the school when a Negro was enrolled. . . .

OK, so you haven't seen a Negro student on the campus, but if you go over to the registrar's office and if you are able to gain access to the records, you will find a Negro's name on file. It happened this way: The University signed a contract with the government to teach night courses at Shaw Field. And it just so happens that a Negro was among the airmen who chose to take the college courses.

He is being taught by a university professor, is listed in university files, and will receive credit from the University of South Carolina for credits earned. It's technical of course, but years from now, when many Negroes will be attending this university, they will find in their orientation books that the first Negro student was enrolled in the Fall semester, 1951.

Another columnist, Gus Manos, was particularly outspoken (*Gamecock*, November 20, 1953).

Segregation is wrong. Its practice is sinful, hypocritical, and backward. It represents the antithesis of the great concept of the brotherhood of man. It opposes all that is democratic, decent, and religious. It confines a specific group of people to an intellectual and spiritual prison. It condemns them to a low standard of living which they can rise over only after overcoming tremendous obstacles. . . .

The idea of separate but equal facilities is a materialistic and hypocritical one. No matter how equal the educational facilities; no matter how equal the number of seats on the bus, no matter how equal the restrooms and water fountains, one great fact remains which overshadows all: In providing separate and perhaps equal facilities, we will be depriving these people of something more important than money can buy. This is human dignity, one of the most treasured gifts of mankind. . . .

We are appropriating huge sums of money to build and support two separate and equal school systems in a state whose educational standard is still among the lowest in the nation. We should be concentrating all our financial and other efforts to building one truly fine school system for the children of the state.

Not all students agreed with the vocal *Gamecock* staffers. Flynn Harrell responded in a guest column (December 4, 1953).

There is an old axiom, "You can judge a cause by the men back of it." Today there is a relatively small group of white northern politicians and Negro leaders who seek to abolish segregation for cheap political purposes. We who live in the South and are familiar with our way of life are far better able to cope with our particular problems than are the NAACP agitators who occupy office suites in downtown New York and who base their opinions on the distorted stories appearing in the Negro Press and the Daily Worker.

Many persons defend segregation on the grounds that it is not contrary to the constitution, nor is it going against the wishes of our creator who separated the peoples of the earth into the various tribes and further divided them into the various tongues.

Today there are still many evils which we should correct. We must continue to educate the people of both races, particularly must we show the Negroes that they shouldn't vote as a block (watch Ward 9 in Columbia). . . .

Segregation is essential to our peculiar way of life. We must provide separate facilities for both races. We must lay aside all political and racial prejudices and work together to insure our continued peace, prosperity, and happiness—the Southern way of life.

Eventually a single, courageous faculty voice was heard on the issue of integrating the schools and colleges. However, for his public support of integrated education, Dr. Chester C. Travelstead, dean of the College of Education, was removed from his position by the Board of Trustees, marking a dark time for both racial equality and academic freedom. The *Gamecock*, December 2, 1955, reprinted Travelstead's letter of May 20, 1955, to Gov. George B. Timmerman, Jr.

You have said: "Never before has anyone seriously proposed that the children of two biologically different races be compelled to mix socially." I suppose you are referring to the Negro and Caucasian races. If so, it should be pointed out that science has not concluded that there are fundamental biological differences between the Negro and the Caucasian. The blood which was available for your use and my use as Navy lieutenants in World War II was not labeled either "white" or "Negro." The only distinguishing labels were by blood types, which are determined irrespective of race. . . . Variety in many ways is apparent among members of the same race. Therefore, we do not eliminate biological differences by putting one race in one school and another race in another school.

. . . I will appreciate your serious consideration of my views in this matter, and I will be delighted to discuss it with you at your convenience.

In a speech before summer school students and faculty in 1955, Travelstead called for an end to segregation.

It is my firm conviction that enforced segregation of the races in our public schools can no longer be justified on any basis—and should, therefore, be abolished as soon as practicable. Even though, as a white Southerner, I have, since early childhood, taken for granted the practice of segregation, I can find no justification for it now. The fact that we have practiced segregation on the assumption that is was right and just does not make it right and just.

The Board of Trustees responded.

The Executive Committee of the Board of Trustees is of the opinion that it is not in the best interest of the University to renew your appointment as dean of the school of education. It wishes, however, to give you the benefit of appropriate notice of termination. Therefore, you are advised that your services will end at the conclusion of the fiscal year 1955–56.

Jack Bass was one of the first students to respond in print (*Gamecock*, December 2, 1955).

Did the executive committee of the Board of Trustees, who decided on Dean Travelstead's dismissal, actually read his speech?

Dean Travelstead did criticize attempts at circumvention of the Supreme Court's decision which declared segregation in public schools unconstitutional. . . . The whole speech was nothing more than an intelligent approach, using reason rather than emotional outbursts, to the most serious social problem of our time.

He stated in detail the alternatives open to South Carolina and the future of its public educational system and questioned the wisdom and possible consequences of several—especially the proposed adoption of a system of state-supported private schools.

Perhaps Dean Travelstead foresaw the result of his speech when he stated that the silence by the professional education organizations in South Carolina might indicate "a great reluctance to speak one's views—reluctance because of fear of embarrassment, ridicule, or reprisal."

Yet he spoke, and it was an admirable display of courage and moral integrity. And yet he was fired, not for having this opinion, but for expressing it openly.

Not only was this rash and short-sighted act of the board of trustees a blow to academic freedom and freedom of discussion, it was a damaging blast at the very basis of the foundation of this or any other university—intellectual integrity.

The next issue of the *Gamecock* (December 9, 1955) published letters of some students who approved of the Board of Trustees' action. Fred LeClerq, a freshman from Denmark, S.C., was one of several supporters.

Just how far does academic freedom extend? Would it be far reaching enough to protect a professor if he were a communist? In 1953 Rutgers University dismissed several members of its faculty who were alleged communists and who invoked the fifth amendment when questioned in senate hearings. I believe integration to be as diametrically opposed to the welfare of this state as communism is to the welfare of the nation. For this reason, I certainly think Dean Travelstead's dismissal was both justifiable and commendable.

Three USC alumni, then students at the Medical University of South Carolina, wrote a letter of support (*Gamecock*, December 16, 1955) but did not feel free to allow publication of their names.

We would like to go on record as disapproving the infringement of academic freedom and freedom of speech executed by the University's board of trustees in firing Dean Travelstead. . . .

One of the qualities we valued most in our professors was their personal opinions. It is our belief that a man's personal opinions make him a teacher and a man of stature, whereas a man who simply spoon-feeds popular ideas originating on a local level is merely a disseminator of information.

Chester C. Travelstead assumed his new position as dean of the school of education at the University of New Mexico on February 1, 1956.

6

Years of Protest,
Years of Growth

The sixties began with the long-resisted integration of the University, and then the attention of the Carolina community turned to the great theme of growth: more students, more faculty, more dormitories, more classroom buildings, more athletic facilities, and, necessarily, more bureaucracy. As Pres. Thomas F. Jones went about changing the institution from "a creaky old provincial school" into a large research university willing to measure itself against national standards, so too did USC students partake in the social upheavals sweeping the nation. They joined in the Civil Rights movement, reacted for and against the war in Vietnam, avoided the draft and got drafted, tested the definition of "good taste" in campus journalism, experimented with illegal drugs yet remained true to beer, wore their hair longer and their skirts shorter, demanded a voice in University affairs, questioned the curriculum, and always rooted for the Gamecocks and complained about parking.

STUDENTS AT PLAY: THE WAY THEY WERE

The *Gamecock's* motto was still "Crowing for a Greater Carolina" and its logo still an old-fashioned rooster. A back-to-school photo essay (September 16, 1960) explained with complacency and confidence what being a Carolina student meant.

This is Carolina—you're part of it now. You stood in the lines to make it official and now you're meeting friends to make it fun. You're being impressed by our leaders and perhaps you're even beginning to feel a pride in our school. But you have barely begun to understand Carolina. Some of you will rush and feel the frightened exhilaration of pledging. You'll "turn it on" at parties. You'll attend Religious Emphasis Week, Bob Stevens' basketball games, and Mr. [Clarence Eugene] Crotty's plays. One night you'll see the University's loveliest compete for May Queen and the same night see the tapping of the latest set of campus leaders. Spring will bring you track meets and Derby Day with its stunts and its shapely Miss Venus. You'll participate in University Day and see the May Queen again plaster the new Student Body president. But all these things will simply be short recesses from all the long, serious study sessions and quick naps.

Derby Day and Miss Venus? Pat Conroy, knowing that truth is stranger than fiction, described this unique Carolina event in his novel *Beach Music*.

I wrote almost all the copy for three straight yearbooks and Mike took more photographs than anyone who had ever worked for the *Garnet and Black*. In one photograph, Mike had caught the essence of the annual Miss Venus contest, where coeds from the sororities dressed in tight blouses, short shorts, and high heels, and paraded across a stage wearing paper bags over their heads. It was a traditional way to judge the Carolina woman who possessed the most desirable body; the jury was a leering batch of fraternity boys famous for their testosterone level. Mike's photograph captured the bagged, anonymous heads of this girls' lineup, their strained, pigeon like bosoms stuck out and shoved toward the camera's lens, for the pleasure of one grotesque, ogling face of a fraternity boy, appreciating breasts that seemed to stretch out into infinity. I captioned it "The Teat Offensive." When President Thomas Jones invited us to explain the play on words Mike and I both insisted it was a printer's error. . . . For us, the *Garnet and Black* was part epistle, part Rosetta Stone, Hallmark card, Socratic dialogue, and census report. It was a bright accumulation of life assembled from the formlessness of ten thousand lives thrown together in a great bouillabaisse and simmered for four years.

Johnny Gregory, Class of 1968, captain of the football team, and 1973 graduate of USC School of Law, married Zeta Tau Alpha's Miss Venus contestant of 1971, Betty Lumpkin, Homecoming Queen of 1970. Gregory remembered the heady days of the mid-1960s.

A man simply cannot have a better college experience than I had. When I think of those fall Saturdays—first I would go to my 8:00 am history class with Dr. Charles Coolidge. Now there was a great professor! Next I would go to the stadium and have my ankles taped, play a football game at 1:00 o'clock, take a shower, say hello to my parents, then join the brothers for a gathering that night.

Fraternities dominated campus life. The Sigma Chi's sponsored Derby Day every year, and on most weekend nights they would end with breakfast at Arthur's Goody Shop in Five Points, so Arthur was one of the judges who picked the best legs and named Miss Venus. In 1966 when the fraternity was put on probation and couldn't take new members, they listed their pledges as Buddy Budweiser and Sammy Schlitz and the like. I was a Sigma Nu, and we had a beer-drinking relay race with the SAE's. The Sigma Nu's won because they drank their beer warm. One year when our members were presidents of all four classes, *The Gamecock* ran a headline, "No Nu's is Good Nu's."

Football games enlivened fall semester. William C. Barksdale, Jr., Class of 1964, remembered the great Sigma Nu prank, when the brothers charged the field dressed as Clemson players at the Carolina-Clemson game in 1961. Barksdale was number 29 that day.

None of us knew what to expect. We had been rehearsed and admonished to avoid conflict if it should break out. Gordon Roman had been the point man on the project. Coach [Marvin] Bass and company had provided white uniform pants, helmets, shoes and pads. Somehow orange jerseys had come from a cooperative high school. Tuck tape of orange hid the garnet stripes on the helmets.

When the big day arrived, we went to the game in a chartered bus as was our custom. We were all decked out in three piece suits with coolers filled with ice and beverages, dates on our arms. We were there early. Excitement was in the air and the boys of Sigma Nu knew why!

At the appointed time we left the stands and slipped into a changing room—it was the first time in the uniforms for us and the fit on some was suspect. We crossed our fingers, dressed and started our passage to the Clemson entrance. Fans along the way cheered us "Tigers" on.

When we burst onto the field there was a brief pause and then the Clemson band struck up Tiger Rag. I remember a sea of orange in the northeast corner of the stadium—rat hats on Clemson rats.

We started innocently enough in formation with the side-straddle-hop. But, when the cow milking spoof and the twist began, we knew the jig was up! The music stopped. The orange hats poured onto the field and the fight was on! It was some brawl—the game was delayed by half an hour. We had fooled Clemson! How sweet it was.

Campus life went on in its traditional way as students lived in dormitories and worried about their roommates. Eve Horne, "Society Writer," passed on some of the lore of the college experience (*Gamecock*, February 14, 1963).

Misery Is

An instructor who is nine minutes late.
An alarm clock at 7:00 a.m.
A term paper.
Russell House coffee.
Discovering your fourth cut is your fifth cut.
Being a second semester senior with a 1.9 g.p.r.
History 11—for the third time.
The fourth quarter of a USC football game.
Trying to say goodnight to your date in South dorm
    lobby.
A roommate who is pro-Kennedy when you are for
    Goldwater.
A roommate who is a recruiting member of the BSU.
Seeing your pinmate with someone else.
Someone bumming your last cigarette.
Watching a couple make out from your dorm window
    on Saturday night.
Wearing madras on a rainy day.

An anonymous poet expressed beatnik malaise and echoes of Ferlinghetti
in the *Gamecock* (May 15, 1964).

On Leaving This Place

I'm tired.
Tired of puppets instead of people,
Of people with crew cuts and tweed coats,
pipes and Picasso buttons.
People who drop soliloquies carefully
labeled intelligence.
I'm tired of people who play the dating game
like touts at the race track,
Tired of seeing people used because
it's only a game.
Of people who turn making out into a social
grace and a woman into a piece of beef,
Of watching sincerity fester into smoothness.
I'm tired of cynics who call
themselves realists,
Tired of minds rotting in indifference,

Of people bored because they're
afraid to care,
Of intellectual games of ring-around-the-rosy.
I'm tired of people who have to be entertained,
Tired of people looking for kicks with a
bottle in one hand and a cigarette in the other,
Of girls proud of knowing the score and
snickering about it,
Of the girls intent on learning the score.
I'm tired of sophisticated slobs,
Tired of the drunkards who are never
more than tight,
Of people who tinker with sex until it's smut,
Of people whose understanding
goes as deep as "neat."
I'm tired of people who scream they hate it
but won't leave because they're lazy,
Tired of people with nothing better to do
than glue their days together with alcohol.
I'm tired of people embarrassed at
honesty, at love, at knowledge.
I'm tired. Yeah, very tired. So long, Carolina.

FROM COEDS TO FEMINISTS

Carolina's "coeds," subject to relentless rules for ladylike behavior were
beginning to tire of what a columnist called "Trite Regulations" (*Gamecock*, March 18, 1960).

There is a rule that no phone calls may be accepted or placed after 11,
and wrath will fall upon you if you're caught violating this necessary rule.
It seems that placing a call in a closed booth after 11 p.m. will disturb the
girls who are chatting and romping around from room to room, making
their nightly visits.

Another major problem is the positions in which girls study. Instead of
sitting up straight with both feet flat on the floor, most girls like to strike a
comfortable position, while digging out knowledge from books and notes.
But this isn't proper or lady-like. Many girls have been reprimanded for
crossing their legs over chairs or tables. Aren't we uncouth?

Why the lobby is "off limits" for bermudas is still a mystery to us. Girls
are allowed to wear them in the sorority rooms, but the lobby rule remains

a puzzle. Would the house mothers have us go back to "hobble" skirts and bustles?

Men questioned the rules too; at least Tom Olrick did in a letter to the *Gamecock* (October 28, 1966).

A few weeks ago, I was informed that the reason why I, or any other USC male, never saw the weaker sex in shorts or slacks was that there is a school rule against it. I was further informed that the women of Carolina could wear the aforementioned articles of apparel providing that they also were "draped" with an overcoat.

After a good deal of reflective analysis (about 10 seconds), I came to the conclusion that I couldn't conclude why there is such an absurd rule. I sincerely believe that the male populace of USC is being deprived. Like any other normal American male, I appreciate the sight of a well filled pair of bermudas.

I would like to know the sin against a female in shorts. I can hardly begin to believe that a moral issue determines this ruling. Off with the raincoats! Long live shorts! Women of Carolina take up the cry! The men of Carolina are firmly behind you.

Toni Metcalf Goodwin, B.A. in English 1963, and M.A. in English 1966, remembered the dean of women and the days of dress codes as not entirely restrictive.

Dean Elizabeth Clotworthy lives in my mind's eye as one of the strongest women I have known. I guess I was somewhat in awe of her, even a little intimidated, although she was never aloof. But she was not, in today's parlance, someone you would ever think of "hanging with," and jeans and tee shirts were not part of her wardrobe. But in the mid 60's, when I was at USC, they were not part of any coed's wardrobe, at least not on campus. That was the time of the well-worn London Fog raincoat which we all wore to cover up whatever did not meet the dress code (which was only for girls of course).

The term "role model" was not part of our vocabulary, but that was what Miss Clotworthy was—a model for the changing role of women on campus. She encouraged us to go beyond the traditional avenues open to females then—nursing, teaching—by making sure we were recognized for what we did, especially if we were involved in leadership or challenging roles. She praised academic achievement, membership in groups that had been all-male, any accomplishments we made; for me, it was being on USC's Debate Team.

She was the advisor for Alpha Kappa Gamma, an honorary society for senior women, and we used to meet in her pretty apartment on campus. I remember the tea, the porcelain plates, the silver, the flowers, but especially feeling so glad to be included in this group. I think we believed we really could do whatever we imagined; life has since taught some of us otherwise, but I have never forgotten that liberating experience.

Gradually, the raincoats —and more—disappeared. From high in Capstone House, poet Kay Boozer saw a different scene (*Crucible*, December 1971).

Window Scene, X-rated

nine stories away
from ground people I
am nine stories away
from a night silent park
the window through which
I moment dream
up frames a full moon
down frames the park
a fecund couch for lovers come
to lie on
cushions of yielding grass,
security from moonlight
given by cooperative oak-dogwood walls
windowed to the park
I stand here now
waiting
voyeur to
the ritual.

Reluctantly, the Board of Trustees gave up parenting. A student writer described the event (*Gamecock*, January 25, 1973).

Conservative Board Bends toward Liberal Coed Dorm

The University's Board of Trustees approved a proposal for a residence hall to house both men and women on restricted halls of the same building.

Some board members were appalled with the idea of men and women sharing the same building, though restricted by elevators programmed to stop on certain floors. Their complaints were about the atmosphere. They didn't want to subject young women to a "slum area."

Their failure to realize they were dealing with men and women caused them to act as overprotective parents—irrationally. But the times are changing, and even with 11 middle-aged and old conservative white men, the board is bending with the changes.

Next, Carolina "coeds" insisted on equal rights (*Gamecock*, February 12, 1971).

Rejected Page Suing Senate—Claims Hiring Discrimination

Vickie Eslinger, one of two Carolina coeds who were recently denied jobs as pages in the state Senate, is suing the body on the grounds that it discriminates against women in its hiring process.

Clerk of Senate Lovick O. Thomas, who has final authority on the hiring of pages in the Senate, reviewed their applications several weeks ago, however, he rejected them, telling Miss Eslinger "the Senate is a place of business and consequently no place for a woman."

Thomas suggested that they should apply for jobs as tour guides. "I laughed when he told me that," Miss Eslinger said.

A First Step toward Diversity

In the early sixties integration was at last coming to Columbia. When African Americans held sit-ins at local lunch counters, some USC students were both interested and sympathetic. Selden K. Smith (Ph.D. 1970) and Hayes Mizell, both graduate teaching assistants in the Department of History, attended sit-ins in the Kress store and Woolworth's on February 17, 1961. Smith later recalled their being called in by Deans [Wilfred H.] Callcott and [Robert H.] Wienefeld.

Dean Callcott had a really scrawny neck and used to pull nervously on his collar. That's what he was doing when he said to us, "It has been brought to our attention that you and Mr. Mizell were in that dime store. In the interests of your own personal safety, we don't want anything to happen to you. Now, were you in that dime store?" He asked us this two or three times, so finally I said to Dean Wienefeld, who taught a course in the French Revolution, "Dr. Wienefeld, if the French Revolution were going on, wouldn't you want to go and see what was happening?" Wienefeld came to class on the hottest and muggiest of summer days, wearing a coat but showing not a bead of sweat. We said he had freon in his veins and called him "The Grim Reaper." He pointed his bony finger at us and said,

"No sir, I would not cross the damn street." I said, "Well, it interests me." That was the extent of the discipline—just that conversation.

Ted Ledeen, Director of the YMCA on campus, got the liberal students organized. Along with Hayes and me was Charles Joyner, Dan Carter, Bob Ackerman, and John Duffy.

When President Jones came, he and Hyman Rubin, Sr. started the Luncheon Club which met on campus on the first Friday of each month. There was no agenda; it was just an opportunity for black and white men to get acquainted in a social setting. In the 1990's, the club began to admit women.

In the fall of 1962 Henrie Dobbins Monteith, an African American woman, sued for admission. "Negro Girl Seeks Admission to Carolina" ran the *Gamecock* headline. Thus, desegregating the University was the first test of Tom Jones's leadership; all agreed he passed high. Perhaps he was helped by the brave *Gamecock* editor, Joan Wolcott. Her editorial response to Gov. Ross Barnett's resistance to integration at the University of Mississippi appeared on October 2, 1962, and asked Carolina students to conduct themselves with dignity.

Violence has played a large role in the Mississippi integration episodes and those who have witnessed the Ole Miss campus expressed sorrow and concern for the extensive damage there. The abrupt halt of classes and the general uneasiness in that area speak poignantly for a calmer approach to Southern integration. Chaos is not a desirable state for any campus or town.

It is our fervent hope that if integration comes to the USC campus, it will be met with rationality and wisdom on the part of those concerned. We are not peacemakers but we desire no scars to mar our beautiful campus or to blemish the heart. Urging others to take one stand or another by driving poster-decorated cars or tacking up signs with messages "written in blood" is not our approach to the problem. We want no hotheads stirring up trouble at our state university. With intelligence, faith, and regard for our fellow students, the integration problem can be settled in the spirit of which our Carolina Community was founded.

September 13, 1963, or I-day as it was called by the administration, went smoothly and peacefully. African Americans Henrie Dobbins Monteith, Robert Anderson, and James Solomon enrolled in their classes according to a carefully orchestrated plan. Twenty-five years later, Anderson remembered that time (*Gamecock*, November 21, 1988).

My father had died in May of that same year, so the experience I had was doubly traumatic. I was personally in the process of grieving. I was the only one out of the three of us who lived on campus. I felt isolated. I grew up in a segregated system. However, when you've got parents like mine, they protected you from the impact of racism. So for me, coming to Carolina was the first experience of being impacted by racism. For many years I denied the impact of those experiences and those traumas. I remember walking across the Horseshoe, and there was a young man standing in the window with a broom stick. He said, "Nigger, we've got you now." This is a memory that never left me, a symbol of all the experience meant to me. I hope that if we have learned anything from it, that no individual, no group, can be made to experience that kind of pain, that kind of trauma. And I think as individuals, as Southerners, and as Americans, we should cut out this cancer called racism.

Henrie Monteith Treadwell recently remembered her experience.

The most interesting fact surrounding my entry into the University of South Carolina is that if "they" had just had the courage to admit me, a child of taxpaying citizens of the State of South Carolina, without requiring a court's intervention and order, I likely would not have ever passed through the portals.

Many individuals in South Carolina, White and African-American, mobilized quickly once I announced my intention to actually enroll to insure that I had "friends" and supporters. The encounters with the well-intentioned often left me with the clear impression of people who wanted to help, but who did not always understand. One young man, in a "prepping" meeting asked me what it was like to "look in a mirror and see a Black face staring back at me." I learned patience, understanding, and forgiveness. I could have been, maybe should have been, hurt or insulted by this "educational" process by which I learned, but I developed a stronger sense of mission, purpose, and commitment to the elimination of divisiveness, misunderstanding, and inequity. And . . . I had a loving and supportive family and an enormous network of "drummers" who had decided that we should shift the paradigm of business as usual in South Carolina and march to a different beat.

Entry into the University, the day of enrollment, was not a major event in my life even though it was a signal event for all of South Carolina. Entry was just one more small step on the path to equality for all citizens of South Carolina. I hardly saw the press, the security people, or those who wished for me to go away, to disappear. There were those Whites who meant well, I suppose, who said to me "It's all right for you to go to the University; you are from a good family. It's those others that we do not want at the University." I always smiled and took guidance from an inner spirit that must have been provided by The Almighty. Who were "those others"? Those "others" included me in so many ways, on so many days. I enrolled for "those others," and for myself. Wanted or unwanted, I decided that "we" had a right to be at the University of South Carolina.

The dynamite sticks thrown in the yard of my uncle and aunt, Henry and Martha Monteith, did nothing to deter us. We saw this assault as yet another truly misdirected and uninformed attempt to stop the move to the future. The hate phone calls were viewed as a nuisance, but not a deterrent. In fact, the dynamite, the phone calls, the actually-insulting, but perhaps well-meaning, comments all strengthened my resolve. If we had simply been viewed as people with the same rights that Whites took for granted, we might have left them to themselves . . . to their detriment, I think. Currently, I view daily the transition of America from a White to a community of color. The future was drumming at the heels of South Carolina in 1962–63, but only a few of us were listening.

After enrollment into my classes I saw myself as just a student. Yes, I noticed the security. Yes, I endured harassing phone calls on campus. Yes, I endured little parcels left at my dormitory door. I enjoyed knowing that those who planned the harassments took more time planning to bother me than I spent eliminating the acts of hate, or disrespect, from my mind. No one could invade my privacy or my pride, and I thank my family for imbuing me with the force of will that made it possible for me to laugh and just move on to the next classroom assignment. I knew that many of my professors did not embrace the principles of segregation, of the old confederacy. So the classrooms were safe, if not always extremely nurturing, places.

The cafeteria was always a warm place for me even though I ate alone most of the time. The cafeteria help were mainly African-American and they looked after me. I continue to believe that where a "family" does not exist, one can be created. The men and women who prepared and served the meals, and who cleared the tables, were my friends and supporters. A part of the African-American ethos in that time meant that we were always there for each other. Today, in many ways we are still there for each other when others choose to be absent. Importantly, at the time, I did not need more, as members of my community were there for me in whatever way that they could be.

Am I satisfied with my decision to enter the University? Absolutely!!! So many worked so very hard to prevent the integration of the University of South Carolina from following the path witnessed in other southern states. I succeeded in doing my part because so many men and women of all colors worked hard to insure that I could persevere and achieve.

The Orangeburg Massacre and the assassination of Martin Luther King, Jr., galvanized faculty and students. Tom Terrill, who taught the first Afro-American studies course, The Negro in American History, wrote to the editor of the *Gamecock*, April 18, 1968.

Friday afternoon, I lectured or, more accurately, I led a discussion at a nearby Negro college. The recent tragedy in Memphis set the background. The blunt questions of the students made the experience far from pleasant: why do white men hate black men, why should I fight, for a country that classifies me as I-A for Viet Nam and second class at home, why will whites let us cook for them but not associate with them? I felt very white, very inadequate, and very ashamed.

But millions of agonized words, such as these, are wasted unless there is action, and Carolina students can act.

(1) You can give money to the Metropolitan Education Foundation which will provide education projects for children from poor homes in the Columbia area.

(2) Carolina sororities and fraternities can cease their segregated practices, and the university should not support those groups which refuse to change their racist habits.

(3) Carolina white students can make a sincere effort to find out what the feelings and grievances of Negro students really are. Don't go on guessing in ignorance. Ask in a genuine spirit of seeking to know and understand.

(4) All Carolina students can refuse to patronize segregated institutions.

(5) Carolina students can actively demand quality education for all people in South Carolina.

The Association of Afro-American Students emerged as a political force in 1969, asking serious questions about the University's development plans and requesting an Afro-American Studies program. They circulated mimeographed broadsheets like this one from 1968.

Black Power

Let's take a look at the University of South Carolina. We hear people in Columbia talking about all the good the University is doing for the community. The question that we raise is: which community? It is clearly evident that the good being done is for the white community. We contend that USC is HURTING THE BLACK COMMUNITY WITH ALL ITS "PROGRESS." Probably the biggest example of this is the coliseum. USC moved 700 BLACK families so Carolina could have a basketball court. The families were placed into another slum. This also happened in the case of the tennis courts across from Booker Washington.

Why did the student government give a memorial service for the students at S.C. State College if they didn't condemn the actions of the police? WHY DID THEY WANT TO HAVE A MEMORIAL SERVICE FOR MARTIN L. KING WHEN A LARGE NUMBER OF CAROLINA STUDENTS HAD A PARTY ON CAMPUS CELEBRATING HIS DEATH?

IS THIS RACISM?

Are we going to stand by and let these acts be committed against our brothers?

We are in rebellion,

B.A.D. (Black Afros for Defense)

Luther Battiste, Class of 1971 and an International Studies major from Orangeburg, served on the Student Government Committee for Curriculum Review in the College of Arts and Sciences. Their final report recommended an Afro-American Studies program. Battiste talked about black students' experiences when he participated in a panel on student life (*University of South Carolina Magazine*, Fall 1970.)

During my three years at Carolina I have matured because of USC's community of people who are by no means homogeneous. Being exposed to people unlike myself has been a positive factor mainly because I have become more aware of myself as a person—a Black person. This I regard as one of the greatest fruits of my education. Overtly racist teachers do exist on this campus; but they are balanced, I must admit, by teachers who are sympathetic with the problems of Blacks. Because of the lack of Black teachers and administrators, Blacks on this campus find themselves lost in a sea of whiteness.

In courses related to the liberal arts, Blacks are generally completely overlooked. During my freshman year, passages relating to Afro-Americans were often not discussed because of fear of controversy. But if the University invests proper personnel, money, and interest in the new Afro-American studies major, a better rapport can be established between Black students and administrators.

Social life for Blacks on this campus amounts to what a small group of Black students can provide for the other students. Often Blacks hitch hike to Allen and Benedict colleges just for social functions. Such loneliness can only be diminished by recruiting Black students. In a state that is 40 percent Black, 300 Blacks out of 15,000 students hardly seems realistic.

THE ACADEMIC LIFE

Carolina students participated in an exchange program with the University of Warwick in England. One British participant, Peter Shellard, drew some educational comparisons (*Gamecock*, April 14, 1967).

In the first place, a British university attempts to inculcate in the student the idea of self-discipline. Therefore we have a great deal of time and freedom to do our work, sometimes, admittedly, too much time. However, you feel the need to be continually kept up to the mark with quizzes and tests.

In addition your system assumes a "well-rounded" man to be more beneficial to society than one who, as in Britain, has spent three years at college specializing in his chosen field. Your system, I believe, fails to produce the scholar, the genuine article as it were.

Student attitudes at USC, I thought, were passive to all but local and immediate topics; I rarely heard or participated in discussions on national events. This I put down to the conservatism and provincialism of South Carolina.

I disliked the fraternity system because I felt it throws too many people of the same background and interests together when the principle of a university is to encourage the mixing of many people from all walks of life and backgrounds.

But if the fraternity system, like football, satisfies your characteristic craving for "togetherness" then good luck to it!

On the social side, I felt there were too many unnecessarily strict rules. Surely learning how to use freedom must be a principle of a university, for, theoretically, responsibility follows from the use of freedom.

This is true anyway for the majority of students in England, but the petty restrictions on the USC campus destroyed the idea of freedom.

In sum then, the people of South Carolina are among the friendliest I have met, but USC unfortunately doesn't instill in the student the kind of qualities that a British university does—ones that I personally feel are of more use in later life.

In the early 1970s an alternative, off-campus publication, *Common Sense*, provided student journalists—who were increasingly impolite—with an outlet for criticism, satire, and stories on rude and risky topics—at least for four issues. Harry Hope described Carolina professors in *Common Sense*, October 1971.

A Student's Guide to Professors

Snow the Girls

Flashy dresser, well-groomed, good model for a Playboy ad, which he reads religiously. From behind his office door come strange sounds and giggling after classes. Probably a fraternity guy in his college days. He's only in it for the sex. Doesn't care about grading—although he is not averse to helping out a nice-looking coed get an "A."

The Professional Liberal

He feels guilty for the sins of his race and tries to reverse all the prejudices of his forefathers through his work with the ACLU and his weekend demonstrations. Then he wonders why he angers blacks with his "I will fight for them and give them their rights" attitude. A bad case of the Harvard Guilt Complex is usually the problem.

The Little Old Lady Instructor

She has taught junior high school for forty-seven years before getting her master's degree. She still thinks she is teaching eighth grade. She holds spelling quizzes in class and reads Robert Browning's torrid love poems aloud. Very horny. Found outside the student union building doing "recess duty."

The Campus Minister

He represents liberalism in its most disgusting form. A former athlete, he is always trying to drag unwilling souls to the Sunday night fellowship meetings, always trying to "be cool" and "rap with the kids" so that they might "get high with God." He wants to "talk their language" as if students are too dense to read the King James Bible or appreciate Bach's "Magnificat."

Central Casting's Professor

This is the type once considered typical of all professors: forgetful, sloppy, carries two briefcases and a load of books everywhere. All he knows is his field of study. Usually has tenure so feels very safe in his incompetence.

Freak/Revolutionary

You can't tell this one from the students. Usually comes to class stoned. He is always trying to start the Revolution in his class. He was probably a beatnik in his college days. Very rare in the South, and probably an instructor.

Overworked Grad Student

In addition to teaching four introductory classes, he is usually trying to finish his thesis or dissertation, provide for his wife and three small children, and finish out his service in the National Guard. He is also on the lookout for a job, which is hard to find because although his species is very plentiful, it has a high mortality rate.

Carolina students, as always, adored some of their professors. Among them was Jack Ashley, renowned for his course on Milton (*Garnet and Black*, 1970).

Dr. Jack Ashley is a teacher of great enthusiasm and imagination. He dives deep into his subject and, with a challenging grin, invites you to swim with him. He investigates his undersea world with the delight of a little boy, peering through a crystal diving mask for the first time. And you feel the delight, you look through the mask too, and the murky, grey world of words flashes suddenly alive, new and fascinating. A man of great knowledge and great dedication, with the power to dramatize, stimulate, and teach.

I always hated cutting his class.

I loved doing his paper.

His test was such a blast.

And, in his home he served us strawberry shortcake.

STUDENT ACTIVISTS

By the midsixties students stopped obeying and started demanding. First, they wanted to be heard, starting with letters in the *Gamecock* (February 11, 1966).

Dear Mr. [Sig] Huitt:

The student at Carolina often wonders where his place is in this computerized institution. One solution was supposed to be the formation of Student Government to represent student opinion to those who administer the University. We learned rapidly, however, that concern for student opinion was either totally absent, or based on an intricate system of administrative politics. It seems like a card game, and the student gets lost in the fast shuffle.

The heart of the problem seems to be that while the University spends great sums of money, and staffs itself well, solely for the benefit of students and the solution of their problems, the individual student and his problems are neglected in the machinery of administration.

We have repeatedly found frustration, closed doors, and interested but helpless people in our pursuit of student concerns. We have gone to the bottom and worked up, and to the top and worked down, with the same result. Other offices to try, other busy people to see, other problems left unsolved. We wonder if this is not the most bureaucratic of bureaucracies.

This entire complex lies, as we imagined it would, on the dollar sign dynasty, and political pedagogues of the legislature and some alumni. From the system comes the disproportionate balance of power among Athletics, Administration, Faculty, and last, and certainly not least, the students.

We are not trying to tear down the reputation or greatness of our University. If we did not care deeply about its welfare, we would not criticize or even take the time to write.

All we desire is that these problems be brought to light and that students begin to think twice about the University situation. Carolina, when, oh when?

Thorne Compton
Vice-president of the Student Body
Jim Mulligan
Treasurer of the Student Body

Students also wanted the administration to share their views and concerns, as University Union president Vickie Eslinger spelled out in a letter to President Jones (November 19,1969).

I would like to bring a matter to your attention: the lack of support and lack of interest of the higher Administration in many student activities. I am referring in particular to the October 29 lecture by Dick Gregory (a black comedian and civil rights lecturer) sponsored by the Lectures committee of the University Union. This was undoubtedly one of the most successful lecture programs ever presented at USC—due entirely to the students because of an obvious absence of University Administrators.

I realize that Mr. Gregory is a controversial speaker. But if the feeling does exist among some of the Faculty and Administration (and obviously it does)—that public opinion might frown on their appearing to support such a lecture—then I question the right of those particular people to try to educate anyone. If they didn't come to the lecture because they are "tired of" or "don't like to discuss" or "aren't interested" in what they thought Mr.

Gregory was "probably" going to speak on, then I question their <u>ability</u> to educate anyone. If these same people who didn't come to the lecture are the ones who so loudly profess "interest" in their students, then I question their sincerity and marvel at their open hypocrisy.

We, the students and the University union, would appreciate the Administration's support and interest in controversial programs without regard given to "what will the press/neighbors think if I go."

"Student Senate Passed a Resolution Wednesday Supporting United States Policy in Vietnam," announced the *Gamecock* in November 1965. But when Gen. William C. Westmoreland came to campus in the spring of 1967, his detractors spoke out. "Picketers Interrupt Ceremony," wrote Ginny Carroll (*Gamecock*, April 27, 1967). The years of student protest and activism began.

As about 29 sign-carrying pickets stood outside Rutledge Chapel, University administrators presented the degree of Doctor of Laws to the commander of U.S. forces in Southeast Asia.

Immediately after the degree presentation, Dr. Thomas Tidwell, assistant professor in the Chemistry Department, stood up, held aloft a sign, and proclaimed, "I Protest: Doctor of War."

The larger demonstration was outside the chapel, however, where pickets milled in a circle, carrying signs protesting American involvement in Vietnam. A few of the several hundred students who cheered Westmoreland on his arrival at the Horseshoe reacted strongly to the pickets with boos, hisses and cries of "Get them, kill them."

Part of the 150-man police force on guard outside Rutledge converged on the threatening clash and shepherded the demonstrators away from the chapel area.

Carl Stepp, editor of the *Gamecock* in 1969, attended an antiwar rally and wrote about conflicting campus passions and his own confusion (September 22, 1969).

Denim and Tweed

The rally had been going on for a couple of hours, with the loud music and the kids sitting on the floor and thinking—hoping, too—that they were in, man; living. And the outsiders timidly stepping inside and listening and watching, not sure what to think, whether to love or hate.

It was a kind of paradoxical, perverted way of education with the educators compromising for the "public opinion" and "appropriation" and "good of the whole school" guys. And the kids—the AWARE-types—looking for the Answer and the Way and trying to love and maybe being mixed up and maybe, just maybe, being right and ahead of you and everybody. And it was kind of funny when the leader said he felt sorry for Tom Jones, the president, and his position. You could just bet the president felt sorry for him. And you felt sorry for the world, in such a screwed-up state of love-hate, pity-everybody, political prostitution.

It was all confusing. You hated the War, but couldn't stomach the "let's destroy this whole country" bit. You respected the administration, but couldn't like their policy of containment rather than live-and-let-live.

It stayed confused all day. The war, the soldiers, the Establishment-haters, the gung-ho guys with their emotional blindness and right-wing non-patriotism.

You wanted to love them all, and the little burned children, and the University president slipping along that thin line of state University responsibilities. You wanted them to love each other and you couldn't tell—the bad words and scowls and talk of peace and gentleness and harshness all came together and you wondered just what the hell it would all bring.

You didn't know. You just didn't know.

In May 1970 the student unrest sweeping the nation came to USC. Pat Conroy, in his novel *Beach Music*, captured the changing campus atmosphere.

Then, in 1968, there was the Tet Offensive, the assassination of Martin Luther King, the murder of Robert Kennedy, the Chicago Convention, a whole coloratura of horror in transit along a time line.

As Ledare continued I remembered that our campus had been quiescent, indifferent, as students took over administration buildings at Columbia and Harvard. But hints and markings of change began to appear without the presence of any rhetoric or forethought. We started wearing our hair longer, grew mustaches, and the first beards began to appear. A gradual dressing down had begun subliminally and an SAE boy in a suit began to look odd, a museum piece drifting as flotsam along fraternity row. The daughters of small-town insurance adjusters and Baptist ministers began to dress like hippies and stopped wearing makeup except on weekend visits home. Except for Secession, no trend had ever had its birthplace in South Carolina. But the tumult on the other campuses and the antiauthoritarian tenor of the times could be measured by the length of sideburns creeping down the faces of Carolina men.

Long hair meant drugs and hippies to local police whose presence on campus and in Russell House helped turn the campus into a riot zone. On the seventh of May 1970, following Kent State, students took over Russell House, and Conroy's characters participated.

If the deaths had occurred at the already-radicalized Harvard or Columbia, there would have been some context, some force of mitigating circumstances. But the gunning down of thirteen students in the idyllic heartland town of Kent, Ohio, at Kent State, a college far more deferential in its acquiescence to authority than even the University of South Carolina, was inconceivable. It was clear to us that the government had declared open season on anyone opposing the war. On that single day, in the milling, insurgent coming together of the students of America, all the dangers of solidarity were set loose. Even the most docile and passive of students felt the hot breath of mutiny in the air as we walked toward the Horseshoe. Grievance would soon turn to rage and meekness turn mean, then majestic. What was happening in this blind migration of students toward the open space between the library and the Russell House was taking place on campuses all over America. Intellect and reason had gone underground, civility hibernated, and insurrection took the lead. Yet none of us knew where we were going.

While some students protested the war, others were in it. Twins Bob and Thom Salane, both champion debaters, graduated from Carolina in 1969. Thom was called up in the last draft for Vietnam, August 1969, just after marrying Linda Burton, also Class of 1969. In October, Bob wrote to Thom, in basic training at Fort Jackson, about campus matters.

To bring you up to date on campus activities, I don't know anything. We law students are above such petty and common strife. Seriously, the campus seems to be waiting for tomorrow's Vietnam Moratorium when the "leftist," John Scott Wilson-types and McCarthy-Kennedy forces clash with the YAF-Young Republican-RSVP'ers under the able direction of Richard Hines. My money's on the YAF'ers! It's difficult for me to awaken to any such "cause" at this time.

We should have very few problems with basketball. I'm really looking forward to it. Roche is 1st string All-Am in most of the magazines. In all the pre-season polls, the 'Cocks are picked <u>no worse</u> that #3! Tom Riker is picked as one of the top 10 sophs in the country and Kevin Joyce is the #1 freshman. We are seeing the start of a DYNASTY at USC.

Thom Salane, still in Vietnam in 1971, was ready to come home. He wrote to his wife, Linda, in March of that year.

March 15

I came back in off guard duty last night after getting plenty of sleep—at least 6 straight hours. About 9 pm something set off a trip flare (they are flares wired to the strands of barbed wire. If anything is in the wire it will tug the wire and ignite the flare.) We looked and couldn't see a thing. Usually an animal will get into the wire and set if off then run off. Usually we see it run off but last night nothing! So I loaded up the machine gun and called in to report it. The tower called back in about 5 minutes and said that the tower reported seeing a man out in front of our bunker. They sent an officer and truck load of men out who stayed there for a while, and then left. Nothing else happened but I kept saying to myself "Please God, not now, I'm too short!"

March 19

The unit has put me in for a decoration. I don't know if I'll get it, but if I do it will be either a bronze star or an Army Commendation Medal. I guess it's quite an honor because only about four or five men were recommended for it. Now aren't you proud of your husband. Hum bug. I'd like to tell the army what they could do with their damned medals. . . .

I heard on the news today that Carolina lost to Penn in the NCAA semi-finals of the regionals. I just hope they have better luck next year. I just wish for a change that we didn't have to say "wait til next year." Maybe when we get back there and start rooting for them?!

Well, it's only 93 days to go til I'm out of the Army. I find myself getting a real short-timer's attitude. All I can think about is going home. I'll surely be glad to get there.

JONES UNDER SIEGE

Alums were shocked by accounts of campus activism and blamed Pres. Thomas Jones for whatever students were saying, wearing, smoking, drinking, or thinking. They did not hesitate to let him know.

October 30, 1968

I am very concerned about the radical groups and/or organizations that are becoming more and more disruptive on the USC campus.

As head of the University, it is your responsibility to keep it as an institution of education, not as a festering ground for unshaven, unwashed cruds such as have been seen and heard from as of late.

Whether you realize it or not, there is much growing public opinion on what is happening and why you are allowing it. If for some reason you are afraid to take a stand openly, and denounce such un-American organizations as AWARE/S.D.S., and if you are afraid they will eventually take over your campus as they did at Columbia University, then you should consider retirement, as that is what they will do in the very near future, thereby forcing you into retirement.

May 16, 1969

As an alumni of U.S.C. I was greatly disappointed to read that the Board of Trustees at U.S.C. has agreed to permit students to have alcoholic beverages in their dormitories.

My son has been registered to attend U.S.C. this Fall but now I'm beginning to wonder if I haven't made a mistake in enrolling him at Carolina. I thought the purpose of the university was to give a student an education and not teach them how to drink, or encourage it.

I assume that the next thing that will be allowed is for the men and women students to share the same dormitories. This would be a next logical step according to "lame brained" Board of Trustees way of thinking. They apparently want to do only as the other schools do.

I personally think Carolina is better than any other school and should be the "Leader," not the "follower."

P.S. I am a past contributor to your Educational Foundation Fund!

April 13, 1970

After viewing the late news on television last night, I, as a loyal alumnus of the University, am thoroughly disgusted with the way our University is being downgraded by the caliber of so-called students allowed to attend the school.

I demand that these dissidents be expelled from the school, and allowed to go from here to California, or to some other state unlike ours. When I attended the University, things were so simple that no one could fail to understand the rules under which one was allowed to continue to attend the school—there were certain rules and regulations; one obeyed them or got out—it was as simple as that. And I am fully convinced that society would improve considerably if we went back to that simple system.

My husband and I attended the University—we sent our daughter to the University—but I want to state most emphatically that under no circumstances would we allow our granddaughter to attend under the present conditions.

April 28, 1970

Tuesday of this week I went to the Russell House to purchase tickets for the Bob Hope Special and I was sorry that I had an out-of-town guest with me.

The students in there were unbelievable; I realize that they have freedom of dress; and that the University is not to act as policemen or take the place of parents. Further, Dr. Jones, I have a sixteen year old who wears "Mod" clothes and keeps up with the latest fad, and I too have raised my hemline, but this is not what I am concerned about. These students looked half dressed, shabby, dirty and most unattractive.

Jones was blamed by students and for students, but after the campus uprising, his fans came forward and expressed loyalty and praise.

Dear Dr. Tom,

For many days now I have tried to find time to drop you a note and add my name to the thousands who give you our SOLID SUPPORT!!!! You have done an excellent job at USC, and we appreciate!!!!

You know, it seems to me that institutions always seem to treat their conformist very well; but the man doing something better, something different, something that changes the status-quo—that man stays in a little trouble. I'm grateful that you are at times in trouble, it shows me that you are doing a good job!!!

Sincerely,

Rhett Jackson

Jones resigned in January 1974. Carl Sessions Stepp, B.A. 1970, M.A. 1972, and now a professor of journalism at the University of Maryland, remembered the man he used to criticize and came to admire.

Considering the big fight we had, it sometimes surprises me how fondly I remember President Thomas F. Jones.

Jones was an almost larger-than-life character on the Carolina campus of the late 1960s. Falstaffian and full of himself, he loved bow ties and big cigars, and beamed a high-energy force field into every corner. But he was also a serious scholar and educator in the classic sense, and he helped transform Carolina into a better place.

Our first run-in was small. In my junior year, I interviewed Jones for a story on the integration of the Carolina faculty. Jones suggested that, instead of directly reporting the change, The Gamecock should run a photo that just happened to include a black professor. He felt like that would signal the change without making a big issue of it. Our editors disagreed, and we ran a modest story on page one. Jones was gracious about it.

Our last fight was a doozy. I was called out of English class one day in the fall of 1969 because The Gamecock's printer had alerted Jones that we planned to publish the f-word. As Gamecock editor, I had approved a story on a confrontation in which, as I recall, a demonstrator had shouted the f-word to a police officer, who shouted it back.

Jones was grave. He didn't want the word in the paper, and he made what I took to be threats to try to expel me if it appeared.

This, too, seems quaint now. But it was a huge issue then. Ultimately we agreed to avoid printing the full word; we used f—. Even that was controversial. Loads of people objected to even the toned-down version. Conservative students mounted a "Stepp Out" campaign, unsuccessfully, to get me fired.

Jones never took any action against me, and we remained cordial. As Gamecock editor, I had a standing hour-long meeting with him each week. I looked forward to it. He was immensely inspirational, full of passion for knowledge and the university. I often sat in awe as he gazed into the distance and ruminated on his grand visions for the school.

Like many intellectuals, he was an awkward mingler and could seem aloof from students. He cultivated a certain imperial image (for example, there was a custom that everyone stand up when he entered the room) that as a student I found off-putting. I was disappointed he didn't speak out more forcefully on the day's issues. But he set high standards, hired good people, and threw himself into the work. In a state with a poor record for supporting education and a high proportion of meddlesome politicians, he succeeded in pushing Carolina forward.

Eventually the powers that be brought Jones down. He famously said at the time that friends come and go but enemies accumulate. Looking back, I would say that Tom Jones accumulated more friends than he might have realized.

The 1974 "Carolina Lampoon" section of *Garnet and Black* awarded Jones's successor, William Patterson, a Turkey of the Year Award, "for making sure that no one would ever be able to tell that Thomas F. Jones was ever here." Kathleen O'Quinn lamented the demise of the Contemporary University, one of Jones's educational innovations (*Gamecock*, July 30,1974).

Having witnessed the university system as both staff and student during my three year residence at Carolina, I have never seen it in such an uproar. Which department/person will be the next to go? There's an air of anticipation for the dust to clear . . . and all for a return to the dark ages.

I find it inconceivable that Contemporary University is "in choppy water." In December I will be awarded a B.A. in Spanish, the majority of the course work being restricted and repetitious. My CU project on Mexican women was definitely the highlight of my undergraduate work, moving me into many projects outside the university sphere.

There is NO substitute for a coordinated, contracted project between several faculty members and a student, all excited about a previously unexplored topic.

Remember what we're here for? Let them switch the administration around until their house is in order, but don't let this valuable program be dropped—just because of disillusionment on the part of those that don't care and/or don't understand what it's about.

THE WRITING LIFE

The University continued growing—from 15,000 in 1970 to its current 26,000 in 1979—and that meant new faculty members in every discipline. James Dickey joined the USC English department in January 1969. "I'm not a teacher who writes; I'm a writer who consents to teaching," he said. His presence in poetry classes and writing workshops inspired students for many years, among them Pat Conroy.

May 3, 1974

Dear Mr. Dickey,

Someone gave me a copy of your poems 1957–1967 as a gift the year I went to teach on Daufuskie island. Long before I entered your classroom in Columbia, you were my teacher. Long before I ever saw you, I was searching for Jane McNaughton's in my own life, listening for dead conches in my ear, hoping for sharks in my parlor, and preparing for the day when I would translate the shadows and voices of my own life into words and stories. You were my teacher because your words rang truer to me than any writer that ever lived. I came to your classroom to have a face, a voice, and a presence to connect to the words. I received much more. From you, I received a gift: a relentlessness about finding the single word— the one absolutely right word—that fits, that is so right that a phrase or a sentence is diminished by its absence. I also learned a great deal about passion in writing, about attempting things that I am not yet able to do, about daring, gambling, and groping for regions beyond one's ken or reach.

I wanted to tell you all this in person but the situation was too contrived and the herd of blue haired ladies made it impossible. Thanks very much for the telegram about the movie. My wife had it framed when I returned from California.

In the book I am writing now, seven things I wrote while in your class remain fully intact. The rest of the book is leaden with your influence. I tell you this because of your reverence for the relationship between the teacher and his students. I also tell you this because I carry you with me as I write. Much of the new book will stink of youth; much of the writing will be flabby and unmuscled. But some of it will sing and I hope you will see your teaching in the song. I am grateful to you from my heart.

Your student,
Pat Conroy

As Carolina's graduate programs expanded, graduate students taught more and more courses, especially the inevitable Freshman English. Michael P. Dean wrote a poem about his initiation into teaching, published in the *Crucible*, 1973.

Upon First Teaching Cummings

cummings I said
dropping
my voice into lower case
was a great poet

twenty befuddled heads
dove into the whitewashed
sea of the text peering
about anxiously to find
proof of my dogmatic
statement

one by two like submarines'
periscopes they surfaced
above the wave and began
launching torpedoes of doubt
into my straight ahead course

undaunted I depthcharged them
with Buffalo Bill (now defunct)
and Cambridge ladies in upholstered
souls until the bells declared truce

tomorrow I shall begin by saying
Ferlinghetti is a great poet
I thought and then remained
silent behind a peak of papers
clouding my dreadnought desk

THE WORKING LIFE: IS ANYBODY STUDYING?

The traditional college student—eighteen years old, living in a dormitory, and having bills paid by Mom and Dad—became scarce. Older students entered college after years at work and younger ones lived at home or in apartments and paid their own bills. Most students held jobs, both on and off campus. *Garnet and Black* (1977) writer Felicia Mitchell surveyed the campus job scene.

Working Working Working

Several years ago a shy freshman asked a professor to sign a drop form. He asked her why she was dropping his class and when she told him she was taking too many hours and working he answered, "But I feel being a university student is a full-time job in itself."

Being a student can be a full-time job, but many students find working an economic necessity. Here at USC about 1300 students are involved in the college Work-Study program; 80 per cent of their salary comes from the federal government and 20 per cent from the department in which the student works.

Honors College student Daniel J. Burch says, "Most students find they have plenty of spare time after doing their studying and usually end up wasting it. Working and going to school helps me organize my time well and may be beneficial in the future."

Can a person handle two full-time jobs? Alan McGill, a senior majoring in English, is assistant manager of the Carolina Theater. He has learned how to handle money and office paperwork, as well as how to work with large crowds. His work, however, does interfere with his studies because he usually works late. If that professor said to him, "But Mr. McGill, I consider being a university student a full-time job," he would reply, "Feed me! Clothe me! House me!"

STREAKING THROUGH THE SEVENTIES

After the turmoil of the Vietnam years, students happily returned to campus-centered pranks and pastimes. Randy Newcome reported on one in the *Garnet and Black*, 1974.

The Rise and Fall of Collegiate Streaking

For the past several years, life on the South Carolina campus has been truly in the traditional southern style: slow and easy. Nothing of any significance has stirred the student body since the riots of 1970.

But on March 1, during student government elections this spring, Bud Man, a candidate for presidency of the student body, introduced into his campaign a new attention-getting tactic called streaking.

Streaking is the art of shedding one's clothes and making a mad dash from one designated area of campus to another. Bud Man began his streaking exhibitions through the Towers area and after several escapades had gained the attention and favor of a number of Carolina men. Within days, streaking became a fun, new fad and officially joined the ranks of other well known college antics, such as goldfish eating, stuffing of phone booths, fire alarm battles, and panty raids.

The first large group of streakers (200) raced the campus of the University of North Carolina. As a direct result, South Carolina was challenged. Not to be out done, a mass streak was planned by fraternity row to begin on the Carolina campus at 10:00 P.M. on March 8.

Clothes were shed, huge lines of streakers formed, a crowd of over 5,000 onlookers assembled as *out of the night streaked the five hundred*. The parade began with a procession down the Bates House ramp led by a gallant Olympian carrying a burning broom. The crowd parted like the Red Sea and 508 streakers shot by.

Cries such as "That's my brother with the shoes and tie on" and "Hey, Phil, it was nice seeing you buddy" rang through the crowd with assorted whistles and cat calls by delighted coeds and conservatives.

Music from "The Stripper" blared from the window of Burney and the crowd cheered as trou were dropped from the top of tall trees and the roof of the new information booth.

That night, the University of South Carolina officially took the lead in the national streaking competition.

Before the drinking age was raised to twenty-one, students welcomed themselves back to school with an all-night beer blast, reported by Bob Craft (*Gamecock*, September 17, 1973).

Beer Bust: Passout as Tribal Rite

The band could be heard through the walls of the Armory above the rumble of the car engine. The Armory parking lot was filling with cars, drivers searching for a place to park. It looked like a sixth grade movie about salmon going upstream to spawn and die.

But nobody's gonna die here tonight. Nobody's even going to get punched. Some spawning might get done, but not on the premises.

This is the SGA beer bust to "kick off the season wrong." With 60 kegs of SCHLITZ, "SGA buys only the best!" and the band HUH, it was all set to go.

And going it was. If the band had been any louder, the building's bricks would have been shaking from their mortar, dancing an architectural frug.

Eight or nine taps going non-stop. No place to sit down, the tables fast filling up with people and spilt beer.

In front of the bandstand, about 50 people dancing and carrying on, sweat putting a reflective gloss on their skins that shows up nicely against the colored stage lights.

Pleading from the stage, a woman's voice with a buzz-saw edge, "Could you please drink a little bit less? There's plenty of beer, but we want it to last!"

Surrender by SGA, at 11:30, 20 more kegs are brought in. The tap keepers' shirts are wet from sweat.

"Great party, Rita."

"I'm glad you enjoyed yourself," she says.

Courtship rituals changed, yet stayed the same, as illustrated in the "Mind/Body" section of *Garnet and Black*, 1977.

Carolina Summer: Loving You

We can sit in the grass together;
we can perform ad-lib-one-act
plays on the steps of the psychology building; we can
smoke a joint on Green St. We
can swim at the Natatorium, or
take a weekend at the beach. A
Carolina summer is for being with you.

We can sit naked on the porch
at night; we can camp at the lake; we can hike the
mountains
or watch television while the sun sets. A Carolina summer is
for holding you.

We can stroll through Gibbs
Green; eat McDonalds burgers

on the Shoe; sip some brew at
the Second level. A Carolina summer is for talking with
you.

A Carolina summer is for loving
you.

GAMECOCK ATHLETICS: WHO'S COACH? WHAT CONFERENCE ARE WE IN?

The state of the Gamecocks affected the fate of their coaches, and USC fans paid attention. The *Garnet and Black* (1980) called the protests following head basketball coach Frank McGuire's retirement "Shades of the Sixties."

Rumors that head basketball coach Frank McGuire would not be allowed to continue as coach during the 79–80 season sparked angry reactions by members of the USC basketball team and student body. Team captain Mike Doyle said, "The team unanimously agreed that if coach McGuire is fired, we will not play."

Amid a profusion of "Keep McGuire" stickers and posters, students staged a rally in support of McGuire. The all-night protest consisted of a camp-out in front of USC President James Holderman's office and march of 500 students. "The issue is much more than basketball, it's a test of student rights," Doyle said.

But McGuire was gone. An anonymous die-hard Gamecock fan kept a diary recording the end of an era. His entry dated February 24 appeared in the 1980 *Garnet and Black*.

Last night was one of the most emotional games in any sport I have ever seen. A near-capacity crowd showed up in the coliseum for McGuire's last game on the bench.

Western Kentucky, a 20-game winner, was the competition, and they ran into a fired-up Gamecock team which raced to a big early lead. But things tightened up near halftime, and they stayed that way. We rallied to tie it at 54 with 5:39 left; for the rest of regulation and the entire first overtime, the crowd stood and watched as the teams refused to allow a single point to be scored. Then, as he has so often, Hodges took charge in the second overtime, and some accurate Carolina foul shooting near the end sealed Frank's 550th career win, 73–65.

One by one the seniors came out of the game to a standing ovation and gave the coach a big hug when he got to the bench. It was a joyous, tearful game, and it was the best possible way for Frank McGuire to end his career. His last team was a disappointing 16–11, but they had a lot of exciting games, and that last night was magic. I'll always remember that season and the night Frank went out with a double-overtime win.

When the Board of Trustees fired football coach and athletic director Jim Carlen, students again raised their voices, sometimes loudly. Carol McColl, a junior English major, wrote to the *Gamecock*, January 20, 1982.

I was shocked, saddened and angered by the blatant breach of decency, not to mention ethics, practiced by the illustrious Board of Trustees in December as they once again revealed their incompetence, ingratitude and total lack of humanity. The fact that the Board chose to ax Coach Carlen is further evidence of dirty politics within the university. Their refusal to state a specific reason for Carlen's dismissal is highly suspicious: what can they have to hide?

I am extremely perturbed by the fact that as a paying contributor to the upkeep of this university, I am not allowed to know the "top-secret" machinations of the hallowed board. This secrecy and the suspicions which it arouses only serve to reinforce my conception of the Board of Trustees as a group of money-grubbing, treacherous, old leeches who are perfectly willing to destroy anyone who might get in their way. How much longer can we continue to cater to the caprices of these blood-suckers? If they are allowed to escape totally unscathed from this potential controversy then there is truly no justice in this world.

Nor were students silent when Carlen sued for the fulfillment of his contract. Christopher W. Caswell, a marine science student, joined the chorus of complaints (*Gamecock*, February 1, 1982.)

I would like to join the long march of students complaining about the manner in which the economic difficulties of the University have been handled. The administration needs to be reminded that when you lose your money, you sell the Buick to buy food rather than sell all of your clothing to buy a Mercedes-Benz.

Carolina's new car comes with many of the latest options including an expanded stadium, so more people can watch the football team lose; trips to China for Dr. Holderman and others; and the latest in luxuries: a well paid but unemployed football coach.

Because the administration has elected to be frivolous with what little funds it has available, labs are now dying of malnutrition for lack of proper equipment and students are starving for computer time.

Cheerleading became a varsity sport, and *Garnet and Black* (1980) applauded the results.

1979–80 was a year of changes for the Carolina cheerleaders, according to head cheerleader Donna Rice. Only Rice and Sissy Tolly returned from the squad of the year before, so there was drastic personnel turnover.

The varsity squad appeared at all twelve football games and every home basketball game. Rice and company also helped get things rolling at pep rallies, including the big one for the Clemson game on the State House steps.

One thing that did not change was the Carolina cheerleaders working hard to keep up the spirits of Carolina fans. From their collective gymnastic skills to their considerable dancing talents, the team was a consistent source of enjoyment at the games.

7

Going Global, Getting Wired

CAROLINA PREPARES FOR A
THIRD CENTURY

Pres. James Holderman, committed to making the University of South Carolina an international presence, directed everyone's attention to global affairs. This meant taking trips and setting up exchanges, holding conferences and receiving ambassadors, inviting actors and composers and media moguls to campus, hiring the famous as visiting professors, receiving visitors as powerful as the president and as exalted as the pope. Holderman turned University affairs into an elegant, decade long party, and everyone who was invited had a wonderful time. Sometimes even students got to attend.

THE PARTY BEGINS

Tom Coyne reported on President Holderman's plans for a Chinese exchange program and on the student body president's reaction (*Gamecock*, November 7, 1980).

"This was a groundbreaking trip," Holderman said. "USC is now at the forefront of the U.S. Chinese relations."

Student Government President Larry Kellner calls his recent trip to China "surprising" and "fascinating." Kellner said trips to Peking University and Shansi University were the highlights of the trip.

"At Peking University I had the opportunity to talk with four Chinese students. I felt like they weren't holding back at all. They talked about their complaints, and they were very curious about our television equipment. I was very surprised at how well their English was. Most of them had taken only two years of English, but they were very fluent."

The group also visited the Great Wall, the Ming Tombs, the Great Hall of the People, and the Forbidden City.

Arthur Tai, Class of 1982 and a Rhodes Scholar in 1983–84, participated in the USC–Shanxi University exchange program in his senior year. He wrote about his experience to "Scoot"—Scott Lawson, Class of 1983 and an earlier exchange participant. Tai traveled with Mi Hanfu, who later came to USC for graduate work in the College of Education (M.Ed. 1985, Ph.D. 1988).

February 1983, On the Road, China

A day and a half on the North-South Express makes Bulldog Wang and the foreign experts building seem pretty nice. By the way, did I tell you about the after hours escape? [Exchange participants were locked in nightly.] Ropes from the second floor balcony. Yankee ingenuity strikes again. I haven't had a seat since Zhengzhou—another forgettable site—but Mi and I have staked out a locked exit area between cars. . . .

Before coming out, I knew intellectually how rare it was to have a chance to study in China, but as I travel about this country I now know first hand how unique it really is.

I say that Zhengzhou is forgettable, but I don't think I'll ever forget it. After scouring the immediate area near the train station, I settled on a noodle shop, which anywhere else in the world and with any other option available I would have passed on. Ordering four liang of noodles which came served in the usual chipped bowl with the usual bits of mystery meat floating in the soup, there was no place to sit, or squat, then a stool came open outside where the shop spilled out into the street. I sat down with relief. But before I even got the chopsticks to my mouth, two beggars crowded up and just stared. I forced myself to eat a bite or two, but no matter how I tried to control my thoughts, it didn't help. Even with my eyes closed, I knew they were there and could feel their stare down to my gut. As if on cue, all of us at the table got up, leaving the twosome to finish the scraps. I didn't eat for another half day.

Scott, I've yet to come to terms with this experience. Why? What can be done? Who ought to do it? All these questions were so different and so easy when we were seated in Gambrell. Gone are the easy answers. I remember the first time I came face to face with poverty. The solution then, or at least my conscience's answer to the question of responsibility, was a collection of canned goods and clothes. The passage of time and the scale of the problem demand a different response. At the deepest level, there is a sense of hopelessness magnified because we can't forget what we've seen or continue believing in the paradigms which no longer seem valid.

You told me that you couldn't go anywhere here without drawing a crowd curious to see a Yank up close. I've taken up the challenge to move about unnoticed. My cloth shoes and army greens go a long way, except they're too new, and I haven't mastered the forward tilt, arms-behind-the-back, lingdao [leader's] walk. Evidently, I walk like a laowai [old foreigner]. People still know I'm not local, but it sometimes gets me just the extra time necessary to glimpse an unprocessed expression, witness an unrehearsed emotion, or visit a Chinese home which wouldn't welcome me otherwise.

THE GUESTS ARRIVE

Students and parents delighted in the famous visitors' coming to campus. *Gamecock* columnist Amy Delpo listened to Bill Cosby (June 11, 1986).

Wearing tennis shoes and a Carolina sweatsuit underneath his academic robe, comedian Bill Cosby was greeted with cheers and applause as he rose to address the USC graduating Class of 1986.

"This day that you receive your paper is a great day," he told the graduates. "All across America people like you are being told to go forth. As a parent, I am concerned as to whether or not you know where forth is. Forth is not back home."

Jeff Shrewsbury, editor of the *Gamecock*, rhapsodized about the ultimate visitor (September 14, 1987).

Wow, what a weekend.

The pope, drinks and football. What else could a red-blooded, wholesome American boy ask for in a three-day span?

At The Horseshoe, there were only 13,000 people, but they yelled like they were twice that.

I guess you have to see the pope in person, but when the man speaks, it seems like a holy nugget will fall from his mouth at any minute. He is just the sweetest speaking little man I've ever seen. And he's cool too.

He got out of his pope cruiser and strutted up to the stage and winged it with the students. His voice seemed to cut through the crowd. He's as far from menacing as you can get, and it amazes me anyone could want to do him harm.

THE VOICES OF DISSENT

Those students not invited to the party began to complain—sometimes with satire and keen insight. Paul Perkins, a journalism major, wrote a letter to the editor (*Gamecock*, April 15, 1985) about visiting professor Jehan Sadat, widow of Egyptian president Anwar Sadat. Later he won-

dered about her salary, wondered enough to file a Freedom of Information lawsuit that he won.

What a feather in our cap to have Mrs. Anwar Sadat teaching us. Would it be possible for President Holderman to acquire Chairman Mao's wife also? Being one of the "Gang of Four" had to be a fascinating experience.

An entire workshop of such women might get us the attention we've been craving. "The Wives of Famous Third World Strongmen."

To provide some sort of balance, we could later invite Margaret Thatcher's husband to visit. He could lecture on the role of Great Britain's men.

Charles Terreni, a graduate student in Government and International Studies, had another suggestion for gaining fame (*Gamecock*, April 4, 1986).

Due to a strange twist of fate, USC has the chance to recruit a new faculty member of unique qualification—the Hon. Ferdinand Marcos.

Mr. Marcos has recently retired from a distinguished career in public service. Over his 30-year tenure he gained experience in a wide variety of fields. Mr. Marcos would be eminently deserving of a faculty chair in the department of government and international studies at USC, and I would venture even further in suggesting that he be asked to serve on the Executive Central Committee of the Byrnes International Center.

Imagine the worldwide recognition this university would gain by hosting Mr. Marcos in his asylum years. USC would at last be a household acronym in countries all over the world. Other distinguished personages would probably consider spending their golden years on our friendly campus. Duvalier could be next!

CPU's "Breakfast with the President" could take on a whole new meaning. Also, our distinguished addition to the faculty might be persuaded to train the platoon of security personnel that follows Dr. Holderman around.

Columnist Andy Duncan contributed some sniglets, "words that don't appear in the dictionary but should" (*Gamecock*, January 20, 1986).

bushoff: to visit a university with much ceremony and publicity, under heavy security, meet no students, say nothing of importance and leave in your motorcade for the airport as quickly as possible.

holdermania: the delusion that Caribbean diplomacy is of more interest to USC students than finding a really good parking place.

jimboob: a fatuous remark made by a high-ranking member of the USC administration. Example: Have you heard the latest *jimboob?*

When students connected the cost of the international invitations with their own rising tuition, their voices turned to rage. *Gamecock* editor Jeff Shrewsbury gave Jehan Sadat "the financial genius award" (November 7, 1986).

Jehan Sadat has to be one of the smartest people on earth, and President Holderman must think USC students are some of the stupidest. Mrs. Sadat got somebody to pay her over $300,000 for teaching a single course for three semesters. Maybe, instead of teaching a class on Egyptian culture, she should teach a class in creative finance.

Where does Holderman get off raising our tuition when he's getting duped into paying that kind of cash to someone who wouldn't have been asked to teach a class if her husband hadn't been assassinated?

And what about those expenses?

Right now, the only recognition USC is getting from Jehan Sadat is a snicker from around the USA that we were stupid enough to shell out those kind of bucks, and even more dumb to try to cover it up.

Daniel Lane, a senior in criminal justice, likewise vented his rage (*Gamecock,* November 10, 1986).

I am an angry man. Very angry. I just finished reading that USC paid Ms. Sadat $207,000 in salary and $107,000 in expenses. USC also paid Bill Cosby $25,000 for an hour or so of his time, and $25,000 to Henry Kissinger and over $20,000 more on several other "visiting dignitaries."

Now, Holderman has informed us that our tuition is going up, again. In case you've lost count, our tuition has gone up every semester since Spring, 1983. This time, however, it's going up $600. I grow very tired of supporting Holderman's ego with my tuition money. His Caribbean Conference is definitely in the top three biggest wastes of USC history. Let's face it folks, how many of you can name one of the leaders that came to that conference? How much did it do for Holderman? Get the picture?

Joseph Ford, a junior in mechanical engineering, was just as angry (*Gamecock,* November 10, 1986).

Come on Jim, give me a break! I'm tired of every semester hearing how much money the state is cutting from the university's budget. I'm tired of being hundred-dollared to death by your bleeding heart "the state will not give me any money" routine.

Holderman, I think you have a lot of gall to even think about asking the students of USC for more money, when you go wildly spending dollars on your new art center, Roost renovations, and guest speakers, not to mention Sadat's salary. Furthermore, I find it hard to believe that USC's tuition is more than twice that of the University of North Carolina.

You say everything you do is for the university. I think you are confused about what the university is, because it is not Sadats, buildings, or guest speakers. The *students* are the university.

***Gamecock* columnist Stephen Guilfoyle wanted to know how to become one of the president's interns (August 26, 1988).**

I'm interested in becoming—and I know I'm not the only one—a USC intern. I want to make thousand of bucks each semester and travel the country and the globe.

But I've never known how, strange as that is. I always knew the president had interns, but never just what it took to become and be a Holder-clone.

Do you meander over to the administration building and tell the president's secretary, "Hey, I want to rap with the prez, doll, about this discount travel program for select students."

Or do you have to go to one office, fill out an application in triplicate and return it to another, take a blood test, take a urine test, take a lie detector test. . . .

Or do you just kind of think and wish and hope and pray and meditate that your karma will eventually reach the nirvana of working for President James Holderman?

From Carolina to Canterbury

In spite of and amongst all the visitors, student life went on, changing naïve freshmen into wise seniors. More and more students participated in exchange programs and relished the opportunities for European travel. Alexa Maddox from Rock Hill wrote faithfully to her parents, keeping them posted on her increasing worldliness, even on her scramble for a fake ID.

September 9, 1986

It's strange, I never thought that I would ever just not be able to write, but these past 2 weeks have shown me that even avid letter writers do have times when writing doesn't seem natural. Daddy's letter made me really sad. I guess it's because you don't talk to your dad about the same things you do your mom. Also, I know he's having a hard time with my leaving so that doesn't help the homesick situation. I hope college always gives me this "campy" feeling because it makes leaving home a lot more fun, if not easier! I guess if I weren't adjusting to school so well, I wouldn't say this, but I think I was ready to go to college and become a little more independent. And you can rejoice that you helped prepare me to be able to make the transition from stage to stage smoothly. I hope that if I have children, I'll be able to help them in that respect as you have us.

I'm glad I finally got this first letter home written. It'll be easier next time, I'm sure. The first letter has to be full of news and feelings. All the other ones do, too, but it just seems like the first one is a big deal.

I'm trying to think of a way to get a fake I.D. Jennifer has an extra license to do hers. There has to be an easier way than getting someone's birth certificate. This is so retarded—I just want to go and dance.

September 14, 1987

It's me again. School is feeling okay now—like an old soft shoe.

I went to anthropology today and I'm guessing it's going to be interesting based on what I've seen so far (mostly black men wearing gourds tied to their privates). Anyway, since the Pope and all the moms left, I've been trying to catch up on my reading and the like. I have to say the Pope is a pretty fun guy. I'll remember that for a long time.

In her sophomore year Alexa took Henry Price's famous and terrifying course in copyediting.

October 28, 1987

Wow, I'm drained. Today I found out I was "below THE LINE" in editing class, so I went to find out what exactly that meant. This time, Dr. Price was quite helpful. I had upset myself so much by the time I got to his office, that I started tearing up. He seemed really concerned and said he hated having a course that made people have "emotional outpourings" (ha ha). I just let the proverbial dam burst; it had been building up. He told me I would have to be in a catatonic state to fail the course, and that he knew I could do much better. It's up to me to study and practice enough to get above the low C I have now. I told him how I'd never had to study for journalism before—he seemed empathetic—and he nursed my ego a little. I am learning a lot (even if the class is boring and frustrating), and I realize that's what's important. I'm not taking this class over again, that's all. Then we started talking about other stuff. I asked him about studying in England, and he seemed to think it was a really good idea. Maybe I should switch to him for an advisor.

October 5, 1988

I'm sitting at my desk facing the window which looks down the hill and out over Canterbury and the Cathedral to the left. It's a wonderful view, so I might have to move my desk back facing a concrete wall if I find myself looking out the window instead of working too much. I also have the picture of the view from my window at home taped up; both are quite different, but equally special.

I'm anxious to get into my classes and start meeting some interesting people. Exchange students are weird because they're already accustomed to university life, but yet they're new to this university. I haven't met anybody who is terribly antagonistic toward Americans, but apparently the Univ of Kent is notoriously leftist. A lot of people wear leather here and have mohawks. I don't know how they can afford to dress like that.

Went to a service at the cathedral and the archbishop was there. He looks just like the pope.

June 12, 1989

This is what Amsterdam looked like to me—watery and wavy and slightly out of focus. Maybe I was breathing some of the fumes from all the joints being smoked. No, it really does seem to shimmer, all bluey and gray.

Next week I'm off to the Glastonbury music festival. It'll probably be really good because it's the last time our "group" will all be together at once.

I've just been learning to play cricket—so now you can tease me back, Daddy. I would've said you were crazy had you told me I'd be playing cricket and going fishing while I was in England. I guess people have done stranger things for a boy/girl.

March 23, 1990

You should see the springtime here—all the new leaves are out and I have azalea bouquets all over the apartment. I went over to the Presbyterian Church and sat in the big, quiet graveyard reading. The air was so clear that everything looked 10 times a brighter hue—the whites of the tombstones and dogwood blossoms, the pink church and the blue sky with not a cloud in it. No one was around and I read Virginia Woolf out loud because it seemed exactly the right words for that time and place. If I could write like any author I would choose her.

The search continues for job prospects—I've been asked to send a resume to Public Interest Research Groups and I'm writing other places and getting more info. each day, it's exciting to know that these people and places exist.

STUDENTS PARTY ON

While ambassadors and foreign secretaries and heads of state—not to mention members of the Board of Trustees and state legislators and business leaders—partied on, so too did USC students, sometimes in new ways. Paula Wethington announced, "This Party Is for You" (*Gamecock*, December 9,1985).

If you're tired of studying and need a break Saturday, a backrub party may be just the thing to ease those aching muscles. "Everybody wants a backrub, especially before exams, " said Shelley Long, party planner for the Association of Honors Students.

Music will be played as people form a continuous chain to give and receive a backrub at the same time. Admission: $2.

A new party animal appeared (*Garnet and Black*, 1983).

Despite the preppies with their button-downs and loafers, Carolina was invaded with a new breed of students called punkers. Their weapons were buttons, boots and bandanas. No true punker appeared without a collar turned up, and real punkers had high standards: Group Therapy or die.

Every Thursday night Group rocked. The lines wound around the building, and students didn't mind. They knew they had to be there early because after eleven o'clock, it was hopeless. Then, the doormen allowed a person inside only when another left—not often. Once in the spell of Group, most punkers left for one reason only—closing time.

Sun worshipers colonized new territories (*Garnet and Black*, 1983).

Sunbathing was a social event, especially on "Blossom Beach" during P.T.H.—prime tanning hours. The "beach," the top floor of the Blossom Street Parking Garage, was a convenient place to socialize over beer and music and to spy on passers-by below. There, students could pack all their necessities into cars and avoid traipsing across campus with an armful of supplies—beach towels, blankets, lounge chairs, radios and coolers. They could adapt tail-gating from football season to sunbathing in style.

Gamecocks made the top ten partying list (*Garnet and Black*, 1982).

Swamp mixer, Old South, White Rose, Sunrise mixers, Medallion Ball, Rose Ball, pledge parties, Luau mixers, champagne drop-ins, Homecoming, and Greek Week—these were just a few of the parties at USC that earned us standing as one of the top ten partying universities in America.

The Greek Week party lasted for six days and included two band parties, a field day, a banquet, a follies, a rally, and parties on the fraternity quadrangle. Greeks competed in a chariot race, a new game called flour power with contestants searching for colored coins in a huge bag of flour, a wheelbarrow race, and the sisters' beer keg–tossing contest.

When a thunder storm arrived, suddenly two hundred Greeks were playing in the mud, another hundred were on the quad sliding, and another hundred were playing in the Thomas Cooper reflection pool which was cleared by campus police.

A Worldly Student Body

As USC's research ambitions grew, so too did the number of its graduate programs. Students from all over the world came to study in every discipline, and they had to learn campus customs quickly. Daisy Boatwala came from Bombay in 1990 to study for a master's degree in English.

When I arrived in Columbia from India and walked from the gate with passport in hand, I noticed a huge board with the picture of a red rooster and bold lettering saying, "WELCOME TO GAMECOCK COUNTRY."

My, I thought, symbol of the South. Maybe, I'll see more of this pastoral, rustic setting. Then, in the baggage area, again a lighted showcase said, "CITY OF THE GAMECOCKS."

Signs really get you into cultural tutoring; I began to suspect that the South was big on poultry as an export product. In any case, that rooster seemed to be demanding respect.

Rooster Land, I thought. Hey! No one told me this side of America. In India we look upon U.S.A. as the big nuclear power country.

A volunteer from the Columbia Council for Internationals got me settled in the Holiday Inn for the night. The receptionist asked me if I had a Master Card or a Visa.

"I have a visa," I replied, pulling out my passport, and wondering what could be the matter.

"Oh, good!" he said, not looking at me, clicking away at his computer, "What's the number?"

"Number? My passport has a number, but I don't see any on my visa."

"Oh no, no! I said, Visa Card—a credit card." He was grinning.

"I just arrived from India," I said, feeling annoyed that I looked like a fool, "And in India we don't have cards to deal with." He smiled and accepted cash. I noticed he had a leather bag on a table nearby, with the red rooster on it. I was getting used to seeing those red feathers, though it was spooky.

The next day I set out to find U.S.C. First I found the "S.C. Bookstore" with the red feathered friend on one of its walls. A license plate on a parked car said, "I Am A Gamecock at Heart." I passed them by, but I was beginning to think there was a political ideology behind this symbol.

As I walked on, it seemed the South seemed to lack people. Where were they all? In India, only the death of a politician or a curfew would look like this! Maybe it had something to do with the rooster—"gamecock holiday" or something.

Then I saw a cubicle that said, "Touch Matic," and another that said "C & S," and yet another, "NCNB." Two girls came out of one. Both wore shorts and T-shirts that said, "S.C. Gamecocks."

Back at the Holiday Inn, I asked the receptionist, hesitatingly, "Say, Rick, what exactly is a Gamecock? Is it social or political?"

"No! That's the symbol of our sports team. We take great pride in the Gamecocks. Football is the greatest self-expression of American youth."

I was feeling much better. The intimidating rooster with the ruffled feathers was not equal to the Nazi swastika. Good, this was still a free country. But, just imagine, football!—at the airport, on license plates of cars, on T-shirts, just about everything. East and West, I thought. My, I had a lot to learn about U.S.A. And I had only just begun.

Joanna Daiwo arrived in 1994 from the Solomon Islands to enter an M.Ed. program in higher education studies in the College of Education. In a letter to her parents, August 1994, she described her early days on campus.

The people I have met so far are very nice, friendly and interested in the country I am from. I find though, that many of the people I have talked to have no idea where Solomon Islands is situated. A few people I have talked to think it is in Africa. I think when people see other people with dark skin, they automatically think he or she is from Africa. African Americans are people whose ancestors came from the continent of Africa centuries ago, and most of them have dark skin like us. I know what you are thinking—black people in America! I know the only Americans you have seen are white. Yes, I have seen many dark skinned people here. Solomon Islands is a very small nation really compared to the United States of America.

. . . Yesterday, Thursday, I decided to explore the city of Columbia alone. Columbia is the capital of South Carolina, like Honiara to the Solomon Islands. They do not have many public buses. I guess with everyone virtually having a car or vehicle in this place, there is no need to have public buses around. As a visitor who can't drive, I find it hard to move around easily. Columbia is huge compared to Honiara. There are lots and lots of big buildings and they have traffic lights on every road. There are lots and lots of big shops or stores here, which are filled with many different kinds of things. . . . People are friendly everywhere you go. Some people have stopped me on the street to ask where I am from.

Beginning of Week 4

In some situations, I have to ask my way around as one could easily get lost in these big buildings with many rooms. Although all rooms are labeled, I found myself one day entering a different classroom in the first week. I had missed the notice informing students of the change of the class venue. I left the room as soon as I realized I was in the wrong class. I am getting more and more busy each day as the semester weeks fly by. My schedule is increasingly getting bigger. There are various tasks to carry out. For example, academic papers, journal articles, books to read, and assignment papers to organize and write up for due dates. I only have two examinations to sit this semester, and I am pleased about that. Sitting examinations has not been one of the favorite elements of my whole education journey.

More than 200 USC alums have joined the Peace Corps, serving around the globe from Romania to Mongolia, Botswana to Nepal, Costa Rica to the Solomon Islands. Jason Coleman, a 1998 graduate, wrote to Crys Armbrust, assistant principal of Preston Residential College, from his Peace Corps post in Zambia (July 29, 1999).

Greetings from the bush. I dealt with screaming babies all day. I'm becoming a bona fide farmer, with blisters on my hands to prove it. I tilled my garden by hand yesterday and transplanted about 30 cabbage plants. My chicks are now chickens and my dog is no longer hand sized. I gave him a rabies shot last week, and he never even flinched. I suppose I'm pretty good at giving injections.

I have a meeting with the village on 9th Aug. about my hospital project. It's going to be lots of hard work and headaches, but I think if people will actually work, it can be successful. I've asked to attend the 1st International Conference on AIDS in Sub-Saharan Africa in Sept., but I don't know if that's yet been approved.

I've just started reading Pat Conroy's <u>Beach Music</u>—it makes me think about good ole SC. We've got a culture unique to us that I neither realized nor appreciated until my abrupt removal from it.

You should get some type of grant and come and see me under the auspices of research. Or just come. I think you of all people would truly appreciate "life in the bush." I've come to love it. No drama. No bs. Pure nature. It has certainly changed my outlook on life and has me thinking long and hard about what is really important to me.

Another Peace Corps volunteer, Anne Knight, an Honors College student in the Class of 1998, wrote from Burkina Faso to the *State* (December 19, 1999).

A landlocked country in West Africa, Burkina Faso is not large, or powerful, or even ethereally beautiful. Yet something in the natural architecture of its flat-line savannas and shady thorn trees is reflected in the easy smiles and work ethic of its people: a straight-forward, unpretentious integrity.

The name of the country means "the land of the upright people." Generous and genuine, the people seem frequently amused by me, as I confound their sense of what is right and normal. You want to ride your bike for exercise? they ask. You don't know how to cook leaf sauce? Why aren't you married?

I am here for two years, and already I know it will be difficult to leave. Who would have thought I could so easily acclimate to taking bucket baths instead of showers? Who needs air conditioning when the breeze rifles leaves on the ground as if they were popcorn bursting from their kernels?

But every day I think of new things I love about home. I think of Walmart Supercenter on Forest Drive, where my college friends and I would go at 2 a.m. to peruse the vast offerings of a competition-driven market. (So many shades of nail polish, so little time!)

And I think of my college education, which I took for granted.

Here the Burkinabe students painstakingly copy lessons from the board, because their notebooks are their textbooks.

Every day I note another thing to appreciate: the special hand shake between friends; the students' show of respect by standing as the teacher enters the room; the good humor that spreads from person to person as if friendliness were a communicable disease.

Before I left Columbia, an acquaintance said to me, "You're going to be eating monkey over there." Well, I've not yet seen any vendors of monkey meat, although I understand that some people—poor enough to buck society's dictums—do eat dog.

I've heard it's very tender.

Emily Streyer, Class of 1999, spent her junior year in England and Eurailed on the continent—a set of experiences she turned into a novel for her Honors College thesis. One summer she worked in France, sending postcards home.

June 9,1998

Work is going better. Get to practice my French during the breaks, although I still have good days and bad. I'm learning how to swear properly in French and trading the similar gems in English. (It's a multi-lingual workplace). The food at HRC Café is good, but I never quite understand why Americans come to France to eat at the Hard Rock Café. What grand differences between "tourist" and "traveller."

July 28, 1998

I finally went to the Louvre last night. I figured I couldn't return to the States having visited Paris 3 times and lived there 2½ months and say I <u>didn't</u> go to the Louvre. Yes, I did see the Venus de Milo, although I don't understand why it's so celebrated. I found many other ancient Greek sculptures I liked better, and they weren't broken. (But some were broken in rather amusing places—it's no wonder the Greeks were essentially bumped out of the limelight by the Romans when their soldiers ran around with nothing but a helmet on . . .) Saw the Mona Lisa. I do see why that one is famous—it's something different from what everyone else was doing.

August 5, 1998

I have been asked if I am German, Italian, English (most frequently), and on three separate occasions, <u>Brazilian</u> (although the only possible explanation is that I met three separate people on crack), but never have I been asked if I'm French. Today I went to the post office to buy stamps, bag worn across one shoulder in typical French fashion, <u>baguette in hand,</u> and before I opened my mouth, one of them said, jokingly, "Sorry, No English!" I said with mock indignance that je parle Francais! and the conversation moved amiably from there. I can't say, though that I'll ever regret that I'll never be French.

LEARNING IN NEW WAYS, NEW PLACES

Some constants held true during two centuries of undergraduate life. Students procrastinated, made excuses, crammed for exams, stayed up all night writing papers, complained about some professors and worshiped others, passed and failed. But a revolution in pedagogy occurred as well:

the student became a researcher. In the 1990s USC students actively participated in research projects with faculty members, gathered data in laboratories and in the field, served as interns in businesses and agencies, presented papers at professional conferences, and published articles. They joined their teachers in the quest for new knowledge, and they learned about the world of work by working there.

Caroline Parler spent the summer of 1998 participating in the Research Experience for Undergraduates, sponsored by the National Science Foundation. During her internship at the University of Colorado, she worked on photopolymerizable polyanhydrides for orthopedic applications—new materials to repair broken bones. She kept in touch with her parents in Irmo via e-mail. In the spring of 2000 Caroline was awarded a Rhodes Scholarship.

June 2, 1998

we're killing our rat today. he had an implant put into him 4 weeks ago—i didn't realize that the poor little sucker was going to have to croak for us to get it back out again. i'd actually like to sit in on it just to get a feel for how the stuff works when it goes inside a living thing. might be kind of gross, though—hope I don't get too squeamish.

June 23, 1998

right now i'm in the middle of making a bunch of samples to start studies on later today. amy (my mentor) has a big presentation to make in august, and the data that we're taking now is hopefully going to be what she presents. if the results turn out good, there may even be the possibility of a paper coming out of it, so i have a chance of being published!

July 24, 1998

i am on some kind of natural high. it's been a great day. my stuff on the rotovap worked all day. this synthesis that amy's been trying to do for two years finally worked—and i was the one who did it. my boss, kristi, was there to witness it, and she gave me a high five for pulling it off. she also asked me about grad school and said that if i wanted a job out here again next summer, i had it. it's payday. i'm going dancing in denver tonight at this place called polyesters that's all 70's and 80's music.

August 8, 1998

i'm so excited! i just printed out a draft of my poster presentation, and i think that it's going to kick butt! i'm really proud of the work i've done so far. still have a lot to do, though—not to mention the entire paper to write—i'm tackling that tonight.

i had a great time on saturday night. we went back to the karaoke place and my song got picked so i got up there all alone, but the crowd really cheered me on, and i got lots of compliments. i even talked to the hot waiter whom i had spied there the first night i was in boulder. we went to one other place after that, and as it turned out, the guy at the door was an ex-USC football player. small world, huh?

Martha Wright, a journalism major in the Class of 2002, spent the summer of 2000 in Washington D.C. as a communications intern for the National Organization for Women and kept a journal recording her experiences.

I was eager to intern at a place whose application cited a "fast-paced, feminist environment." Still, on the first day, D.C. did its best to intimidate. I got turned around on both the Metro and the street before a D.C. native took pity on me. I barely made it to the intern meeting, at which I was one of four young women who were the first batch of summer interns. Like beauty queens, we introduced ourselves by location. Astor, from Hong Kong; Stephanie, from California; Holly, from New York; and Martha, from Lexington, South Carolina. They looked at me quizzically, perhaps searching for the stalk of grass that was supposed to be between my teeth.

That we covered a lot in a little time with our orientation session was no surprise; the huge headache I had afterward was. There were some disappointments. Travel to the national conference in Miami wouldn't be covered by NOW—interns were free labor, so I thought there would be some form of compensation. Ditto for conference registration, all meals, and a hotel stay. All the costs were up to us; not a boon for the student budget. Each intern was required to work 32 hours a week. By lunch on orientation day, I felt this "internship" was mislabeled. It was more like a "Pay to Work" program. Back at my Virginia relatives' house later, I sat in a warm bath and wondered why I'd turned down summer jobs that paid so I could travel to an unfamiliar city and work like a rented mule.

But the second day, I started to remember why. On Day One, each intern had been paired with a staffer. On the second day, I was the new member of the communications team, which keeps NOW in the news. Suddenly, I was where I belonged. We do press releases, we keep up with politics, we get to be experts on who says what and where. We call reporters, editors and broadcasters to send coverage to rallies and protests.

We even get to invent quotes by Patricia Ireland for press releases, an action journalistically impure for print majors but apparently OK for Public Relations purposes. Working on the communications team ensures my writing, information gathering and copy editing skills won't go into hibernation during the summer. Rebecca Farmer, once an intern and now head of media relations, offered me work immediately. And in doing so, she helped me recall why I'm here: to do something that really matters to the organization as a whole and keep everyone stocked with the information. There are regular duties and spur-of-the-moment assignments, like giving NOW President Patricia Ireland background on the person who's interviewing her on MSNBC later in the day.

So now I'm a month in. On my lunch breaks, I walk up one block and turn right onto Pennsylvania Avenue, passing the currently-under-renovation U.S. Treasury and the always-under-investigation White House on my way to Lafayette Park. And there, I, imagining myself a D.C. native, sit on a bench and watch the real tourists go by.

Amy Coppler worked as an emergency medical technician while she was a student at USC. CeCe von Kolnitz wrote about Amy's job (*Garnet and Black Quarterly,* November 1995).

They do the work of a basic EMT: bandaging, splinting, stabilizing patients, assisting paramedics, and sometimes driving the ambulance. "I don't think anyone can ever say it's a boring job. You never know what you're getting into until you get there. You never know what to expect," said Amy. When Amy goes to work, she wears combat boots, a pair of trauma shears strapped to her side. "If someone's been in a car accident, sometimes you'll have to cut the leg off their pants to get to the cut or if there's broken bone and it's sticking out." She has to wear clear plastic safety glasses and latex gloves, "in case someone's spurting blood" and a safety belt to protect her back. "I'm learning to lift people that I'd never imagined I'd be able to lift."

Amy has already been accepted to the Medical University of South Carolina where she'll start school in the fall. "It's nice to have a job where you have to think. You just get more out of it—to hear how you got someone to the hospital on time. You don't get that by taking Senators chips and cokes when they're hungry. It might sound overdramatic. But someone's life could be in your hands."

For many USC students, working one's way through school meant only drudgery. Donna Delia wrote about her job on the night shift (*Portfolio,* Spring 1995).

Clocking in and clocking out. My part time job was as monotonous as these two functions. My life was held by each click of the clock—hanging in limbo until 7 a.m., when the night shift at Wal-Mart was over. Customers who shop between 11 p.m. and 7 a.m. are the people we don't often notice. A class of people who represent the world and how it has changed over time.

The fight to stay awake began when I trudged into the trenches of the shoe department to survey the damage from earlier in the day. Even though it was after eleven, customers still filled each aisle. It was the beginning of November, and everyone had just gotten paid. Military, state and welfare checks all came out on the first, and so did the people. They lined up like ants, grabbing shoes and throwing them onto the floor to try on.

Close to 1 a.m. the three old men who came in every Friday night sneaked up and tried to scare me. Each time they came in, they would joke about their weekend passes from the mental hospital. Sometimes, I almost believed them.

Around 2 a.m. a mother, who didn't look much older than 25, asked me where the cheapest shoes were for each of her kids. I wondered how this woman could bring her kids out this late at night. We dug through a shopping cart of $2 clearance shoes and found four pairs of canvas oxfords for each of her little girls. For the mother, I found a pair of black sneakers clearanced out to $6. She told me she needed the shoes for her new waitressing job she was starting the following night. $2 an hour plus tips and four kids to feed. I hoped that wasn't her only job.

From 6 to 7 a.m., I sat in the back and worked on my homework. The words blurred on the page and my arm felt too heavy to write. I thought about my job and how I hated it. At least I'm going to school, I thought. I would hate to have to work here for the rest of my life.

Some USC students have turned campus jobs into careers, even achieving star status, like Leeza Gibbons who came back to Carolina and talked about her days at USC in an interview with Stephen Brown (*Garnet and Black Quarterly*, May 1995).

When I won the Sarah Ida Shaw Award, named after the founder of Tri Delta, it was the biggest deal. I remember being in the lobby of Capstone. I was having lunch with my dad, and I checked my mailbox and got the letter that I had won. It was such a rush. That's one of the most memorable moments that I had from my time here. Another was sleeping in the studio for the student radio station! I used to have to sign on at 5:30 in the morning, and I was always afraid that I would oversleep. So I would spend the night in the lobby—I was panicked—and wake up every 10 minutes. And I'm sure that nobody was listening except my mom.

I skipped graduation. I had a job and started to work—they had to mail me my diploma. I was in the real world and there was no looking back. So those three years passed pretty quickly—very quickly—sometimes, it' really like a blur . . . and drawers full of parking tickets. I'm sure I still owe them—I'm surprised they let me back on campus.

Scholarships for entering students increased dramatically, drawing highly qualified students to USC. Some South Carolina students, however, having set their hearts on far-away campuses, had to come to terms with staying home—just as Carolina scholar Sharon Panelo did ("Looking for Love in All the Wrong Places or, How I Found Happiness at a Southern University," *Garnet and Black*, February 2000.)

I had a fetish for WASPy uppercrust universities. I lusted in my heart for their accouterments—the wooden floors, the arched doorways, the idyllic quads, the very buildings that reeked of old money. I succumbed to the myth of the New England university, believed that affluence bred intellect and was convinced that no one could ever have any decent thoughts on physics and poetry if they weren't in the Northeastern United States.

As I write this, I am in my second semester of the University of South Carolina and, rest assured, the irony is not lost on me. But now, some of the people I've met here have made significant impressions on who I am, how I think, how I perceive. I think of all the components of this university—the students, the faculty, the buildings, even the landscape—and I come up with a series of images, flickering in a loop like a pale marble movie. These images form a procession of vignettes marching towards one unavoidable conclusion: I like this place.

I've learned I don't need vaulted ceilings or carved stone bosses or friends named Muffy in order to stick my hand into the heart of this university and pick and choose which social, academic, and intellectual portions I partake of. I have found happiness amidst the lush foliage and hospitality of a public Southern university. Admittedly, sometimes it's hard to take a university seriously when it considers "You can't lick our 'Cocks'" a valid sentiment of school pride. But a friend once told me that the trick to surviving at USC was to seek out little pockets of happiness throughout the year. It's like a game, a fun game, picking out the finer points of this school, looking for subtleties—in the way someone turns a phrase, in the way the sun filters through a set of branches—and finding out for yourself that the wrought iron and moonlight and magnolias of this campus are better than any cold Gothic stone Yale can offer, and that the students here are not all miscreants or intellectual zeroes. Whether my affair with USC is mere feigning and my friendships here mere folly is another question, but the present is my only reality, and I'm grateful to have it here.

THE ELECTRONIC REVOLUTION

Suddenly, geographical boundaries dissolved as the Internet made every university, department, and faculty member public information. Students could find anyone in the world from anywhere—and they did. Professors never knew who might appear on their terminals.

To: stancyk@biol.sc.edu

Dear Dr. [Stephen E.] Stancyk,

My name is Debi Klemas-Khalil. I am a 1974 alumna from the Marine Science Program. I was delighted to reach the website this morning and find you and Dr. [Bruce C.] Coull at USC. I called my kids over to the monitor to show them your pictures and CV.

I was equally excited to see that Micropholus gr. is still thriving in the coastal waters of South Carolina. I am thriving in the country of Bahrain in the Persian Gulf. My husband, Ali Khalil, is also a graduate of USC from the Physics Dept. He is completing his fifth year at the University of Bahrain.

I am interested in furthering my expertise in Marine Science. As you can see from my attached resume, it has been a while since I actively pursued my first and lasting interest in the ocean. Do you offer any overseas graduate study? You may be amused to know that I still have my copies of Gross's text as well as Barnes' Invertebrate Zoology.

Students took to communicating by e-mail with friends everywhere as prolifically as they had once used pens and paper. Sarah Hammond, a Preston resident and Honors College student, Class of 2002, wrote to a playwright friend in Arkansas about local events.

Subj: from the latest guru on rubbernecking

Date: 1/8/00

Today was the big confederate flag rally on the state house grounds. I'm not sure what the aim of this rally was—seeing as how the flag is already on top of the state house, I guess it's a preemptive strike against any possible sentiment of removal that might be buzzing in the Old Boy network of our legislature. Looked like a picnic. Old Southers—white haired, red haired, bald haired—all milling around like at a bake sale, clutching these enormous rebel flags. It looked sort of like the Fourth of July, except at maybe a Confederate campsite a century ago somewhere WAY back far away from the front line. Old men with scraggly beards were decked out in rebel uniforms. Their grandsons had matching uniforms. Families walking around, mama with a big flag, dad in uniform, and junior with a small version of mama's flag. I swear. It's craziness. There were at least two black people in the rally carrying rebel flags along with the red-necks. What's the deal? Who needs Y2k, we got Armageddon right here in Columbia.

-lavinia giblets

Subj: lunar eclipse tonight, pack up your valuables
Date: 1/20/00
I went to that rally on Monday. Forty-six thousand people were here in Columbia at the State House. It was a thing like nothing I have ever seen before. I feel like I've been cheated, having missed out on the sixties, and I think this little soiree under the Confederate Flag was the closest I'll ever get. People don't gather in mass groups like that for reasons like that any-more. People gather for things like New Years, football games, rock con-certs—but I've never been to any of those things with forty-six thousand people there. Humanity chokes me up. And it was so sedate, like an enor-mous church service. There was lots of singing, lots of preaching, lots of speaking. People together thinking one thought, thinking good thoughts—general feeling of good will—a feeling that SEE, WE HAVE A COMMON . . . something. A dream, a goal . . . even if its something like "get the Con-federate flag off the state house"—which some think is petty (I don't)—even if it's something like that . . . the fact that we are all there to DO that was amazing.

So many people. Not enough white people, but hey. . .I'm a bleeding heart liberal, and not just that, I'm naive, too. I guess I gotta learn to deal with the world not living up to my expectations.

-lola shoelace

Students gave up long distance and e-mailed their parents daily, some-times hourly. Jessica Mann, a freshman from Roanoke, Va., and member of Preston Residential College in the fall of 1999, went online to write home.

Subj: fun day!!!
Date: 8/18/99
Hey mama and everybody, I had an absolutely fabulous day today!!!!
First there was chick-fil-a and then I went to my new job from one to five
and then had dinner—not bad. Then came Aloha Carolina where I took
the leap and joined in an all male beach volley ball game—you know it!!!
Boys galore and I was the only girl—met lots of cool guys—most older than
me and I can't remember any of their names. But the whole thing was awesome. They closed the gates to block the road in front of the Russell House
and then filled part of the street up with sand and we played right there!!!!!!
Very cool.

Subj: classes cool try #2
Date: 8/19/99
My film teacher probably hates me now because she asked who among
us came to the class for entertainment and pleasure and of course I raised
my hand because I enjoy and take pleasure in everything but of course I
was the only one who raised my hand and she had meant something totally
different because she promptly said that this class wasn't all entertainment
and fun and if we thought that we should leave. I felt like an ass but oh
well—I will work hard and show her I am a great student—I'm not too worried about it.

Subj: hey MAMA—And DADDY!
Date: 10/21/99
I am having a hard time getting things done because I am in great need
of sleep and I keep falling asleep amidst anthropology and global issues
(like drug cartels) and end up having wild and crazy dreams about tribal
drug wars. I am REALLY behind in film but I am hoping I can wing it
tomorrow in class and then get caught up this weekend while everyone is
at the Homecoming game and festivities.

Subj: I want some email!
Date: 1/19/00
I got ALL my work done last night after I talked to you, I was VERY
proud, I read ALL my econ, wrote my French paragraphs and I read for
Ancient Civ. about Egyptians, they were pretty cool . . . I could be an Egyp-
tologist except it's just too damn hot and I am not that interested in being
killed by some ancient booby trap or curse or something. Plus, Ian, the

Italy professor guy, said that as soon as you uncover history, you are destroying it, so I don't think I want to do all that.

Subj: GOOD MORNING!!
Date: 2/5/00
I am TRYING to read my International Relations, but all we are doing is political theory and I have decided that I HATE politics. No political science for me, although, that is probably EXACTLY what Int'l Rel. is anyways, but I will get over it, it is just a phase.

Subj: (no subject)
Date: 2/10/00
I learned what a paradigm is today in Int'l Rel. although it is still a little vague, but then again—from what I gather—so is a paradigm! I love my prof. He said "some people think of wars and weapons and corrupt political leaders while others see a beautiful, diverse world full of interesting and beautiful cultures." And ya know that is US! I am so glad that I see the world that way! It is so much more uplifting! So anyways, he said that we are victims of our expectations and our ideas and experiences and, of course what we have been taught by parents and teachers and the media, but that we should become very critical about anything that people say (their opinions on int'l politics). What he was getting to and what I am getting to is that we (me!) must look at the changing politics of the world and not always follow the "group" thinking/popular beliefs, but question them and decide "OK, so that is what someone thinks, but is there another way to look at this?" or something along those lines! So anyways, as you can see, I am psyched about the class!

SOCIAL LIFE: CAROLINA STUDENTS UPHOLD THE TRADITION

Michele Holmes, Class of 2001 and an Honors College student from Woodruff, S.C., won an honorable mention in the Richard Gunter Writing Awards (Spring 1999) for her account of life as a freshman, "The Bus Stops Here."

No one tells a freshman girl how to party. She jumps on the bus with her friends and tries to enjoy the ride. In the end, no one tells her how to break herself of the desire to party, the insatiable craving for just one more chance with just one more guy. No one tells her how to stop getting on the bus.

We wait all week for Friday in hopes that a weekend's worth of parties will erase our stress. Tonight, the girls on the second floor tell everyone in

McClintock that two fraternities, Sig Ep and Sig Nu, are throwing a huge party at Madder Hats. The fraternity brothers always allow girls free admission and alcohol. Of course, all of us decide to go. It is our duty as first-year students to get involved in campus life at the University of South Carolina.

One girl says that Mike will be at the party. I have fifty things I want to tell him, but I will probably only manage to say, "Hi." The last party he ignored me, but tonight will be different; I have a good feeling. I'm going to walk up to him and start talking. Who says girls can't approach guys?

My friends and I walk to the corner of the Bull Street garage to join the other freshmen girls from Patterson, Wade Hampton, McClintock, South Tower, and the Towers. The freshmen guys from the Towers and LaBorde also gather like a herd of cattle on Bull Street. One guy, who is wearing khaki shorts and a white shirt that reads "Eat Me," says to a group of girls, "This summer was so awesome at Myrtle Beach. We got tore up every night." We all have similar stories of our senior trips to the beach.

Our eyes widen as the school bus turns at the corner; we depend upon the bus to take us to and from Madder Hats. The bus driver yells over the laughing and talking, "Shut the hell up, Kids!" Suddenly, I'm in the fifth grade again on the big, yellow school bus. At 11:15 we arrive at the party palace, a small ugly building set in a dark corner of the earth. We confidently march into Madder Hats, our second home as freshmen. We feel sexy, and our hormones pull us deep into the heart of the party. The crowd moves us to the bar. I grab a beer, sip it, and wince. Standing on the bottom rung of a barstool, I search the room for Mike. There is no sign of him or his buddies.

A guy from one of my classes comes up behind me and grabs my arm. "Hi, my name's John. Don't you sit next to me in English?" Behind him, the band walks onto the stage lined with Christmas lights. The band member are young; they're a local group with a name like "Greasy Sprockets" or "Oily Hinges" or "Greasy Oilers." The way his eyes scan my entire body makes me uncomfortable. Where is Mike when I need him?

Many guys, holding long pool sticks, stand around the pool tables and challenge each other in front of the girls. Each new game begins with the loud crack of the balls in the middle of the table. The loud chatter and laughter from the party heightens the excitement of each game.

As I move away from the guys, a feeling of disappointment settles over me. All the other parties I have attended were a lot like this one. Why exactly had I come? I feel like a drug addict losing his high. I am ready for the night to end. At least I'm not drunk and miserable—just miserable. I promise myself that I won't come here again. A feeling of relief overcomes me when the bus pulls up beside us.

Suddenly, Mike is at the bus. "Where were you all night?" he asks me. I'm speechless. Where was he all night? He says, "Look, I've got to go, so I'll see you here tomorrow night, right?" I smile and nod, and then he leaves with his friends. I'll be back now. Tomorrow will be different; I have a good feeling. It's an addiction, I tell myself, as I get back on the bus.

Freshman girls partied too much, and the sophomore slump made its perennial appearance, captured here in the terms and tones of the late twentieth century by poet Erin Bush, Honors College graduate, Class of 2000.

How Things Fall Apart

When the girl I thought was my best friend
asked me if I could really be sure
that all my belief in God was more
than just a handy psychological projection
and I realized I had no answer, I fled her room
into the night, climbing up the marble flood lit steps
of the columned theater down the block from my dorm
looking for some hidden message in the empty
streets, the yellow flickering lamps.
I lay on my back in the middle
of the green commons between
the dormitories. That was the year
that everything turned upside down:
this same girl, who I lived with a semester
and thought I knew, took me out for coffee
and told me she might be a lesbian.
Josh, my sweet and troubled friend, had
a psychotic breakdown and was hospitalized
for three weeks.
Anna C. lived down the hall, dated dark-haired suicidal
    poets,
and had late night binge parties where everyone lay
on her beanbag chairs and argued drunkenly
about mathematics and Tori Amos.
Anna R. was cutting herself
hard and deep, writing her shame on her body
and she spent long periods of time hiding

under Anna C.'s desk, next to the wall.
I was angry at God for letting my friends
have these fissures inside which made their lives
into small, daily hells.
I was meeting Michelle every week,
who was willing to say that life and even faith
could go on. And she was an occupational therapist,
working with a little girl who had cancer
and might not live, so I figured she
knew something. The next semester
I found myself sinking—I could barely
bring myself to do school work. I fantasized a lot
about razors and barbed wire and blood.
I led an "outreach" Bible study with a guy named Stan,
but no one except Christians ever came.
There were many surreal moments when I sat in front
of the group asking questions about a verse, thinking
do I believe in anything at all? My philosophy class and
my anthropology class shook me up—
I wondered if anything could be true, and how could
I say that people who followed other religions were
all wrong, and I was reading lots of angry feminist
theologians, who made me angry too, and I wondered
if I would have to leave the church and dance around
trees to the beat of the goddess if I wanted to be truly
free . . .
The whole world was unraveling around me—
I had no answers.

Garnet and Black (April 2000), confident in postmodern literary sophis-
tication, sponsored the 2000 Worst Poem Contest. David Jones handily
won the twenty-five dollar prize.

First Sight

Loves [*sic*] pure light shown brightly round the stars,
I wish she was the one I call my own.
Her beauty grows like greatly polished cars
And loves [*sic*] connection surely could be sewn.
At first I thought she was a stupid whore,
But when we talked the brains she had were great.
I wish I could only talk to her more,

I think what brought us together was fate.
I think she felt the same about me too,
I thing [sic] I will ask her to marry me.
One like her is not abundant but few,
My heart is filled with great amounts of glee.
Her brains and beauty go well hand in hand,
I'm leaving now to buy a wedding band.

Freshman Allison Smith, Class of 2003, reflected on her college experience.

I'm not exactly the same girl that left Orangeburg. So what is different? I've learned that college isn't about changing everything. Thus far for me, college has been a realization of who I already am. I didn't change my ideas by coming here—I changed how I think. I guess I've learned that friends are the one thing that really make it all worthwhile. Sure, I'm going to find my place to fit in. It's just going to take some time, and it isn't going to be as far from where it was in the past as I thought.

Students Write Back

Students like to complain—about food and parking, roommates and cockroaches, credit hours and credit cards. But they are also generous in praising their professors—who are likely to save and cherish their kind words.

September 29, 1986

Dear Walter [Edgar],

What a pleasure to hear from you.

Now that I am teaching on a college level I often relate a story to my "wide eyed" freshmen. It's all about a first semester freshman who thought an American history class would be a breeze. (Since he had been taking American history so many times in high school.) Once he found out that he was in trouble with the class, he was sure that a sad song would at least get him by. Nevertheless, the history professor flunked him like a hot rock. The moral of the story being that once you reach college you are responsible for your own actions. A corny story, but one that has personal meaning.

I may not have learned much about history in your class, but the "lesson in life" is one I will not forget. I've tried to catch up on the history since.

With respect,
Mark Flowers

Subject: Thank you very much
Date: August 17, 1998
Dear Dr. [Larry] Stephens,
I know you do not remember me, but I was a student of yours in 1982. The opportunity to say thank you never came to pass while I was in school, but now the opportunity has presented itself—so . . . Thank you very much!!

You were one of the major reasons I stayed in the computer industry. I started working for GTE (Phoenix, AZ), then moved to Siemens AG (Boca Raton/Orlando, FL) and now I work for an up and coming company called DPT (Maitland, FL). Our main products are SCSI [small computer system interface] and RAID [redundant array of independent-inexpensive disks] Controllers.

Have a great day and thanks again.
Wayne Blankenship

Dear Dr. [Thorne] Compton:
I wanted to write and tell you how much I appreciate your kindness to me this semester. As you could tell, I knew nothing about the subject when the semester got started and I have to admit I only took this course because my boyfriend was in it. Well, guess what? I ended up liking the course better than I did him! Your willingness to be patient with those students who didn't know anything at the beginning and to explain even the most stupid things was very important to me—it got me through the course.

Just so you know—even those of us who didn't get A's appreciate this course—and I'll keep going to theatre (I even spelled it right!).

Thanks so much
Angé

Bibliography

MANUSCRIPT COLLECTIONS

Amistad Research Center, American Missionary Archives. Tulane University, New Orleans.
Bailey, C. R. Correspondence, 1877. Fisk P. Brewer Papers.
Brewer, Fisk P. Correspondence, 1877. Fisk P. Brewer Papers.

Museum of Education. University of South Carolina, Columbia.
Garnet and Black, 1899–1972. College Yearbook Collection.
Saxon, Celia Dial. Biographical file, 1920–1960.

Robert F. Woodruff Library, Special Collections. Emory University, Atlanta.
Conroy, Pat. Correspondence, 1974. James Dickey Collection.

South Caroliniana Library. University of South Carolina, Columbia.
Ayer, Cornelius K. Correspondence, 1815–1825. Lewis Malone Ayer Papers.
Barnwell, Robert W. Correspondence to Board of Trustees, 1836–37, 1856–1862.
Blanding, Mrs. Louis. Correspondence, 1840. James Douglas Blanding Papers.
Blanding, William. Correspondence, 1838–1840. James Douglas Blanding Papers.
Boyd, Lauren Watts. Diary of Expenses, 1886–1890.
Buchanan, John C. Correspondence, 1883. Robert Means Davis Papers.
Bull, William A. Papers, 1808–1810.
Butler, Lilian. Correspondence and Scrapbook, 1885–1890. Butler Family Papers.
Charles, Sarah, Correspondence, 1826. Charles Family Collection.
Clariosophic Society. Minutes and Records, 1808–1935. Microfilm.
Cooper, Thomas. Correspondence to Board of Trustees, 1821–1830.
Craft, Katie Lou. Correspondence, 1932–1936. James Franklin Miles Papers.
Crosland, Edward. Correspondence, 1860–1870. Edward Crosland Papers.
Crosland, Edward. Papers, 1838–1870.
Crosland, George. Correspondence, 1860–1870. Edward Crosland Papers.
Dabbs, Eugene Whitefield. Papers, 1881–1920.
Dabbs, James McBride. Papers, 1912–1916.
DeSaussure, Henry William. Correspondence, 1808–1815. William Ford DeSaussure Papers.
Euphradian Society. Minutes and Records, 1826–1935. Microfilm.
Forum Club. Files, 1926.
Green, Edwin O. Papers, 1905–1915.

Hammond, James Henry. Diary, 1910.
Hankins, John Erskine. "Carolina Memories and Notes, 1920–1926." Unpublished memoir.
Henry, Robert. Correspondence to Board of Trustees, 1833–1855.
Jones, Iredell. Correspondence, 1860–1865.
Kennedy. Robert MacMillan. Correspondence, 1938. Fitz Hugh McMaster Papers.
Kohn, August. Journals, 1888–1889.
Kollock, Cornelius. Correspondence and Scrapbook, 1915–1920.
LaBorde, Maximilian. Reports to Board of Trustees, 1855–1865.
LeLand, Samuel Wells. Diary, 1851–1865.
Maxcy, Jonathan. Correspondence to Board of Trustees, 1812–1820.
McIver, William. Correspondence, 1882. Robert Means Davis Papers.
McIver, William. Correspondence, 1836–1837. Watson Family Papers.
Meetze, George Elias. Interview with Elizabeth Cassidy West, 3 Feb. 1999. Typescript.
Miles, James Franklin. Interview with Herbert Hartsook, 7 Feb. 1986. Audiotape.
Moore, Andrew Charles. Papers, 1882–1928.
Moore, Thomas John. Papers, 1861–1864.
Preston, William Campbell. Papers and Autobiography, 1817–1902.
Rice, James Henry, Jr. Papers, 1912–1933.
Sellers, John Calhoun. Correspondence, 1912. Edwin O. Green Papers.
Shand, Gadsden. Interview with Elizabeth Cassidy West, 15 Oct. 1997. Transcript.
Stone, Agnes Butler. Correspondence. Butler Family Papers, 1925–1932.
Warren, Mortimer A. Correspondence to Board of Trustees, 1874–1877. State Normal School Curriculum File.
Whetstone, Nathan. Correspondence, 1850–1856. Whetstone Family Collection.
Wilson, Charles Coker. "Fifty Years' Progress," 1926. Unpublished memoir.
Woodruff, Benjamin. Interview with Elizabeth Cassidy West, 11 Nov. 1998. Transcript.
Woodruff, Ruth Hunt. Interview with Elizabeth Cassidy West, 11 Nov. 1998. Transcript.

South Caroliniana Library, Modern Political Collections. University of South Carolina, Columbia.

Hollings, Ernest F. Interview with John Duffy, 7 Dec. 1989. Transcript.
Johnston, Olin DeWitt Talmadge. Papers, 1914–1930.
Lourie, Isadore. Interview with Herbert J. Hartsook, 18 Mar. 1994. Transcript.
Williams, Marshall B. Interview with Herbert J. Hartsook, 6 Dec. 1995. Transcript.

Southern Historical Collection. University of North Carolina, Chapel Hill.

Elliott, John Barnwell. Correspondence, 1859–1863. Habersham Elliott Papers.
Harllee, William Curry. Papers, 1860–1862.

Haskell, Alexander. Correspondence, 1866–1867. Edward Porter Alexander Papers.

Hutson, Charles. Correspondence, 1861–1864; "My Reminiscences," Unpublished memoir, 1910.

Miles, William Porcher. Papers, 1860–1862.

Wallace, Daniel. Correspondence, 1845–1849. Wallace and Gage Family Papers.

University Archives. University of South Carolina, Columbia.

Baker, Leonard T. Presidential Papers, 1931–1936.

Currell, William S. Presidential Papers, 1914–1922.

Douglas, Davison M. Presidential Papers, 1927–1931.

Holderman, James B. Presidential Papers, 1977–1990.

Jones, Thomas F. Presidential Papers, 1962–1974.

McKissick, J. Rion. Presidential Papers, 1936–1944.

Melton, William D. Presidential Papers, 1922–1926.

Patterson, William H. Presidential Papers, 1974–1977.

Russell, Donald S. Presidential Papers, 1952–1957.

Smith, Admiral Norman M. Presidential Papers, 1945–1952.

PRIVATE COLLECTIONS

Armbrust, Crys. Letters, 1998.

Compton, Thorne. Letters, n.d.

Daiwo, Joanna. Letters, 1994.

Easter, Bert. Periodicals, 1930–1940.

Edgar, Walter. Letters, 1986.

Hammond, Sarah. Electronic mail, 2000.

Maddox, Alexa. Letters, 1986–1990.

Mann, Jessica. Electronic mail, 1999–2000.

Parler, Caroline. Electronic mail, 1998.

Safran, Michael. Gamecock sports memorabilia, 1925–1990.

Salane, Thomas, and Linda Salane. Letters, 1969–1971.

Smith, Whitney Allison. Essay, 2000.

Stephens, Larry M. Letters, 1998.

Streyer, Emily. Postcards, 1998.

Tai, Arthur. Letters, 1983.

Waring-Tovey, Helen Anderson. Scrapbooks and photographs, 1938–1943.

Wienges, Othniel. Scrapbooks and photographs, 1942–1944.

Wright, Martha. Journal, 2000.

INTERVIEWS BY THE EDITORS

Barksdale, William C., Jr. 8 June 2000.

Butler, Mary King. 17 May 2000.

Fant, James. 4 May 2000.

Jackson, Rhett. 8 June 2000.

Smith, Selden K. 20 Mar. 2000.
Waring-Tovey, Helen Anderson. 26 Jan. 2000.
Williams, Frank. 16 May 2000.

Books

Armes, William D., ed. *The Autobiography of Joseph LeConte*. New York: Appleton, 1903.

Conroy, Pat. *Beach Music*. New York: Doubleday, 1995.

Dabbs, James McBride. *The Road Home*. Philadelphia: Christian Education Press, 1960.

Grayson, William J. *James Louis Petigru: A Biographical Sketch*. New York: Harper, 1866.

———. *Witness to Sorrow: The Antebellum Autobiography of William J. Grayson*. Columbia: University of South Carolina Press, 1990.

Green, Edwin L. *History of the University of South Carolina*. Columbia, S.C.: The State Co., 1916.

Hollis, Daniel Walker. *South Carolina College*. Vol. 1 of *University of South Carolina*. Columbia: University of South Carolina Press, 1951.

———. *College to University*. Vol. 2 of *University of South Carolina*. Columbia: University of South Carolina Press, 1956.

LaBorde, Maximilian. *History of the South Carolina College from Its Incorporation, Dec. 19, 1801, to Dec. 19, 1865; Including Sketches of Its Presidents and Professors*. Charleston, S.C.: Walker, Evans, and Cogswell Co., 1874.

Lesesne, Henry H.. *A History of the University of South Carolina, 1940–2000*. Columbia: University of South Carolina Press, 2002.

McKissick, J. Rion. *Men and Women of Carolina: Selected Addresses and Papers*. Columbia: University of South Carolina Press, 1948.

Morris, Jan, ed. *The Oxford Book of Oxford*. London: Oxford University Press, 1978.

Patterson, Giles J. *Journal of a Southern Student: 1846–48*. Nashville: Vanderbilt University Press, 1944.

Proceedings of the Centennial Celebration of South Carolina College. Columbia, S.C.: The State Publishers, 1905.

Remembering the Days: An Illustrated History of the University of South Carolina. Columbia, S.C.: R. L. Bryan Co., 1982.

Reynolds, John S. *Reconstruction in South Carolina, 1865–1877*. Columbia, S.C.: The State Publishers, 1905.

Sterling, Dorothy, ed. *The Trouble They Seen*. Garden City, N.Y.: Doubleday, 1976.

Stokes, Allen H., Jr., ed. *A Guide to the Manuscript Collection of the South Caroliniana Library*. Columbia: University of South Carolina, 1982.

Tolbert, Lisa, ed. *Two Hundred Years of Student Life at Chapel Hill*, Southern Research Report Number 4. Chapel Hill, N.C.: Center for the Study of the American South, 1993.

Towles, Louis P., ed. *A World Turned Upside Down: The Palmers of South Santee.* Columbia: University of South Carolina Press, 1996.

Underwood, James Lowell, and W. Lewis Burke, Jr, eds. *At Freedom's Door: African American Founding Fathers and Lawyers in Reconstruction South Carolina.* Columbia: University of South Carolina Press, 2000.

PERIODICALS

Carolinian, 1891–1938.

Charleston News and Courier, 12 Jan. 1889.

Columbia State, 8 May 1911, 25 Apr. 1926, 19 Dec. 1999.

Crucible, 1960–1978.

Gamecock, 1908–2000.

Garnet and Black (annual), 1899–1992.

Garnet and Black (magazine), 1997–2000.

Garnet and Black Quarterly, 1993–1997.

Washington, D.C., New National Era, 16 Apr. 1874, 9 July 1874.

Portfolio, 1980–1994.

South Carolina Collegian, 1883–1888.

University Carolinian, 1888–1891.

University of South Carolina Magazine, 1965–1971.

Yorkville Enquirer, 21 May 1866, 24 Sept. 1866.

OTHER MANUSCRIPT SOURCES

Barksdale, William C., Jr. Personal recollections. Unpublished typescript, 2000.

Boatwala, Daisy. Personal recollections. Unpublished typescript, 2000.

Bush, Erin. "Inheritance." Honors thesis, University of South Carolina, 2000.

Goodwin, Toni Metcalf. Personal recollections. Unpublished typescript, 2000.

Holmes, Michele. Unpublished essay, 1999.

Moore, Andrew Charles, ed. *Roll of Students of South Carolina College, 1805–1905.* Pamphlet printed in Columbia, S.C., 1905.

Roper, John H. "The Radical Mission: The University of South Carolina under Reconstruction." Master's thesis, University of North Carolina, 1973.

Stepp, Carl Sessions. Personal recollections and unpublished electronic mail, 2000.

Treadwell, Henrie Monteith. Personal recollections and unpublished typescript, 2000.

University of South Carolina Alumni Association. "War Years Reunion: Where Were You on December 7, 1941?" Proceedings of Reunion, 5 Oct. 1995. South Carolina State Museum, Columbia. Typescript.

White, Pamela Mercedes. "Free and Open: The Radical University of South Carolina." Master's thesis, University of South Carolina, 1975.

Index

African American students, 37, 55–58, 61, 63, 65, 162, 165, 177–86, 192, 212, 222; African American sues for admission, 178; Afro-American Studies program, 181; Association of Afro-American Students, 181; B.A.D. (Black Afros for Defense), 182; first African American medical student, 57; NAACP (National Association for the Advancement of Colored People), 165, 166; Southern Regional Council, 136; three African Americans enroll in classes, 178–79; Henrie Monteith Treadwell, 179–81. *See also* Civil Rights movement

alumni: *Alumni Record* (alumni magazine), 80; USC Alumni Association, 144, 148; War Years Reunion, 144

athletics, 98–100, 102, 134, 144, 152, 184, 186, 189; athletic facilities, 170; baseball athletes against city teams, 97; "Coed Athletics," 121–22; Faculty Athletic Committee, 100; South Carolina Athletic Association, 100; Woman's Athletic Association, 122. *See also* coaches; sports

bars, 79, 97, 160; Billy Maybin's O, 17–18; Gambling House, 16; Group Therapy, 210; Madder Hats, 225. *See also* drinking and partying

Beach Music (Pat Conroy), 171, 188

beauty contests: Homecoming Queen, 152, 171; May Queen, 170–71; Miss Venus, 171–72

Board of Regents, 64

Board of Trustees, 2, 3, 9, 13, 14, 15, 17, 20–22, 24, 25, 35, 36, 40, 56, 64, 69, 71, 72, 91, 102, 103, 114, 121, 130, 155, 163–64, 167–69, 176, 191, 200, 210

Board of Visitors, 84

buildings and halls: administration buildings, 188, 207; Byrnes International Center, 205; College Hall, 3; College of Education building, 147; Congaree House, 4, 20; Euphradian Hall, 8, 9; Flinn Hall, 104; Goat Hall, 4; Harper College, 8, 96; Maxcy College, 147; mess hall, 100, 105, 138; president's house, 20, 56, 81, 157; Russell House, 173, 188–89, 192, 223; Rutledge Chapel, 13, 15, 20, 26, 31, 32, 38, 52, 53, 55, 56, 58, 65, 89, 90, 92, 106, 108, 123, 129–30, 136, 137, 187; Science Hall, 98; society halls, 92; sorority house, 157, 174; Stanley's Hall, 77; Steward's Hall, 16, 25, 71. *See also* dormitories

campus: Gibbes Green, 157; the Horseshoe, 157, 179, 187, 189, 204. *See also* buildings and halls

Carolinian, The (literary magazine), 84–85, 88–93, 97–102, 129–30, 131, 135–36, 139

celebrations and parties, 20, 53, 77, 154; bonfire, 107; Centennial Celebration of South Carolina College, 8; champagne drop-ins, 211; Clariosophic and Euphradian Commencement Celebrations, 76;

celebrations and parties (*continued*)
Derby Day, 170–71;"fire balls,"
19–20; football victory, 123; Greek
Week, 211; Homecoming, 104,
211; Luau mixers, 211; Old South,
211; pledge parties, 211; student
celebration of the Confederate
cause, 38; Sunrise mixers, 211;
Swamp mixer, 211; swimming parties, 117. *See also* dances and dancing; drinking and partying
cheerleading, 114, 155, 201; becomes
a varsity sport, 201
Civil Rights movement: assassination
of Martin Luther King, Jr., 181,
188; gunning down of thirteen students at Kent State, 189; Orangeburg massacre, 181; student
occupation of Russell House,
188–89. *See also* African American
students
civil unrest: AWARE (student organization advocating free speech on the
USC campus), 191; Chicago Convention, 188; murder of Robert
Kennedy, 188; S.D.S. (Students for
a Democratic Society), 191; Tet
Offensive, 188
Civil War, 37–65
classical education, 1–3, 5–7, 52, 60,
84
Clemson University: rivalry with,
97–102, 115–16, 152, 154–55,
162, 172, 201
clubs: The Capital, 77; Damas
(women's dance club), 119; dance
clubs, 52–53; drinking club, 109;
Forum Club, 66, 96; gaming club,
109; Debate Team, 175; German
(men's dance club), 119; glee club,
136; L'Arioso Club, 77; Luncheon
Club, 178; Shakespeare Club, 53
coaches, 107, 121, 199–200: Marvin
Bass, 172; Francis Bradley, 145;

Jim Carlen, 200; Rex Enright, 145;
Frank Howard, 162; Frank Johnson, 145; Frank McGuire,
199–200; Whitely Rawl, 145
commencement, 13, 60, 72, 143
coeducation, 131, 148, 152, 153, 171,
184, 197; Alpha Kappa Gamma
(honorary society for senior
women), 176; "Coed Athletics,"
121–22; coed dormitories, 176–77;
intercollegiate sports for women
denied, 122; Woman's Athletic
Association, 122. *See also* feminists;
sororities

dances and dancing, 21–22, 33,
52–53, 75–79, 117, 119–20, 134,
152, 153, 154, 198, 201, 208, 227;
College Ball, 75; "College reel," 20;
commencement balls, 76; Damas
(girls' dance club), 119; dance
clubs, 104, 119; "German" (German Cotillion), 76; German Club
(boys' dance club), 119, 120; the
"Hop," 45; June Ball, 119; learning
to dance, 34; masked balls, 53;
Medallion Ball, 210; men inviting
women, 78, 79, 112, 113; Rose
Ball, 211; Shandon Dance, 112,
113; "stag dance," 38; USO State
Ball, 75; waltz, 75; White Rose,
211
dating, 18, 79, 119–20, 135, 144, 146,
155, 157, 172, 173, 226
debate and oratory, 1–2, 8, 10, 53, 69,
70, 85, 90, 91, 92, 93, 97, 123–24,
134, 136, 137, 189; Debate Team,
175; regional oratorical contest,
123
desegregation. *See* African American
students; Civil Rights movement
dormitories, 91, 139, 161, 170, 172,
173, 180, 191, 196, 226; Bates
House, 197; La Borde, 225; Cap-

stone House, 176, 219; coed,
176–77; Eagle's Nest, 79; McClintock, 225; Patterson, 225; Preston
Residential College, 213, 221, 222;
Sims dormitory, 153; South dormitory, 173; tenement dormitories,
153; turned into an infirmary,
126–27; South Tower, 225; the
Towers, 191, 225; Wade Hampton,
225; women's, 104
drinking and partying, 17–18, 28, 31,
56, 109, 112, 117, 119, 160, 172,
190, 191, 197, 198, 204, 210, 211,
224–25; prohibition, 117, 125;
USC makes top ten partying list,
210–11
duel, 25–26, 52

entertainment and amusements: Aloha
Carolina, 223; beach, 198, 225;
bonfires, 114; charity banquets, 53;
circus, 18, 70, 76; concerts, 53,
222; gambling, 16, 97, 117, 194;
hayrides, 155; horse racing, 16;
movies, 117, 120, 145–46, 155;
parades, 97, 101–2, 114, 123, 145,
197; pep rallies, 114, 201; picnics,
45, 76, 117, 118; plays, 53; shell
games, 97; State Fair, 68, 76, 77,
88, 97, 99, 100; sunbathing, 210;
swimming, 117, 143, 198; tandem
bicycling, 135. See also celebrations
and parties; dances and dancing;
drinking and partying

female students. See coeducation; feminists; sororities
feminists, 174–75, 217–18; NOW
(National Organization for
Women), 217–18
fraternities, 74, 76, 91, 119, 126, 152,
161, 171–72, 181, 183, 184, 188,
197, 211, 225; Alpha Tau Omega,
78; Derby Day, 170–72; Greek

Week, 211; Kappa Sigma, 155;
Luau mixers, 211; Old South, 211;
pledge parties, 211; Sigma Epsalon,
225; Sigma Chi, 171–72; Sigma
Nu, 172, 225; Sunrise mixers, 211;
Swamp mixer, 211

Gamecock, The (student newspaper),
90–91, 106–8, 115, 116–17,
118–19, 121–24, 130, 135, 147,
147–49, 151–54, 158–62, 165–70,
172–85, 187, 192–94, 197–98,
200, 202, 204–7, 210–11
Garnet and Black (yearbook), 85, 87,
89–90, 93–94, 103–6, 109, 114,
117, 121, 136, 171, 185, 193–94,
196–201, 210–11, 218, 220, 227
Garnet and Black Quarterly (student
magazine), 218–20
G.I. Bill. See veteran students
graduation. See commencement
Great Depression, the, 105, 119,
132–35, 144, 147

honor societies: Alpha Kappa Gamma
(for senior women), 176; Phi Beta
Kappa, 122
Honors College, 196, 214, 215, 221,
224, 226; Association of Honors
Students, 210

literary societies: 8–12, 15, 61, 69, 73,
85, 104, 110, 123, 125–26, 130,
137, 153; Clariosophic Society,
9–12, 60–61, 75, 76, 90, 92, 108,
124, 125; Euphradian Society, 6,
8–12, 75, 76, 90–91, 92, 108, 109,
136, 137; Parthenian Literary Society, 92; South Carolina Collegian
(literary magazine for Clariosophic
and Euphradian Societies), 75

Maroon Tiger (student publication of
current news and stories), 163

Medical University of South Carolina, 168–69, 218; first African American medical student, 57

oratory. See debate and oratory organizations and associations: American Missionary Association, 62; Army ROTC (Reserve Officer Training Corps), 126; Association of Afro-American Students, 181; Association of Honors Students, 210; AWARE (student organization advocating free speech on the USC campus), 191; B.A.D. (Black Afros for Defense), 182; Columbia Council for Internationals, 211; Debating Council, 131; Educational Foundation Fund, 191; Metropolitan Education Foundation, 181; NAACP (National Association for the Advancement of Colored People), 165, 166; National League for Women's Service, 126; National Science Foundation, 216; Naval ROTC (Reserve Officer Training Corps), 146, 150, 154; NOW (National Association for Women), 217–18; S.D.S. (Students for a Democratic Society), 191; South Carolina Athletic Association, 100; Southern Regional Council, 136; USC Alumni Association, 144, 148; Woman's Athletic Association, 122; YMCA (Young Men's Christian Association), 104, 107, 116, 130, 136, 141, 158, 161, 178; YWCA (Young Women's Christian Association), 104

Peace Corps, 213–14
presidents of USC: Leonard T. Baker, 118, 132–33; Robert W. Barnwell, Jr., 16, 17; Thomas Cooper, 14, 21, 22, 23, 24; William S. Currell, 130–31; Robert Henry, 17, 35; James Holderman, 199, 200, 202, 205–7; Thomas F. Jones, 170, 171, 178, 186, 188, 190–93; Jonathan Maxcy, 5, 13–14; John M. McBryde, 71, 72, 82, 84; Charles F. McCay, 20; J. Rion McKissick, 88, 95–96, 102–3, 133, 147, 154; William Davis Melton, 94; Samuel Chiles Mitchell, 105, 108, 118, 137; William C. Preston, 4, 8, 14, 19, 24; Norman M. Smith, 159, 164; William Howard Taft, Frank C. Woodward, 80–81, 94
professors: E. P. Alexander, 56; William Alexander, 72, 73; Jack Ashley, 185; Havilah Babcock, 131, 132; Robert Barnwell, 6, 9, 15, 16, 17, 48; Francis Bradley, 145, 151; Fisk Brewer, 57, 58, 60, 62, 65; R .T. Brumby, 24; William B. Burney, 72, 132; Wilfred H. Callcott, 177; F. L. Cardozo, 58; Ashmead Courtenay Carson, 79; Thorne Compton, 186, 229; Charles Coolidge, 171; Thomas Cooper, 14, 15, 21, 22, 23, 24; Bruce C. Coull, 221; John M. Coulter, 80; Orin F. Crow, 145; Henry Campbell Davis, 79; R. Means Davis, 14, 71, 72, 79, 80, 82, 83, 94, 95; James Dickey, 194–95; Elbert Daniel Easterling, 79; Phillip Epstein, 72; J. W. Flinn, 92; Robert W. Gibbes, 15; Edwin Green, 54; Richard T. Greener, 59; William Rainey Harper, 80; Robert Henry, 14, 16, 17, 35; Frank Herty, 155; Edward S. Joynes, 71, 84, 104, 139; Maximilian La Borde, 40, 48, 57; John LeConte, 15, 56; Joseph LeConte, 15, 53, 56; Francis Lieber, 6, 14–15; Guy F. Lip-

scomb, 132, 157; William Main, Jr., 59; George McCutcheon, 79; C. D. Melton, 60; William Porcher Miles, 68–69; Andrew Charles Moore, 43, 70, 79, 80–82; Herndon Moore, 110; Josiah Morse, 131, 139; F. J. Moses, 60; Henry J. Nott, 14, 26; Thomas Park, 6, 14; Edmund L. Patton, 66, 71, 84; J. H. Phillips, 81; Henry Price, 208; James L. Reynolds, 52, 56; William J. Rivers, 48; T. N. Roberts, 59; Dan I. Ross, 157; Benjamin Sloan, 67–69, 71, 84; L. L. Smith, 157; Reed Smith, 139; Yates Snowden, 132; Herman L. Spahr, 79; Stephen E. Stancyk, 221; Larry Stephens, 229; Carl Sessions Stepp, 192–93; Isaac Stuart, 6; James H. Thornwell, 14, 18, 25, 26; Thomas Tidwell, 187; Chester C. Travelstead, 167–69; Lardner Vanuxem, 23–24; Charles E. Venable, 39; James Wallace, 14, 30; Mortimer Allanson Warren, 58, 63, 64; George Wauchope, 131; Robert H. Wienefeld, 145, 177–78; James Woodrow, 53, 71, 72; Frank C. Woodward, 80–81, 83, 94. *See also* "Student's Guide to Professors, A"
publications. *See* individual titles

"radical university," 56–61
Reconstruction, 55–56, 62–63
Red Cross, 126, 153
religion, 10, 12, 14, 31–33, 161, 166, 227; American Missionary Association, 62; Bible study, 31, 32, 33, 134, 184, 227; Religious Emphasis Week, 170
residence halls. *See* dormitories
Road Home, The (Eugene W. Dabbs), 139

scholarships, 37, 57, 58, 153, 216, 220
sororities, 119, 152, 171, 181; Alpha Kappa Gamma (honorary society for senior women), 176; Greek Week, 211; Kappa Delta, 161; Luau mixers, 211; pledge parties, 211; Sunrise mixers, 211; Swamp mixer, 211; Delta Delta Delta, 161, 219; Zeta Tau Alpha, 171
South Carolina Agricultural and Mechanical College, 66
South Carolina College, 1–5, 8, 11, 18, 20, 24, 25, 31, 33, 37, 38, 40, 41, 43–44, 48, 52, 53, 66, 70, 76, 79, 80, 90, 91, 93, 94, 97, 99, 104
South Carolina Collegian (literary magazine for Clariosophic and Euphradian Societies), 75
South Carolina House of Representatives, 8–9, 133, 140, 141, 161
South Carolina Senate, 9, 53, 55, 75, 109, 133, 161, 177
sports, 97, 98, 114–17; athletes against city teams, 97; baseball, 97, 111, 116, 124; basketball, 104, 116–17, 121, 122–23, 145, 170, 182, 189, 199, 201; track, 89, 145, 171; football, 96, 97–99, 103, 114, 115, 116, 118, 119, 123, 124, 138, 142, 148, 157, 162, 171, 172, 173, 183, 200, 201, 204, 210, 212, 217, 222; intercollegiate, 103, 104, 117, 122–23; South Carolina Athletic Association, 100; Woman's Athletic Association, 122. *See also* cheerleading
State Normal School, 37, 56–58, 63–65
streaking. *See* student pranks
student exchange programs: China, 202–4; England, 183, 207–10, 215; Solomon Islands, 212–13

student pranks, 196; breaking or stealing the college bell, 20–21; "Great Biscuit Rebellion," 25; Sigma Nu prank, 172; streaking, 196–97
students as soldiers. *See* Civil War; World War I; World War II; veteran students; Vietnam War
"Student's Guide to Professors, A," 184–85

University Carolinian. See Carolinian, The
U.S. House of Representatives, 10, 76
USC School of Law, 52, 59, 60, 61, 65, 91, 104, 105, 109–13, 136, 140, 156, 163, 164, 165, 171, 189;

"History of the Junior Law Class," 117–18; regional oratorical contest, 123

visiting dignitaries: Bill Cosby, 204; Dick Gregory, 186; Henry Kissinger, 206; Pope John Paul II, 202–4, 208; Jehan Sadat, 204, 206–7; Daniel Webster, 14
veteran students, 140, 144, 156; G.I. Bill, 156–57
Vietnam War, 170, 187, 189–90

World War I, 104, 126–29, 145
World War II, 120, 144–69